Postbaccalaureate Futures
New Markets, Resources, Credentials

Postbaccalaureate Futures
New Markets, Resources, Credentials

Edited by
Kay J. Kohl
and
Jules B. LaPidus

AMERICAN COUNCIL ON EDUCATION ★
ORYX PRESS ★
Series on Higher Education
2000

The rare Arabian Oryx is believed to have inspired the myth of the unicorn. This desert antelope became virtually extinct in the early 1960s. At that time, several groups of international conservationists arranged to have nine animals sent to the Phoenix Zoo to be the nucleus of a captive breeding herd. Today, the Oryx population is over 1,000, and over 500 have been returned to the Middle East.

© 2000 by The American Council on Education and The Oryx Press
Published by The Oryx Press
4041 North Central at Indian School Road
Phoenix, Arizona 85012-3397
http://www.oryxpress.com

Published simultaneously in Canada
Printed and bound in the United States of America

∞ The paper used in this publication meets the minimum requirements of American National Standard for Information Science—Permanence of Paper for Printed Library Materials, ANSI Z39.48, 1984.

Library of Congress Cataloging-in-Publication Data

Postbaccalaureate futures: new markets, resources, and credentials / edited by Kay J. Kohl and Jules B. LaPidus.
　　p. cm.—(American Council on Education/Oryx Press series on higher education)
　　Includes index.
　　ISBN 1-57356-360-9 (alk. paper)
　　1. Universities and colleges—United States—Graduate work—Congresses. 2. Continuing education—United States—Congresses. 3. Education, Higher—Economic aspects—United States—Congresses. I. Kohl, Kay Jordan, 1940– II. LaPidus, Jules B. III. Series.
LB2371.4.P68 2000
378.1'55'0973—dc21   00-021939

CONTENTS

FOREWORD

Robert M. O'Neil

A s the new millennium opens, one of the happiest and most productive collaborations in American higher education is that between the Council of Graduate Schools (CGS) and the University Continuing Education Association (UCEA). Improbable partners though they might have seemed a decade or even half a decade ago, these two national organizations have forged an effective and durable alliance that reflects shared concerns and hopes for the future of the sectors for which they speak. Discussions and joint endeavors between UCEA and CGS in the late 1990s have generated a remarkable sense of interdependence and potential mutual benefit—as well as clear proof that the whole which this alliance represents far surpasses the sum of its organizational parts. Indeed, the collaboration and its products, both tangible and intangible, offer a model for other potential partners in an increasingly interdependent academic world.

The papers contained in this volume are an essential product of the UCEA-CGS alliance. Most were presented at a colloquium held in Aspen, Colorado, in November 1998; the meeting was generously supported by the Kellogg Foundation, and it was attended by a remarkable array of academic, business, and professional leaders who share a deep interest in the capacity of American higher education to serve the nation's needs in the coming century.

The blending of backgrounds and perspectives was both deliberate and perceptive on the part of the Colloquium planners. The subject was optimally

Robert M. O'Neil is the founding director of the Thomas Jefferson Center for the Protection of Free Expression and professor of law at the University of Virginia.

suited for a far too rare exchange of views among people from business, government, and the academy. Here, providentially, was an issue in which each group not only had a vital interest, but also the understanding and advancement of which depended heavily on a sharing of insight from just such a cross-sector dialogue. Each sector proved to be an equal as well as an essential partner; no one sector dominated, though there were several topics on which one sector may have had stronger views than did the other two.

In fact, each of the individual sessions reflected a blending of views from government, business, and academia. The quality of the discussions served to remind the participants what a splendid opportunity had been created. The declared focus of the Colloquium—postbaccalaureate futures—might imply an almost irresponsible breadth of coverage. Yet the topic proved eminently manageable, if in certain respects rather eclectic because major themes within the agenda are still taking form.

In logical fashion, the Colloquium (and the papers presented here) began by seeking to project the relevant future in terms both of demographic realities and institutional capacities. Detailed data provided in each major topical area serve as the point of departure for conjecture about the impact of various alternative assumptions and scenarios. Not a single future, but in fact many and varied futures, received close scrutiny. From the outset, one issue proved transcendent: what is the most appropriate balance between traditional, campus-based programs and newer educational media and means of both instruction and certification?

While no definitive or categorical answers emerged—indeed, simple solutions were strongly discouraged—the relevant considerations have never been better marshaled than they were at the Aspen Colloquium. To a remarkable degree, conferees who brought preconceptions or predilections found in the intensive discussion of each of the papers more than ample challenge to easy assumptions about how best to meet a rapidly changing and dynamic set of learning needs.

The benefits of the gathering extend far beyond the compilation of this most useful and timely collection of papers. In the traditional campus setting, deans of graduate studies and deans or directors of continuing education have had surprisingly little contact. Apart from their shared presence at deans' meetings and routine social events, and perhaps a very occasional common task or joint assignment, they have tended to follow separate paths. Many opportunities—most especially opportunities for students—doubtless have been lost over the years because of such rigidities, which may have been even more detrimental to learning than the more widely disparaged departmental and disciplinary boundaries.

Against this history, the discovery that those who guide these two vital dimensions of university life do in fact have much in common and may benefit immensely from working more closely together is a significant outcome of the Postbaccalaureate Futures Project and of the Aspen Colloquium. A new and heartening spirit of interdependence, as well as a sense of mutual esteem, is evident throughout these papers and marks the major contribution of this volume to the vision of American higher education in the new millennium.

ACKNOWLEDGMENTS

T his book emerged from conversations with a large number of colleagues in higher education institutions and the private sector. We are indebted to the authors of the chapters in this volume. They are among some of the most prominent thinkers in their fields. Their willingness to write on topics that we identified enabled us to shape this volume. Unfailingly, all of the authors responded to our requests with thoughtful, provocative essays.

We are especially grateful to those members of the Council of Graduate Schools (CGS) and the University Continuing Education Association (UCEA) who have supported this progressive collaboration between the organizations from the outset. The title of the book, *Postbaccalaureate Futures*, is intended to suggest that there are multiple visions of how different higher education providers will respond to working adults' expanding demand for learning opportunities. This subject has been the focus of a multi-year dialogue between members of our two associations—a dialogue that has challenged assumptions, helped frame the issues surrounding postbaccalaureate education, and broadened everyone's perspectives.

We are deeply indebted to the participants in the Aspen Colloquium for their comments and critique of the contributions in this book. The Colloquium provided an opportunity for leaders from the private sector, government, and higher education to engage in a candid discussion of the issues surrounding the rapid growth in demand for postbaccalaureate education. We are grateful to Mary Burke for her management of the arrangements for the Colloquium.

We would like to thank the W. K. Kellogg Foundation for its generous support. The Foundation's funding not only made possible the Colloquium on

Postbaccalaureate Futures, but also helped underwrite this book. In addition, the Foundation supported three regional invitational workshops focused on developing postbaccalaureate programs to meet workforce needs; these were organized under the leadership of Stanley Gabor, dean of the Johns Hopkins University School of Professional Studies in Business and Education. We are especially grateful to our project officer at the Kellogg Foundation, Betty Overton-Adkins. Her encouragement and interest in this project were invaluable.

There were many individuals whose careful reading of various chapters improved the manuscript. We are especially grateful to Debra Stewart and Robert Rosenzweig for their helpful comments. Jill Bogard of the American Council on Education library helped us unearth many useful sources. We are indebted to Kelly Stern for her skillful editorial assistance and preparation of the index. Jim Murray of the American Council of Education (ACE) has been a source of encouragement and support throughout the preparation of this manuscript.

Our hope is that this book will interest those in the higher education community, government, and the private sector who are concerned with addressing the postbaccalaureate learning needs of the workforce in a knowledge-based economy.

INTRODUCTION

Postbaccalaureate Education— A Work in Progress

Kay J. Kohl and Jules B. LaPidus

D emand for higher education continues to increase—perhaps most significantly among individuals who already have earned a baccalaureate degree. Changing jobs and the need to integrate new technologies into the workplace have given postbaccalaureate learning a particular urgency. The chapters in this book reflect diverse perspectives. Our intent is to provide a vantage point from which to consider the issues, opportunities, and challenges facing higher education with regard to postbaccalaureate education as currently defined and understood. The objective is to provide a better understanding of what is happening in this rapidly changing and growing part of higher education. Distance education, instructional technology, for-profit education providers, and asynchronous learning—themes which dominate much of the current literature—are not the topics of this volume; rather, they are assumed as context.

Developments in postbaccalaureate education warrant close examination because they point to important new challenges, opportunities, and models for higher education as a whole. The idea, however, is not simply to stand back and dispassionately describe a phenomenon that has acquired all the characteristics of a juggernaut. How new technology and expanded demand might shape postbaccalaureate learning in the future and the concomitant implications for higher education institutions are the questions at the heart of this volume.

Kay J. Kohl is the executive director of the University Continuing Education Association (UCEA).
Jules B. LaPidus is the president of the Council of Graduate Schools (CGS).

Written by both higher education and industry experts, the following chapters seek to address some of these questions.

Part 1 focuses on emerging markets for postbaccalaureate education. In Chapter 1, Jules LaPidus introduces the subject by defining what distinguishes *postbaccalaureate* from *graduate* education. All graduate students are postbaccalaureate students, LaPidus notes, but not all postbaccalaureate students are graduate students. As the market for postbaccalaureate education has grown, so too has the diversity of providers and their responses. This has increased the importance of credit and the demand for credentials focused on the needs of professional practice.

In Chapter 2, Kay Kohl explores the nature of the postbaccalaureate learning imperative. Kohl contrasts workforce needs with demographic realities by way of emphasizing that the growing demand for postbaccalaureate learning opportunities should not be seen as a passing phenomenon. Higher education institutions can and should play a role in responding to increasing demands for education by working men and women. The challenges involved in adapting policies and creating programs that take account of learner preferences in an increasingly competitive environment are discussed. Those higher education institutions which are prepared to incorporate postbaccalaureate learners into their institution-wide mission rather than treating such education as a tangential activity are likely to have the greatest appeal to learners and to enjoy more partnership opportunities with business, government, and the professions.

In contrast, many investors perceive a promising landscape for companies in the education business. In Chapter 3, Howard Block discusses why education stocks appeal to investors and how value is determined. He observes that Internet-enabled education holds considerable promise for improving learning and for retaining learners. That said, Internet-enabled education is recognized to be "a new and emerging market" with a host of intellectual property issues and which is primed for consolidation—thus posing substantial investment risks.

In Chapter 4, Stephen Mitchell, James Van Erden, and Kenneth Voytek assert that globalization together with new technologies and shifting labor markets have made knowledge and skills a source of competitive advantage. Companies are viewing the acquisition of knowledge workers in much the same terms as component parts or services. Employers are relying upon a supply chain model, the goals of which are to get the right people with the right knowledge in the right place at the right time so they can contribute to innovation or improved productivity. What colleges and universities must do to continue to be important education providers for business and industry in the face of the Knowledge Supply Chain strategy is the subject of this chapter.

Part 2 stresses the importance of strategic visioning and decision making. All three chapter authors observe that incremental decision making will not anticipate choices that universities need to make to realize the benefits of technology for students of all kinds.

In Chapter 5, Michael Schrage cautions universities that new technology is far less about creating and managing new information resources than it is about creating and managing new relationships. Having the technology does not guarantee that the relationships will follow.

In Chapter 6, Michael Goldstein explores the changed environment of postbaccalaureate education and of the marketplace as a whole that is transforming the resource equation. He outlines a decision-making process for academic administrators to use when making choices in the context of a particular marketplace and the partnerships that might derive from or drive those choices.

Anticipating that postbaccalaureate learners in an information society will want access to digital library resources, Peter Lyman in Chapter 7 describes three kinds of change a digital library might imply: changes in intellectual property, changes in information technology, and changes in social relationships in organizations. All of these, Lyman notes, represent opportunities for innovation in both the form and process of postbaccalaureate education.

Part 3 focuses on the various forms that postbaccalaureate education is assuming today, with particular emphasis on how it is being offered and the kinds of credentials and quality assurances that are being developed.

In Chapter 8, Alan Bassindale and Sir John Daniel stress the idea of postbaccalaureate education being driven by students' learning needs. They describe changes in the nature of postbaccalaureate education in terms of changing patterns of demand, changing methods of delivery, and changes in universities. In particular, they describe mega-universities and comment on for-profit institutions, virtual universities, and corporate universities, as well as the role of different kinds of institutions in serving students. They conclude with a description of The Open University, its philosophy, programs, and practices.

In Chapter 9, Steven Crow is concerned with issues related to quality assurance in postbaccalaureate education—particularly certificates and other non-credit activities. He points out that university faculties have been the arbiters of quality for credit and degree programs and that accrediting organizations have focused their attention on these activities as well. As the number of education providers increases, particularly in the wholly unregulated and undefined certificate area, and as universities also expand their involvement in this area, Crow foresees a need for accrediting associations to ensure that their standards and evaluation procedures are relevant and make sense for these relatively new areas of postbaccalaureate education. To do this, he suggests several approaches involving extensive interaction among the various communities that provide this kind of education, as well as focusing attention on institutional quality assurance procedures.

In Chapter 10, Alice Irby explores the area of postbaccalaureate certificates. She describes the rapid and dramatic growth of this ill-defined sector of education, fueled for the most part by a confluence of factors, including an increasingly knowledge-based economy, the development of information technology, and the need for employees to acquire specialized skills and updating. She contrasts the kinds of programs being developed in universities, which tend to focus on a body of knowledge and the process by which it is acquired, with those being developed in the non-university sector (corporations, professional groups, etc.), where competence to perform in the workplace is the only thing that counts. She concludes with a discussion of the opportunities and problems being encountered in this important area.

In Chapter 11, Donald Langenberg argues that education should be neither episodic nor confined to a certain period in one's life. He stresses the importance of competency—of what one knows and can do—in determining a student's progress through the education system and urges reconsideration of the entire education system, particularly in terms of lifelong access. That gives rise to lifelong credentialing, and Langenberg sees the possibility that degrees and diplomas may be replaced by other forms of recognition for educational accomplishment, such as certificates or portfolios. This becomes particularly important as students accumulate educational experiences from a variety of sources through a lifetime of learning.

Part 4 raises the overarching issues for universities, business and industry, and the public at large. In Chapter 12, Myles Brand focuses on research universities and describes some of the changes taking place as different and more insistent demands related to postbaccalaureate learning impinge on the usual balance of teaching, research, and service. In particular, he comments on the evolving concept of *distributed learning,* by which he means use of a variety of formats for and approaches to meeting student needs. He devotes much of his chapter to the particular culture of the research university and proposes various approaches for adapting to postbaccalaureate learner needs without compromising the unique resource that these universities represent. With respect to faculty roles and responsibilities, he explores a departmental model in which individuals may have different responsibilities (research, teaching, service) at different times and in different proportions. He concludes by commenting on partnership models and provides specific examples from his own institution.

In Chapter 13, David Burnett provides a perspective from the corporate world, particularly in terms of the relationship between employers and employees relative to knowledge acquisition and corporate goals. He discusses the needs of corporations to invest in their employees' intellectual development so that benefits accrue to the corporation. Simply providing educational benefits without using employees' increased knowledge and skills to further corporate goals could have little effect other than to increase employees' job mobility—clearly an undesirable outcome for the employer. Burnett draws attention to the idea that companies develop their own knowledge base and must discover ways to share that knowledge, as well as the company's "culture," with employees for the benefit of the company. He contrasts this with the acquisition of training through arrangements with outside providers—often universities.

In their analysis in Chapter 14 of the public policy implications of the changing contours of higher education, Pat Callan and Joni Finney use the term *system of users* to describe an increasingly diverse set of higher education providers, whose principal characteristic is that students perceive it as an increasingly adaptable and usable resource even though the individual parts are not connected in any formal or even coherent way. Callan and Finney suggest four major factors influencing higher education: erosion of public consensus regarding who pays; intensifying competition; economic stratification; and the influence of technology on teaching and learning. They discuss the role of state government in dealing with these issues—particularly as the issues impact finance, quality assurance, and governance. They conclude by posing broad questions about information and data used in assessing progress, and the public purposes of education.

Finally, in Chapter 15, Kay Kohl and Jules LaPidus sum up and propose some activities to facilitate the higher education community's transition into this rapidly changing and complicated new era.

These 15 essays begin to map the terrain of postbaccalaureate learning in support of workforce needs. The computer and telecommunications revolution and intensified global competition are driving the expanded demand for postbaccalaureate learning opportunities. This demand is enticing a multiplicity of providers, making it difficult for consumers to differentiate among products in the absence of a delineated system. New partnerships among universities and between universities and the private sector are changing the higher education typology. Digital networks are facilitating the emergence of new "learning communities" inside and outside the academy. The long-standing university monopoly on credentialing is eroding in the face of new competition. Technology is making possible new approaches to learning—for example, extra-university knowledge networks—that may be particularly well suited to the postbaccalaureate learner.

As universities try to understand the new circumstances in which they find themselves, four assumptions have emerged that define the bedrock upon which new concepts and new structures will be built.

- Universities have a responsibility to provide ongoing education to their graduates.
- Expanded competition and new user demands require universities to develop postbaccalaureate programs that emphasize learning and performance.
- Universities need to plan how best to take advantage of new technologies to create productive networks, foster the flow of knowledge, and improve learning.
- Although postbaccalaureate education may be viewed primarily as a private rather than a public good, the increasing importance of higher education in a knowledge-based economy suggests that few universities can ignore the needs of their graduates in the workforce and yet retain public confidence.

Universities certainly will be involved in whatever new education systems develop. Given the extraordinary range of institutional type and mission in U.S. higher education, the particular nature and extent of that involvement will vary. But the role of the traditional university as the primary provider of postbaccalaureate education—and thus as the definer of what is an acceptable level and standard for this kind of practice-oriented education—may be changing. Universities, because of the evolution of the new kinds of educational systems described here, may become partners in loosely defined educational coalitions whose structures, objectives, methods, and standards change to reflect current workplace needs. The critical issues can be expressed in familiar terms: the relationship of supply and demand; the relationship of cost and value; and, particularly for universities, the relationship of business opportunity and educational responsibility. Our purpose in bringing together the essays in this volume is to explore these and related issues and to provide some guidance for the future.

PART 1

· · · · · · · · · · ·

Emerging Markets for
Postbaccalaureate Education

CHAPTER 1

Postbaccalaureate and Graduate Education: A Dynamic Balance

Jules B. LaPidus

The purpose of this chapter is to describe and discuss the relationship between graduate education, which traditionally has been concerned with degree programs, and postbaccalaureate education, a broad term for a variety of kinds of education which may or may not be degree related. Perhaps the best way to express the difference between these two kinds of education is to point out that while all graduate students are postbaccalaureate students, not all postbaccalaureate students are graduate students. This has been an important distinction, but as higher education and its relationship to jobs and careers evolve, the two terms are coming into a new kind of balance that is affecting the way people think about their education.

POSTBACCALAUREATE EDUCATION

The term *postbaccalaureate education* usually refers to a level of education that builds upon the foundation provided by undergraduate education. There are several different ways to look at this. Ideally (and perhaps idealistically), acquisition of the baccalaureate degree implies that students possess the general attributes traditionally associated with this degree—that is, the ability to read with understanding, to write cogently, to think coherently and analytically, and to be able to deal with different or conflicting ideas. In some fields (e.g., chemistry, mathematics), postbaccalaureate students are also expected

---

Jules B. LaPidus is the president of the Council of Graduate Schools (CGS).

to have specific knowledge acquired during their undergraduate education. In other fields (e.g., business, public administration), students increasingly are being required to have related work experience. Other types of educational experiences are unrelated to undergraduate education and are considered postbaccalaureate simply because they occur after the baccalaureate has been earned; these will not be discussed here.

Generally speaking, there are two types of postbaccalaureate education: credit and non-credit. Students admitted to graduate programs must accumulate a certain number of academic credits as part of the degree requirements. Courses and other activities for which graduate credit is awarded usually are subject to prior approval by department faculty. At many universities, approval at the college and graduate school level is also required. In some cases, these credits may be earned in "graduate non-degree" status, an enrollment category in which the student has not been accepted into a specific degree-granting program but has been approved to take courses. Most universities have such categories but limit the number of such credits that can be transferred into degree programs. Credits earned in this way might also apply toward certificates signifying the completion of certain requirements designed to prepare the student for some specific activity and to attest to some competency. Activities that earn graduate credit become part of the student's transcript, and this has implications for transfer to other institutions and programs.

Non-credit postbaccalaureate education comprises a wide variety of courses, workshops, seminars, and other educational experiences offered by universities or other organizations (such as professional societies or corporations), the purpose of which is to help students learn about specific topics or acquire specific skills. They may or may not be related to academic programs of study or graduate degree programs. They usually are not part of the student's transcript and do not transfer to other programs.

The question of credit and its value in the academic marketplace has become more important as the number and diversity of education providers has increased. Today, students are likely to accumulate educational experiences from a number of different sources, including corporate universities, professional societies, and for-profit educational enterprises, as well as traditional universities and colleges. Some of these award academic credit; others do not. As students, employers, and education institutions attempt to assess educational accomplishments, either for purposes of application to additional degrees or to demonstrate qualifications for a particular job, problems will arise.

Over the years, the term *postbaccalaureate* has become strongly associated with practice-oriented or professional education. It is almost never used to refer to doctoral education—either the Ph.D. or professional doctorates such as the M.D. or D.D.S. Many people use the term to refer to non-degree academic experiences, such as certificate programs or individual courses, seminars, workshops, etc., designed for individuals with baccalaureate degrees. In practice, however, the master's degree has dominated this part of higher education in terms of numbers of students, numbers of programs, and general program design and philosophy. The master's degree has been a real American success story; approximately 400,000 master's degrees are awarded each year in hundreds of different specialties. To understand what is happening in postbaccalaureate education today, it is important to understand what has been happening to the master's degree.

MASTER'S EDUCATION

Since the 1950s, master's degrees have played an important part in the educational plans of large numbers of people. Surveys of freshman attitudes about educational plans continue to show that the majority of college freshmen aspire to the masters' degree as their educational goal. During the 1990s, the hegemony of the master's degree has been increasingly challenged by shorter duration, less expensive, and more convenient alternatives that do not involve graduate degrees. Certificate programs in particular are becoming increasingly popular, either in place of graduate degrees or as modules that can be applied toward graduate degrees. As the perceived value of different kinds of educational credentials changes, it becomes important to understand what the credentials signify and how they are related.

Spencer, in commenting on the development of the master's degree since 1945, states that

> Unburdened by the imperatives of any tradition to which the academic community was passionately attached and lacking any but the most elemental and mechanical guidelines for structuring the degree, those faculties and administrators responsible for designing master's programs have enjoyed a measure of discretionary authority essentially unique in modern American education. Thus, as tidal changes have swept across American civilization since World War II, the academic community has proven willing, on a campus-by-campus and largely ad hoc basis, to adapt the master's degree more readily than any other level of education.[1]

For the most part, postbaccalaureate students seek specialized knowledge and skills related to jobs and careers. The master's degree has been the primary means of acquiring this kind of knowledge, in a form and with a credential that is reasonably well understood.

Master's degrees are focused on the state and the needs of professional practice, and as they have developed, they have taken on certain characteristics that tell us a great deal about the nature of postbaccalaureate education. Spencer defines five "fundamental realities" that have been incorporated into master's programs: "specialization, professionalization, application, decentralization, and depersonalization."[2] Although these terms may have needed some explanation in 1986, they are self-evident today. Currently, 85 percent of all master's degrees are what have come to be called practice-oriented, or professional, degrees. They are specialized in terms of focus, applied in terms of content, decentralized in that they often are offered through different units in the university as well as by non-university organizations, and depersonalized in that they often seek to shape students according to a predefined template of professional competencies. Employers often subsidize some or all of the costs of this education.

Most students in master's programs pursue postbaccalaureate studies on a part-time basis, usually because they work in the professions they hope to advance in through the acquisition of more education. In many programs, it is common—if not mandatory—to have practitioners as regular or adjunct members of the faculty. Thus, the workplace serves as a practicum for the academic program. Current issues and concerns of practice are brought to the programs directly by faculty, practitioners, and students and tend to influence the nature of those programs; thus, the programs coexist with practice as parts of an adaptive system.

In a broader sense, master's programs are aimed at improving professional practice and provide all involved with the opportunity to step back from day-to-day issues to examine the general context. Not only can this lead to changes in the nature of practice, but it also serves to prepare students to be leaders and change agents in their professions. Those programs recognized as being the best in their fields transcend professional competency and foster professional leadership.

Some students, faculty, and practitioners seek instead to focus not on the practice of a profession but on the current problems and practices of a particular business, industry, or company. This, in turn, can lead to increasingly fragmented programs consisting of courses, workshops, seminars, or other experiences devoted to certain problems of interest to employers and employees. Ultimately, a program may be divided into a number of parts that may or may not be connected, each dealing with highly specific and usually applied subject matter. Often, award of a certificate attests to mastery of a particular segment.

CERTIFICATE PROGRAMS

Postbaccalaureate certificate programs constitute one of the fastest-growing areas in higher education. These programs are attractive to students and employers for a number of reasons. They often are short term, some lasting for only a few days or weeks. They are highly specific and easy to define in terms of what students will learn. They usually are amenable to a wide variety of delivery systems, particularly those involving online or asynchronous approaches, so they are available anytime, anywhere. For many, they are the most flexible, accessible, and responsive educational offering available.

Nevertheless, there are some concerns. Because there is no standardization or quality control, certificates can be offered by any organization that chooses to do so. This can make it difficult for students and employers to assess the value of these programs. Until recently, certificates were offered primarily by education institutions and professional associations, often as part of continuing education programs related to professional certification. In these cases, the imprimatur of the offering organization served as an indicator, and often a guarantee, of quality. Yet the rapid growth in certificate programs and the lack of generally agreed upon standards has attracted many for-profit organizations to the market, with the result that *caveat emptor* may be the best advice for students.

The expansion of certificate programs has led to questions about the need for graduate programs, since compilations of certificates provide much more specific information about what an individual knows or knows how to do. Employers may be less willing to pay for master's degrees, preferring instead to invest their education dollars in training. The result of this kind of fragmentation can be employees who are continually up-to-date on the latest techniques and practices but who have little idea of how, why, or to what purpose things fit together. The lack of this broader perspective in some practice-oriented programs and the difficulty of providing it through collections of unrelated courses are issues of some concern.

The last step in what may prove to be a circular progression is for students and education providers, driven by the desire for closure (or tradition), to develop procedures whereby a certain number of certificates can be applied toward an advanced degree, most likely a practice-oriented master's degree. The idea of "credit banks" where educational credentials accumulated over time and from a variety of different sources can be stored and perhaps "cashed in" when a sufficient number have been accumulated has been considered. The problem is that adding components in a summative fashion ignores the interrelationships among them, with the result that programmatic integrity may be compromised.

AN EVOLVING SYSTEM

Generally speaking, the providers of postbaccalaureate education have been education institutions—that is, universities and colleges; businesses and industrial organizations; and, to a lesser extent, professional societies and associations. In many cases, the development of postbaccalaureate courses and programs has been carried out through close cooperation between relevant parts of this "community of interest" to provide students with the kinds of educational opportunities they have needed at various stages in their careers. Thus, universities have worked closely with the business and industry community to develop both specific and general programs. These have been offered in whatever way seemed appropriate—on campus, on site at the business or industry, on site at an off-campus facility maintained by a university (or several universities or a consortium of universities and industries), or through any one of a variety of synchronous or asynchronous distance learning mechanisms.

A characteristic of this system is that it has been relatively formal in structure. The nature of the education, the structure of the program, and the process for earning credit and receiving certification typically have been determined in advance, and students have had a reasonably clear understanding of what they have had to do and of what options were available. Two factors are affecting this system and creating both new problems and new opportunities: the rapid development of distance education mediated through educational technology and the rise of for-profit organizations designed to use this and other technologies in the provision of educational services.

For years, various techniques have been employed to make education available to people who cannot use campus-based programs. Replacing written materials with audio or video cassettes, or even having students watch televised classes, does not provide anything new or different but may serve to make postbaccalaureate education more convenient. Advances in interactive audio/video technology have added a new component to distance education, making it possible for students to participate in real time in classes being held at remote sites. Access to the World Wide Web has provided a new dimension to distance education by making it available online and thus connectable to and interactive with databases and other sources of information. The use of e-mail also has created an opportunity for students to interact with one another and with faculty. The array of options may seem bewildering to the student, who must construct an integrated package of learning experiences that merits certification. The individual components of a particular educational program may be available in a number of formats and from several providers, and this has given rise to educational brokering services, which provide students with information and counseling as they develop programs that meet their needs.

All these techniques and approaches to providing education have fostered the idea of the virtual university, as well as its extension, the virtual consortium. But most students want real credit that has real value in the marketplace, and it is not clear at present that portfolios or personal Web pages recording miscellaneous educational experiences will replace degrees or other formal recognition of educational accomplishment. A question that remains is whether education providers or "credit brokering" services can develop articulation agreements that will make it easier for students to combine credits earned in a variety of ways and from a variety of sources. In all cases, key concerns will be in four broad areas: the certification of accomplishment and the credibility of the certifier; the perception of quality and value by both worker and employer; the availability of education in terms of time and place (convenience); and, finally, the cost and who will pay.

It is clear that workers' motivation to seek postbaccalaureate education and employers' expectation that workers will have or get it are strong and growing. Just as the period starting in 1945 led to the extraordinary growth in master's degree programs, so the period we are in now, characterized not only by socioeconomic change but also by technological revolution, is leading to growth in certificate and other non-degree programs. Degree-granting and nondegree-granting programs have always coexisted within universities, but for the most part they have attracted different populations of students and have been subject to different forms of administrative oversight. In most cases, different units have offered them, and they have not been viewed as competing with one another. That situation is changing as universities respond to market forces that mandate the tailoring of educational programming to meet students' learning needs.

Some people believe that graduate degrees—particularly the master's degree—will continue to dominate postbaccalaureate education; others suggest that these degrees will be replaced by shorter term, more specialized, and less expensive non-degree experiences. At least for the foreseeable future, postbaccalaureate education likely will be a mix of degree programs and non-degree activities. Students will play a larger role in determining their educational agendas, and the relationship between universities and non-university education providers will shape itself so as to provide effective, affordable, convenient, and educationally responsible ways to meet student needs. Graduate and postbaccalaureate education, credit and non-credit education, degree and non-degree education will continue to coexist, but they will be much more commingled. A dynamic balance will exist among them that will change in response to new opportunities, new technologies, and new educational needs.

NOTES

1. Donald S. Spencer, "The Masters Degree in Transition," CGS *Communicator*, Council of Graduate Schools, January 1986, p. 1.
2. Ibid.

CHAPTER 2

The Postbaccalaureate Learning Imperative

Kay J. Kohl

Efforts to create opportunities for mature men and women to continue learning have been continuous and longstanding in the United States. The Chautauqua Movement of the late nineteenth century pioneered the development of summer sessions for teachers, extension programs, and correspondence schools—innovations adopted by many land-grant universities in the early twentieth century. After World War II, the GI Bill of 1946 further democratized American higher education by offering thousands of veterans the opportunity to earn a college degree. When many veterans opted for professional studies in management, engineering, and technical subjects rather than the liberal arts, institutions had to significantly adjust their curricular priorities.[1] Some four decades later, competition for talent, coupled with the availability of telecommunications satellites for transmitting education, led some high technology corporations to organize the National Technological University, an educational consortium of U.S. universities that joined forces to deliver postbaccalaureate education to highly mobile engineers, scientists, and technical managers at their work sites. By the end of the twentieth century, the rapid growth of online courses developed by both private sector and traditional university providers seemed to promise still further equalization of access to higher education.

Kay J. Kohl is the executive director of the University Continuing Education Association (UCEA).

Many higher education institutions have sought to address the demands of adults seeking part-time postbaccalaureate learning opportunities. Institutions' responses have been shaped by both financial and status considerations. The academy persists in its tendency to dismiss or at best devalue as "training" postbaccalaureate education that is not traditional graduate education. This prejudice is longstanding. As early as 1918, Thorstein Veblen wrote that "'Vocational training' . . . for proficiency in some gainful occupation. . . has no connection with the higher learning."[2] Veblen was particularly scathing in his observations about the training offered by university schools of commerce, which he characterized as "detrimental to the community's material interests."[3] Yet today, there is a growing recognition that higher education institutions cannot exist in a vacuum. The kind of postbaccalaureate learning that a university develops and the way it delivers curricula will be influenced by outside groups—employers, government, or professional societies.

Those who dismiss the need to become involved in postbaccalaureate education may be preoccupied by their institutions' strained finances or unwilling to foster collaborations that might draw away scarce resources. They have yet to confront the fact that job security in the new economy derives not from the promise of lifetime employment in a large company but rather from the quality of an individual's current knowledge and skills. This has profound implications for higher education institutions. The United States' reliance on knowledge to remain competitive in today's globalized, highly technological economy suggests that universities should be contemplating an enlarged role in postbaccalaureate education. After all, the capacity of individuals to change jobs several times and to acquire the new expertise and technological skills that the economy requires ultimately will depend on access to learning opportunities.

The new economy "is a knowledge and idea-based economy where the keys to wealth and job creation are the extent to which ideas, innovation, and technology are embedded in all sectors of the economy."[4] It depends upon a higher education infrastructure to develop and maintain high-quality knowledge workers, a majority of whom already have baccalaureate degrees. The importance of lifelong learning in this new economy thus calls into question some fundamental assumptions about the constituencies, policies, and structures of traditional higher education institutions.

What are the most important drivers pushing higher education institutions to rethink how they respond to postbaccalaureate learners? What are the demographics of the postbaccalaureate population? Can it be argued that this population's size and needs differ significantly from postbaccalaureate learners of a decade or two ago? What is the nature of today's demand for postbaccalaureate learning? How does serving postbaccalaureate learners support or conflict with institutional values? And what kinds of institutional changes might be required of universities that want to serve this constituency?

FORCES BEHIND THE NEED TO RETHINK POSTBACCALAUREATE LEARNING

Aging of the Workforce

The aging of the American workforce, plus the increasing technological component of most jobs, is serving to make employee education a priority. Baby boomers (individuals born between 1946 and 1964) will account for nearly half of the workforce in the year 2000. Because of its sheer size, the baby boom generation will still be a significant cohort in the workforce in 2010. Thus, remaining competitive in a knowledge economy will require organizations to invest in retooling their existing workforce. Employers cannot rely on a sufficient infusion of younger workers to provide needed new skills and knowledge. This represents a marked change. In 1976, individuals between the ages of 16 and 34 accounted for fully half of the U.S. civilian labor force; by 2006, this younger age cohort will be eclipsed by the 35- to 64-year-old age cohort, which will account for 63 percent of the labor force.[5] (See Table 1.)

TABLE 1

CIVILIAN LABOR FORCE, 1976, 1986, 1996, AND PROJECTED 2006

Age Group	Percent Distribution			
	1976	1986	1996	2006
16 to 24	24.3	19.8	15.8	16.4
25 to 34	25.2	29.4	25.3	20.7
35 to 44	18.0	23.1	27.3	23.8
45 to 54	17.7	15.1	19.7	23.6
55 to 64	11.9	10.1	9.1	12.6
65 to 74	2.6	2.2	2.4	2.2
75 and over	0.4	0.4	0.5	0.6
Total 16 years and over	100.1	100.1	100.1	99.9

Source: BLS, Department of Labor, Monthly Labor Review, November 1997.

Changing Occupational Mix

At the same time that the workforce is aging, the entire structure of the U.S. economy is undergoing profound and rapid transformation. The occupational mix in the United States changed dramatically between 1969 and 1995. Office jobs replaced most of the jobs lost in the production or distribution of goods.[6] Knowledge jobs—those held by managers, professionals, and technicians—accounted for 31 percent of all employment in the United States by 1993; they are expected to account for a third of all jobs by 2006.[7]

At the end of the 1990s, digital networks began to rapidly change the way organizations communicated with one another and distributed their products to the public. Business-to-business Internet commerce was projected to reach more than $800 billion annually in 2002,[8] and e-commerce (retail sales) on the Internet was projected to increase from approximately $8 billion in 1998 to between $35 billion and $75 billion by 2002.[9]

Job "Churning"

The need for individuals to continually update their knowledge and acquire new skills is further precipitated by a phenomenon known as job "churning." It is estimated that one-third of all jobs are in flux each year, meaning that they have recently been created or soon will be eliminated from the economy.[10] This "churning" is destabilizing for individuals, even in a robust economy. Career ladders within organizations are disappearing. The nature of the employment market is such that few college graduates can expect to stay with a single employer for an entire career, and most can anticipate a succession of careers with different employers. In this fluid economy, individuals are placed in the position of having to assume responsibility for developing their own learning plans—a task for which many feel unprepared.[11]

New Competencies for the Twenty-first Century

Professionals in fields such as law, medicine, pharmacy, engineering, education, and accounting pursue continuing education at regular intervals not only to maintain licensure or certification, but also because they must adapt their skills to massive changes in their professions' organization and structure. Therefore, the dilemma confronting many professionals is that the pressure to learn is increasing at the very same time that their workload also seems to be expanding.

The shift in the United States from a largely private to a managed care health care system has made it essential for practitioners to acquire new learning. The 1998 Pew Health Professions Commission called for reinventing the regulatory system "to ensure the highest level of practice from professionals". . . which "will mean learning new skills and practicing in new ways."[12] Health professional schools "must lead the effort to realign training and education to be more consistent with changing needs of the care delivery system."[13]

Improving the quality of the teacher corps is another national priority. Comparative international test scores consistently show U.S. high school students lagging well behind their peers in other advanced countries in subjects critical for a knowledge economy, such as math and science.[14] Anticipated teacher shortages due to retirements, reductions in class size, and increased enrollments have further compounded K-12 school quality concerns. In 1999, the U.S. Department of Education projected that the country would need two million new teachers by 2010. The fact that the high school-aged population is growing fastest poses a critical need for teachers with both content and pedagogical knowledge.

One strategy for helping address a teacher shortage is to encourage early retirees and liberal arts graduates to enroll in alternative certification programs. Such university programs may be full or part time but redesigned specifically to prepare college graduates to meet state teacher certification requirements. When the demand for teachers is great, as it is in California, many districts resort to hiring teachers without full certification. This led California State University to launch CalStateTEACH in 1999. This 18-month program provides "emergency permit" elementary school teachers with a bachelor's degree the opportunity to earn full certification by completing an integrated site-based curriculum. Patterned after a successful British Open University program, CalStateTEACH combines personal coaching with online support and self-study.[15]

School districts are not simply having to recruit more teachers, but they also are asking teachers to learn new methods of teaching and to integrate educational technology into their classrooms. As of 1999, three-quarters of the states had established student standards for technology. The issuing of such standards derives from policy makers' recognition that their states cannot attract the better paid "knowledge worker jobs" absent a workforce prepared to function in a digital environment. Tennessee Governor Don Sundquist expressed the sentiments of many of his fellow governors when he said, "We, as governors, cannot fail to have every child participating in the information age. If we fail, we set our workforce and industry back. If we succeed, we assure that jobs are retained in every community and our children have a bright, prosperous future."[16]

The rapid pace of technological change, combined with the high turnover of information technology (IT) professionals and increased reliance on technology throughout organizations, means that employers have needed to invest increasing amounts of money in education and training. Institutions such as Boston University's Metropolitan College deliver their graduate-level computer science certificate and degree programs to IT professionals in traditional classroom settings at the work site, as well as online.[17] Employers go to considerable lengths to secure IT professionals. This includes supporting training, offering bonuses to new IT hires, and lobbying to expand the number of immigrant visas issued to foreign nationals in computer professions. Notwithstanding these incentives, more than 350,000 information technology jobs were unfilled in 1998, for want of qualified workers.[18]

In coming years, the demand for workers with a baccalaureate or higher degree is expected to increase as a result of technological advances and employers' eagerness to increase productivity. According to Merrill Lynch, "Motorola calculates that every $1 it spends on training translates to $30 in productivity gains within three years."[19] The National Center on the Educational Quality of the Workforce found that a 10 percent increase in the average education of all workers within an establishment is associated with an 8.6 percent increase in productivity."[20] (See Figure 1, p. 15.)

Of the 25 job categories which are growing fastest and which are projected to have the highest earnings in 2006, nearly all require at least a baccalaureate degree.[21] (See Figure 2, p. 16.) Many require practitioners to pursue continuing education on a regular basis to maintain competency or licensure. As corporations shift their focus to human (as opposed to financial and physical) capital, they can be expected not only to invest more in their workers' education but also to demand more of their employees.

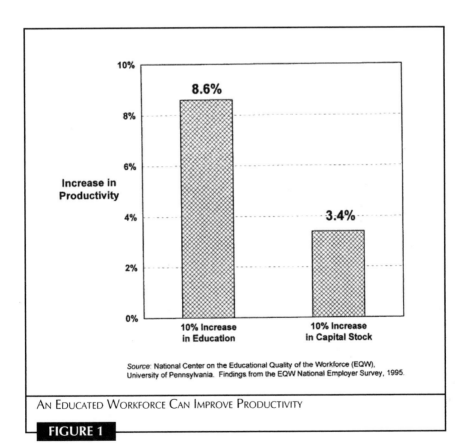

Source: National Center on the Educational Quality of the Workforce (EQW), University of Pennsylvania. Findings from the EQW National Employer Survey, 1995.

AN EDUCATED WORKFORCE CAN IMPROVE PRODUCTIVITY

FIGURE 1

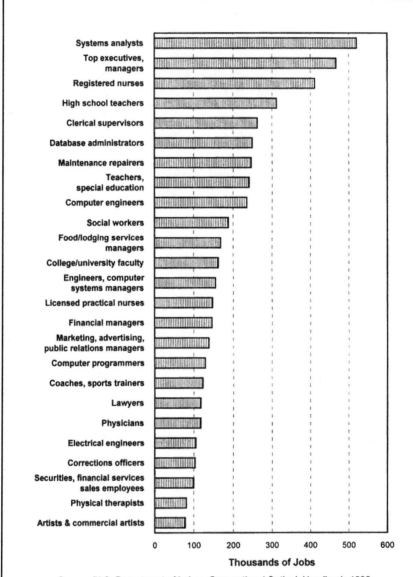

Source: BLS, Department of Labor, *Occupational Outlook Handbook*, 1998.

OCCUPATIONS WITH FAST GROWTH, HIGH PAY, AND LOW UNEMPLOYMENT THAT HAVE THE LARGEST NUMERICAL GROWTH, PROJECTED 1996–2006.

FIGURE 2

DEMOGRAPHICS OF POSTBACCALAUREATE DEMAND

"Non-Classified" Students

It is difficult to determine just how many postbaccalaureate learners are being served by higher education institutions. The annual postsecondary surveys conducted by the U.S. Department of Education focus on students matriculated in degree programs. Moreover, the data combine students enrolled in postbaccalauareate degree programs with those in certificate programs. Thus, it is impossible to learn what proportion of the enrollments are in postbaccalaureate certificate programs and what proportion are in degree programs. Nor is it possible to make the linkage between the age of the postbaccalaureate student and the type of program in which he or she is enrolled. Students who are enrolled in university-sponsored programs that are not credit bearing are not counted at all in official government statistics. Consequently, there is no way to ascertain who is doing what at the postbaccalaureate level. The paucity of data enables university leaders and legislators to more easily avoid coming to terms with the policy implications of the rising demand for postbaccalaureate learning opportunities.

The National Household Education Survey, sponsored by the U.S. Department of Education, is the one study which begins to shed some light on the dimensions of the postbaccalaureate population. In 1995, it revealed that 39 percent of employed college graduates had participated in at least one work-related course during the past year.[22] Those with a college degree were found to be twice as likely as persons with only a high school diploma to pursue work-related education.

Educational Attainment Levels

With more jobs requiring at least a college degree, educational attainment levels in the United States have climbed rapidly in recent decades. In 1970, 12 million Americans had graduated from college; by 1998, that number had reached 30 million. Baby Boomers, as a cohort, have high levels of educational attainment. In 1998, 28 percent had earned at least a bachelor's degree.[23]

A bachelor's degree has become a screening device for many employers. A master's degree is often viewed as a way to distinguish one's self from other job applicants and perhaps to qualify for a higher salary. Even those just entering college anticipate that they will need to earn credentials beyond a bachelor's degree. A 1998 national survey of American college freshmen revealed that 39 percent plan to earn at least a master's degree, and another 26 percent expect to earn a professional or doctoral degree.[24]

The knowledge economy has accentuated the relationship between education and job earnings. Simply stated, those with the most education generally get the best paying jobs.[25] Pay for college-educated workers increased 10 percent in the United States between 1979 and 1995, even as the job opportunities and average earnings of those with less than a college education decreased.[26] What is striking is that the pay gains of college-educated labor occurred at the very time that the supply of college graduates was increasing.

Increased Labor Force Participation by Women

By 1998, slightly more women than men in the United States between the ages of 20 and 64 years old held at least a baccalaureate degree.[27] With the rise of women's educational levels and with more people establishing themselves in the workforce prior to having families, societal norms have shifted. "Working for pay or profit . . . is now an integral part of many women's lives, much as full-time homemaking was for women in previous generations."[28]

Having young children has not slowed the upward trend in women's labor force participation. In 1996, some 77 percent of U.S. women with children between 6 and 17 years of age were in the workforce, compared to only 55 percent in 1975. Moreover, the workforce participation rate of women with children less than 6 years of age increased from 39 percent in 1975 to 62 percent in 1996.[29] Economics remains perhaps the most important reason for women's increased participation in the workforce. Many U.S. families have found it increasingly difficult to maintain the standard of living to which they aspire without two incomes. Also, more U.S. households with children under 18 years of age are headed by women (27 percent in 1997,[30] compared with 10 percent in 1970).[31]

As women have assumed increasing financial responsibility for their families, they have pursued more postbaccalaureate education. By 2007, graduate and professional degree enrollments are projected to reach 2.1 million.[32] This represents an almost 22 percent increase within the space of just 20 years. Much of this growth can be traced to the fact that women are enrolling in graduate and professional programs in ever greater numbers. By 1999, women represented the majority (56 percent) of master's degree students. Today's "typical" graduate student is female, in her thirties, married with dependents, and takes classes on a part-time basis while also holding a full-time job.

Women's overall labor force participation rates are projected to continue to rise after 2000, albeit at a slower rate than in the 1980s and 1990s. At the same time, the composition of the entire American labor force will become ever more diverse, ethnically and racially, in coming decades.

Minority Participation

Postbaccalaureate education participation rates differ markedly among minority groups. Asians boast the largest proportion of college graduates and the highest participation rate in university postbaccalaureate education. Some 42 percent of Asians in the United States age 25 or older had completed a bachelor's or higher degree in 1997, compared with 25 percent of whites and 13 percent of blacks.[33] Among whites and Hispanics, more men than women held professional and master's degrees in 1998; among blacks, women held 64 percent of master's and professional degrees.

NATURE OF THE NEW POSTBACCALAUREATE DEMAND

The demand for postbaccalaureate educational opportunities is growing both because people need continuous learning to stay occupationally relevant and because the population interested in self-enrichment learning activities has mushroomed. Yet the priorities of postbaccalaureate education consumers are not easily accommodated by traditional university programs.

Convenience

Convenience ranks very high with postbaccalaureate students. For most, education is only one of the things they do; it is not the focus of their lives. Many already have demanding work schedules. According to a 1997 Bureau of Labor Statistics study, the number of employees working at least 49 hours a week increased from 13 percent in 1976 to 18.5 percent in 1993.[34] Professionals and managers, as well as those in sales and transportation, were among those working longer hours. Family responsibilities and long commutes contribute to the "time famine" many people feel. In this context, convenience often prevails over cost and institutional reputation when it comes to choosing among alternative learning opportunities.

To say that postbaccalaureate students value convenience in no way implies that they would necessarily choose electronic instruction over a nearby satellite campus offering face-to-face classroom instruction. Most students say that they prefer a traditional face-to-face class over online learning, and thus far, enrollments support this. Still, technology is expanding higher education's reach and is challenging basic assumptions about what curricular structures best promote learning.

The largest consumers of postbaccalaureate education are also those most likely to have Internet access—namely, the baby boomers (54 percent) and Generation X (35 percent).[35] As their familiarity with the potential of asynchronous Internet learning increases, they may be expected to seek out institutions that rely less on a passive lecture format and focus more effort on the creation of interactive and collaborative learning experiences. Universities aiming to capture this market are using their Internet sites not only to advertise their courses but also to develop relationships with prospective students who provide valuable information about what kinds of courses, services, and credentials they are seeking. Adapting to the Internet implies much more than delivering instruction and student services in new ways; it requires that universities adopt a new system mindset.

Modularization

Employers have helped push the modularization of curricula. They have called for "just-in-time" learning packaged in smaller segments than degrees. The postbaccalaureate certificate programs that have enjoyed a recent surge of popularity respond to these criteria. Such programs offer a sequenced, integrated program of study in a narrow specialty area that often culminates in a performance-based credential.

Besides providing learning in convenient-sized blocks, certificate modules can be readily aligned with industry interests and professions' needs. The Boeing Company has developed a network of universities to deliver postbaccalaureate certificate programs to engineers at the work site. The programs consist of select courses carved out of existing master's degree programs. The opportunity to apply credits toward a master's degree at the participating institutions greatly enhances the programs' appeal to Boeing employees.

Many individuals already have at least one postbaccalaureate degree but realize that they need to continuously acquire new learning to remain competitive in the job market. Earning a postbaccalaureate certificate requires a smaller investment of time and money than a degree. Postbaccalaureate curricula frequently are cutting edge, adapted to the requirements of emerging professions. Successful completion of a multicourse certificate program from UCLA, San Francisco State University, or New York University in fields such as electronic commerce or digital design[36] involves acquiring specialized skills as well as an understanding of the theory and applications relative to the latest technologies. These certificate programs prepare students for immediate entry into new career areas and the credentials are widely recognized by employers. Sometimes, an employer will pay the tuition for a certificate program; the further up the career ladder an employee is, the more likely that will be the case.

The most educated employees tend to receive the most employer support for educational activities. Nearly 90 percent of employees with a bachelor's or higher degree were the beneficiaries of formal employer-provided training, compared to 68 percent of those with some college and 60 percent of those who had a high school education or less.[37] These figures confirm that many students in university-based postbaccalaureate executive, master's, and certificate programs are accustomed to their employers' supplying tuition monies.

What these figures do not reveal is who pays for the education of employees who do not receive educational benefits. The most rapid job growth is taking place in small and medium-size firms, many of which do not offer educational benefits. Individuals who need to prepare for entirely new careers often have no choice but to rely on their own resources. It is this situation that prompted Sallie Mae, one of the oldest providers of student loans, to inaugurate a new professional education loan program in 1999. Sallie Mae's program targets the part-time "nontraditional" student borrower who may need a loan to purchase a computer or to pay tuition fees. The decision to inaugurate the program was based on an assessment that increasing numbers of individuals will find it necessary to build on their current knowledge to remain employable and that they will need to make a personal investment to do so.

Employers Embrace Digital Learning

How corporations approach employee education is being transformed still further by information technology. Eliminating the necessity of synchronism makes it possible to deliver course content without requiring that an employee sit in a classroom either at the work site or on a college campus. Reducing time away from the job means potential cost savings for employers. By 2001, more than half of all employer-provided education and training is likely to be delivered electronically.[38]

Universities currently claim a relatively small proportion of corporate education and training dollars. A shift to online education means that higher education institutions aspiring to serve the corporate postbaccalaureate market can no longer be wedded to real-time teaching. Prominent schools of business, such as those at the University of Florida, Ohio University, and Duke University, now offer online executive M.B.A. programs. Though much of the learning is technology mediated, each of these programs also has a residential component, and none is inexpensive. They are geared to the full-time professional, who in most cases can count on tuition being paid by his or her employer.

California State University (CSU) at Chico and Telcordia Technologies (formerly Bellcore) jointly developed a Telecommunications Master of Science degree program designed to help telecommunications professionals keep pace with rapid change and the convergence of technologies. Students learn through live, satellite, and Internet classes provided by Chico and combined with Telcordia labs and seminars. Master's degree projects are overseen by CSU, Chico, faculty. Those who complete the program can expect to enhance not only their skills but also their career prospects.

Often, corporate clients will not buy pre-designed programs. They want universities to customize postbaccalaureate programs for their employees. Content is readily available from multiple sources. In 1999, the University of Georgia and PricewaterhouseCoopers together developed a customized M.B.A. program for the accounting firm's technical professionals.[39] The curriculum includes advanced information technology courses, business case studies drawn from PricewaterhouseCoopers archives, and instruction, which involves a mix of approaches, including on-campus classroom, workplace team learning, and distance education.

Some experts argue that traditional universities add value to distance learning programs by "packaging and delivering content to meet the needs of specific groups of individuals."[40] It is foreseen that "program structure will no longer be determined by content-based disciplines, but will instead be determined by the characteristics and needs of the target population."[41] This perspective implies a departure from traditional academic values, which assume that faculty have complete responsibility for determining a program's organization and content.

In an attempt to avoid possible conflict with faculty, some universities have restricted their partnerships with the for-profit sector to non-credit curricula. But if a university expects to realize substantial earnings from the sale of non-credit postbaccalaureate-level professional courses through a for-profit entity, it may be disappointed to learn that for-credit programs are what consumers want most. However, delivering credit programs to a broad audience beyond the campus makes everything more problematic. An institution will need first to resolve difficult intellectual property issues with its faculty, as well as non-disclosure issues with its private sector partner. It also will need to develop an efficient, round-the-clock student services infrastructure.

Competitive Environment

The expanding population of adults with college degrees, coupled with the availability of new technologies, has attracted increasing numbers of new competitors to the postbaccalaureate market. Private sector providers such as University of Phoenix, Walden University, and Jones International University are now competing with traditional U.S. universities in the delivery of postbaccalaureate education to both corporate and individual consumers. In the 1990s, many nonprofit museums began to redirect their missions from a collections focus to an education focus and used the Internet to acquaint new audiences with their research and resources.[42] The establishment in 1999 of the Open University of the United States forced U.S. universities to confront the prospect of increased competition from international universities on their own turf. Together, these developments highlight the erosion of traditional universities' credentialling monopoly. They also point to a still more significant change—namely, that the educated American public now relies on multiple sources for new knowledge, and the traditional university is but one such source. What has emerged is a great variety of institutions competing to respond to diverse postbaccalaureate learning needs. And in the coming years, the products of these knowledge-producing institutions are apt to look more and more alike.

Historically, liberal arts education has been an important domain of universities. Yet fewer and fewer students are enrolled in liberal arts curricula, perhaps because they are assuming more responsibility for paying for their undergraduate education. Some 37 percent of those who graduate from college today have majored in business, education, engineering, or information sciences. This may not indicate a diminishing interest in the liberal arts so much as a reordering of the sequence of students' university studies. It may be common for future generations to complete a work-related curriculum as undergraduates and then to pursue humanities, arts, and sciences education as postbaccalaureate learners. Certainly, the new business environment places a high value on creativity and the ability to integrate multiple disciplines—talents that tend to be fostered by a liberal arts curriculum.

By 2020, most individuals in the workforce will need to prepare themselves for as many as seven or eight careers. Liberal arts education has the potential to stretch people's minds and extricate them from their parochialism. In arguing for a common core of learning, Todd Gitlin observes, "We badly need continuities to counteract vertigo as we shift identities, careen through careers and cultural changes."[43] Several universities currently offer fine master's of liberal studies degree programs. Yet the imperative to realize revenues from such postbaccalaureate programs frequently has had the effect of discouraging their further development.

Interestingly, the opportunities offered by the Internet may prompt some universities to reevaluate their previous positions and to invest in reconfiguring their postbaccalaureate programs in the humanities, arts, and sciences. Technology has eliminated many of the barriers that previously separated higher education institutions from their far-flung alumni and the public at large. Traditional universities have an opportunity to become prominent providers of postbaccalaureate liberal arts education. Higher education institutions have formidable for-profit competitors, but the public is favorably disposed to obtaining such education from a nonprofit university or museum. An institution's success will depend on its ability to develop a unique identity and to deliver high-quality Internet-based programs. In a higher education market which is becoming increasingly branded and competitive, some universities may decide that their advantage lies in concentrating on the niche markets where they can add significant value.[44]

Meanwhile, other cultural institutions have recognized that potential benefits are to be gained from creating educational offerings for this much more highly educated public. Museums, scientific societies, botanical gardens, public libraries, and performing arts organizations have discovered that sponsoring education programs and developing Web sites can win them important support. City governments, too, have come to see a role for the arts in revitalizing communities and attracting tourism.

ADVANCING INSTITUTIONAL VALUES WITH POSTBACCALAUREATE EDUCATION

Enhanced Curricula

The job churning occurring in today's economy means that traditional university programs in a single discipline often do not respond to the needs of postbaccalaureate learners. Practitioners quickly discover—whether they work in health care, law enforcement, the arts, or another field—that they require knowledge and skills outside their primary disciplines. An interdisciplinary vision is one attribute of some of the best university postbaccalaureate programs. Very often, such programs are developed by faculty in collaboration with relevant employers. For example, a University of Denver master's degree program in environmental policy and management combines courses in science, law, economics, management and applied communications. A museum studies certificate offered by Tufts University uses faculty from the departments of art history, history, and education; a program evaluation certificate integrates courses from the departments of child development, urban and environmental policy, the School of Nutrition Science and Policy, and the School of Medicine. The Pew Commission report recommends requiring "interdisciplinary competence in all health professionals."[45]

Many university leaders advocate elimination of the walls that separate university departments. Traditional budgetary policies often undermine such efforts. For that reason, a potential role of interdisciplinary postbaccalaureate programs is to assist an institution in the development of new working models for interdepartmental cooperation.

Another aspect of many postbaccalaureate programs is an emphasis on performance outcomes. Employers who underwrite much of their employees' postbaccalaureate education want evidence that their investment is making a difference. Practitioners eager to meet licensing or certification requirements seek assurance that the education they pursue will qualify them for their jobs. This is an area of potential conflict if faculty conclude that their right to determine the components of a credentialled university postbaccalaureate program has been appropriated by an employer or professional body.

University/Industry Cooperation

As the lines between the nonprofit and for-profit sectors blur, an ongoing dilemma for universities is deciding when it is beneficial to collaborate with outside organizations and when doing so may compromise their independence.

One advantage of designing education programs for an industry is the exposure it provides university faculty to state-of-the-art practice. The insights gained from such experiences help faculty update existing university courses, with the result that students at all levels benefit.

Another byproduct of providing postbaccalaureate education and training to industry is that it can strengthen a university's relationship with an important corporate research sponsor. Given the unstable nature of federal government funding, universities are actively seeking to diversify their sources of research monies. Indeed, much of universities' prestige tends to be bound up in their capacity to establish a stable funding base.[46] Having such a base has become essential to attracting top faculty and graduate students.

In 1992, United Technologies Corporation (UTC) forged a partnership with Rensselaer Polytechnic Institute to provide education and training to its employees. What emerged was a virtual corporate university, Rensselaer Learning Institute (RLI), which contracts with higher education institutions to deliver courses and degree programs to UTC employees. In 1999, RLI had contracts with some 40 colleges and universities and offered two undergraduate and eight master's degree programs in business and engineering fields. Courses are delivered to UTC employees at their work sites either electronically or in a traditional classroom setting. The incentives for pursuing education at UTC are significant, with the company not only paying tuition but also awarding UTC stock to any employee who completes a degree.

When RLI first began operations, it relied primarily on face-to-face classroom instruction. Since then, its focus has shifted toward asynchronous technology-mediated instruction and to adapting courses to individual learning styles. RLI's goals are to reduce learning transfer time and to increase knowledge retention. RLI also anticipates that as high-quality distance education products are developed, other corporations will become interested in purchasing its services. Together, these efforts are seen as further enhancing the return on UTC's investment in education.

Maximizing Scarce Resources

Partnering with other institutions is one way universities can be more responsive to postbaccalaureate learning demands. Such partnerships can be a vehicle for overcoming state residency and tuition requirements while simultaneously offering important cost savings and quality enhancements.[47]

The Mountain and Plains Partnership (MAPP) was created to assist working health care professionals in underserved urban and rural areas develop the skills needed to assume expanded primary care clinical roles. The program targets nurse practitioners, certified-nurse midwives, and physician assistants who would not be able to complete a campus-based program. MAPP employs interactive video, the Internet, and online library resources to deliver courses to students in Colorado, Wyoming, and the border states. Faculty from the eight partner institutions review the MAPP Online Common Curriculum for quality and compatibility. A key component of the MAPP curriculum involves preparing health care practitioners to meet their state's licensing requirements for writing prescriptions, as they may be the only ones in their community with the authority to do so.

In Arizona, individuals seeking a master's degree in public health can choose from the three state universities' relevant course offerings. Instruction is available in traditional classroom settings as well as via the state's ITFS network. Although the University of Arizona, Arizona State University, and Northern Arizona University all contribute courses, the University of Arizona awards the degree. By agreeing that only one public university in a state will award a given degree, but that courses from other universities will be accepted toward a degree, Arizona's higher education institutions are able to offer health care professionals convenient access to postbaccalaureate education and to maximize the use of scarce university resources.

Developing strategic partnerships with private sector companies can enable universities to minimize many of the risks and costs associated with the creation of a new postbaccalaureate program. But reconciling the values of traditional public universities with those of private sector companies can be challenging. A National Science Foundation grant launched the Joint Arizona Consortium—Manufacturing and Engineering Education for Tomorrow (JACME2T) in 1994. This cooperative venture involved Arizona University, the University of Arizona, Northern Arizona University, Motorola, IBM, McDonnell Douglas (now Boeing), Intel, Hughes (now Raytheon), and AlliedSignal (now Honeywell). Together, the group created a university/industry coordinating structure charged with assessing knowledge and skills needs and creating appropriate learning "products" for manufacturing engineers and managers. The collaboration has yielded many programs, including an engineering master's degree offered by the three universities through a variety of media and a number of postbaccalaureate certificate programs.

Economic Development

States, too, are rethinking their economic development strategies. Instead of chasing new industry with tax breaks, a number of states are focusing on fostering education, entrepreneurship, specialized skills, and technological innovation.[48] The underlying assumption is that those states with a high-quality workforce will be the most likely to attract good jobs and to realize growth across all income groups.

Rather than building new institutions, states such as Illinois, Michigan, Ohio, and Texas are focusing on the development of locally governed university centers served by both public and private institutions in the state. These centers typically are located in "edge cities" near metropolitan areas, where there often is a concentration of affluent, college-educated adults employed in knowledge industries.

In 1999, market research persuaded the Illinois State Board of Higher Education to approve establishment of a university center in a suburb north of Chicago that had experienced significant population growth and that was a 45-minute drive from the nearest public college. The research revealed that potential consumers preferred evening courses that met no more frequently than twice weekly and which were within a half hour's commute. Interest in upper-division and graduate level courses was high. Two-thirds of those surveyed indicated that they would be comfortable taking a course via the Internet.[49]

With three-quarters of the American population now living in metropolitan areas and with many public universities located in small communities, sought-after higher education resources are frequently out of reach. This is both a political and economic issue for universities. Increasingly, institutions need to be perceived as responsive to the education needs of postbaccalaureate learners in the labor force if they are to retain public support.

Strategic Decision Making

Universities' preoccupation with traditional college-age students, coupled with their typically fragmented organizational structure, often makes it difficult to focus attention on the learning demands of postbaccalaureate students. To begin with, it takes commitment from an institution's top leadership. But establishing broad-based support requires much more. There has to be an effort to provide decision makers throughout the university with a common understanding of the needs of postbaccalaureate learners and why these are interrelated with the institution's more traditional roles. It helps to involve regional economists, demographers, and technology experts who can offer compelling data on the environmental forces that underlie the expanded demand for learning.

The familiar Strengths, Weaknesses, Opportunities, Threats (SWOT) analysis is used widely to promote strategic thinking by university decision makers. It's possible to imagine a discussion evoked by the SWOT process being very cost effective if a careful assessment of the investment required and of existing competition were to result in a decision to forego launching yet another online M.B.A. degree. Rich SWOT discussions can help participants identify institutional strengths and potential collaborative opportunities. When this kind of information is combined with an understanding of the market structure, an institution should have an improved chance of identifying program areas with strong appeal to postbaccalaureate learners. Still, creating a new program of high quality—even in an area of purported strength— usually will require that the institution provide sustaining support at the outset. This implies multi-year planning and the willingness to invest, alone or with a partner institution, in programs that may not have an immediate return but which are judged to position the institution importantly for the future. Much of the hesitancy in institutions stems from the recognition that this could require the reallocation of scarce resources to new program areas where predictability, control, and constituencies are uncertain.

CONCLUSION

With the knowledge-based economy intensifying the demand for postbaccalaureate education, traditional universities are being compelled to decide how and to what extent they will respond. Much of the demand necessarily relates to new workforce needs. However, the current higher education system is not structured to accommodate the needs of a lifelong learning society. Universities are important providers of executive education and vocational master's degree programs—often lucrative endeavors. Yet it is postbaccalaureate certificate programs that evidence job-related competence and online courses tailored to changing workforce needs that are increasingly in demand.

Universities are potentially well positioned to respond to an expanding population of college graduates' interest in high-quality cultural and arts programming. But few have done so. Universities have been slow to conceptualize—much less articulate—what role they plan to assume in the postbaccalaureate arena.

Meanwhile, other education providers have taken note of the growing demand for postbaccalaureate learning opportunities. This demand, together with the availability of new information technologies, has attracted a host of new competitors into the higher education market. Partnerships between universities and private sector providers and the creation of new for-profit university-sponsored ventures are further blurring the lines between the private and the public sectors. In a very real sense, the postbaccalaureate learning imperative is compelling traditional universities to reexamine their entire system in the context of the emerging knowledge economy. What functions does the university serve? Whom does it educate? How does it convey knowledge? And who pays?

NOTES

1. Clark Kerr, "Expanding Access and Changing Missions: The Federal Role in U.S. Higher Education," *Educational Record*, 75, 4 (Fall 1994): 27-31.
2. Thorstein Veblen, *Higher Learning in America*. New Brunswick, NJ: Transaction Publishers, 1993, p. 140.
3. Ibid., p. 150.

4. Robert D. Atkinson, Randolph H. Court, and Joseph M. Ward. *The State New Economy Index: Benchmarking Economic Transformation in the States.* Washington, DC: Progressive Policy Institute Technology & New Economy Project, July 1999, p. 3.
5. American Outlook, Hudson Institute, Fall 1998, p. 31.
6. Robert D. Atkinson and Randolph H. Court, *The New Economy Index: Understanding America's Economic Transformation.* Washington, DC: Progressive Policy Institute, 1998.
7. Atkinson, Court, and Ward, *The State New Economy Index,* p. 16.
8. "Keeping Track of E-Commerce," *The New York Times,* 22 September 1999: 58.
9. "E-Commerce: Virtually Here," Merrill Lynch & Co., April 1999, p. 2.
10. Atkinson, Court, and Ward, *The State New Economy Index,* p. 4.
11. New York University's School of Continuing and Professional Studies learned from exchanges with students visiting its Internet site that continuing education students were looking to universities to provide vastly expanded career advising services.
12. E.H. O'Neil and the Pew Health Professions Commission, *Recreating Health Professional Practice for a New Century.* San Francisco: Pew Health Professions Commission, 1998, p. 1.
13. Ibid., p. ii.
14. The "Third International Mathematics and Science Study" compares the 1995 test scores of twelfth graders in selected economically developed countries. The study reveals that students from the United States ranked nineteenth in math tests and sixteenth in science tests—below the international average in both instances. Washington, DC: National Science Foundation, 1998.
15. http://www.calstate.edu/tier3/Executive/TeacherEd.html
16. *American Education at a Crossroads.* Washington, DC: National Governors Association, 1999.
17. For several years, Boston University has been delivering graduate certificate and degree programs in computer science to IT professionals on site at Liberty Mutual Company in southern New Hampshire and at the Foxboro Company in Massachusetts.
18. *American Education at a Crossroads.* Washington, DC: National Governors Association, 1999.
19. Merrill Lynch & Co., *The Book of Knowledge—Investing in the Growing Education and Training Industry,* April 1999, p. 126.
20. Ibid.
21. Bureau of Labor Statistics, U.S. Department of Labor, *Occupational Outlook Handbook, 1998-99 Edition,* Bulletin 2500, p. 4
22. U.S. Department of Education, Office of Educational Research and Improvement, NCES 98-309, October 1998.
23. U.S. Bureau of the Census, Education and Social Stratification Branch. *Educational Attainment in the United States: March 1998 (Update).* Detailed tables and documentation for P20-513. PPL-99, November 1998, pp. 1-5.
24. Linda J. Sax, Alexander W. Astin, William S. Korn, Kathryn M. Mahoney, *The American Freshman: National Norms for Fall 1998,* Cooperative Institutional Research Program, American Council on Education and University of California, Los Angeles, p. 18.
25. Anthony P. Carnevale and Stephen J. Rose, *Education for What? The New Office Economy.* Princeton, NJ: Educational Testing Service, 1998, pp. 22-23.
26. Ibid.

27. As of March 1998, 51 percent of women and 49 percent of men in the United States between the ages of 20 and 64 years had earned a bachelor's degree.
28. Howard V. Hayghe, "Developments in Women's Labor Force Participation," *Monthly Labor Review,* September 1997, p. 43.
29. Ibid., p. 42.
30. Bureau of the Census, U.S. Department of Commerce, *1998 Statistical Abstract of the United States, 118th Edition.* Washington, DC: 1998, p. 65.
31. Bureau of the Census, U.S. Department of Commerce, *1990 Statistical Abstract of the United States, 110th Edition.* Washington, DC: 1990, p. 51.
32. U.S. Department of Education, Office of Educational Research and Improvement, *Projections of Education Statistics to 2007,* NCES 97-382, pp. 40-43.
33. U.S. Department of Commerce, Bureau of the Census, Current Population Reports, "Educational Attainment in the United States: March 1997," by Jennifer Day and Andrea Curry (P20-505).
34. Phillip L. Rones, Randy E. Ilg, and Jennifer M. Gardner, "Trends in Hours of Work since the Mid-1970s," *Monthly Labor Review* (April 1997): 10.
35. http:://cyberatlas.internet.com
36. UCLA Extension, San Francisco State Extended Education, and New York University School of Continuing & Professional Education all offer a variety of certificate programs in multimedia studies.
37. Harley Frazis, Maury Gittleman, Michael Horrigan, and Mary Joyce, "Results from the 1995 Survey of Employer-Provided Training," *Monthly Labor Review,* 121, 6 (June 1998): 3-13.
38. James Van Erden, "How Training Is Delivered," National Alliance of Business Projections, Presentation at American Council on Education Annual Meeting, 16 February 1999.
39. http://www.informationweek.com/744/training.htm
40. Dewayne Matthews, "Transforming Higher Education: Implications for State Higher Education Finance Policy," *Educom Review* (September/October 1998): 3.
41. Ibid.
42. Stephen E. Weil, "From Being about Something to Being for Somebody: The Ongoing Transformation of the American Museum," *Daedalus* (Summer 1999): 229-58.
43. Todd Gitlin, "The Liberal Arts in an Age of Info-Glut," *The Chronicle of Higher Education,* 1 May 1998: B4.
44. Chris Riley, "Will Colleges and Universities Become Brands?" *Planning for Higher Education,* 27 (Winter 1998-99) 13.
45. O'Neil and Pew Health Professions Commission, *Recreating Health Professional Practice for a New Century,* p. v.
46. Patricia J. Gumport, "Graduate Education and Research—Interdependence and Strain," in *American Higher Education in the Twenty-first Century—Social, Political, and Economic Challenges,* edited by Philip G. Altbach, Robert O. Berdahl, and Patricia J. Gumport. Baltimore: The Johns Hopkins University Press, 1999, p. 419.
47. Matthews, "Transforming Higher Education," p. 54.
48. Atkinson, Court, and Ward, *The State New Economy Index,* p. 36.
49. Peter Schmidt, "Illinois Considers a New Model for Providing Higher Education," *The Chronicle of Higher Education,* 29 January 1999: A40-A41.

CHAPTER

Investing in Learning Companies

Howard Marc Block

INTRODUCTION

T he motivation to invest in education companies is not unlike the motivation to invest in any business. Investment decisions ultimately should rest on the evaluation of certain investment characteristics, including risk, return, yield (interest or dividend), liquidity, and estimated growth. The relationship between the current value of a stock (what an investor should be willing to pay) is strongly tethered to expectations of its future value. Its future value, of course, is tied to its future earnings. And future earnings are forecast using an estimated growth rate for the company's earnings.

The relationship between current earnings, future earnings, and the estimated growth rate is often used by investors in setting the price that investors will pay today for the stock. Many investors are willing to pay a price equivalent to current earnings multiplied by the estimated growth rate. A key determinant, therefore, in determining the earnings multiple—the price you'll pay for a stock—is the company's growth rate. Forecasting the growth for the industry in which that company competes is somewhat less tenuous than forecasting growth for a specific company. Therefore, investors should consider the health and growth rate of an industry when determining the price they are willing to pay for the stock. This is as true of investments in higher

Howard Marc Block is a managing director, Banc of America Securities.

education and other learning companies as it is of individual investments in any of a number of options.

GROWTH DRIVERS FOR EDUCATION COMPANIES

One of the primary reasons that education stocks appeal to investors is the apparent health of the education industry. The landscape of learning has never looked more promising for companies in the business of education. The growth drivers in education include, but are not limited to, the following:

- *The increasing popularity of lifelong learning.* According to the 1995 National Household Education Survey, 76 million adults aged 16 and older participated in one or more adult education activities during the preceding year. That number—a 25 percent increase from just four years earlier—encompasses 40 percent of the adult population in the United States.
- *A projected decline in labor-force growth between 1999 and 2006.* Therefore, workers will need to learn more and to learn more often. They will need to adapt to the needs of a highly competitive global economy characterized by rapid technological change.
- *Shortening product cycles.* New products are being introduced and older products are becoming outdated at an increasingly rapid rate. Therefore, businesses must ensure that their customers and employees learn about more products and services more often.
- *Increasing product complexity.* The technological quotient of products and services supporting the economy has increased significantly, driving the need for more readily available "learning."
- *Increasing use of outsourcing.* Businesses are electing to outsource functions that are not their core competencies. Primary outsourcing candidates are staffing and employment services, information technology services, document management, facilities management, and all training and education-related functions.
- *Increasing economic dependence on human capital.* Such dependence encourages an aptitude for managing and productively employing human capital—a task incumbent on our learning systems.
- *Corporate encouragement of employee education.* Corporate America's encouragement, accommodation, and subsidy of employees' pursuit of higher education help corporations attract and retain employees.

These growth drivers—and likely many more—together support investors' inclination to consider education companies.

THE MARKET

Beyond the long list of growth drivers, investors are drawn to education companies for several market-related reasons.

Fragmented Market

Company growth may emerge not only as a result of overall market growth, but also as a result of market share consolidation. Even companies in shrinking markets can grow if they are able to steal share from their competitors. For this reason, investors are attracted to the fragmented nature of the education market, in which no single business has a dominant share.

Favorable Competitive Landscape

A more subtle reason for the appeal of the education industry is that most of the "competitors" are not very competitive. Although the market is fragmented, most of the providers are not-for-profits, which tend to operate under different business principles (if any) than for-profit entities.

For example, Apollo Group employs hundreds of professionals whose compensation is tied to their success in recruiting and retaining students. How many traditional higher education institutions do that? In addition, Apollo Group is sufficiently capitalized to enable aggressive media campaigns—again, unlike anything traditional higher education institutions have ever done.

Who wouldn't want to compete in a market where the "competition" is hardly competitive?

Formidable Barriers to Entry

Investors are drawn to businesses that compete in markets shielded by formidable barriers to entry. Higher education companies enjoy such protection. The barriers common to this market include capital requirements, cost disadvantages, incumbent reactions, economies of scale, customer switching costs, and government policy.

Government policy poses the most formidable barrier to wannabes and upstarts in higher education. Providers must secure state licensing (a daunting challenge in many states). Second, the provider must seek accreditation by either a national or regional body. Finally, the provider must pursue approval from the federal Department of Education to be eligible for Title IV aid.

The government policy burden is constant. For-profit higher education providers generally derive a substantial percentage of their revenues from federally sponsored tuition loan programs and thus are subject to extensive regulation by the Department of Education and the Office of the Inspector General. In general, these regulations govern the amount of revenue that can be derived from federal financial aid programs (90 percent), the financial strength of the company, student record keeping, and course program quality.

THE BUSINESS MODEL

Higher education businesses enjoy an enviable business model which serves as a magnet for most investors. The model is characterized by the following:

- *Recurring revenue* from "customers" who typically enroll for extended time periods; this also leads to increasing profitability. Serving students costs less money as the relationship matures because the up-front costs of marketing and admissions need not be incurred again.
- *Opportunities for operating leverage* created by a centralized, fixed cost structure and expanding profitability from the capacity to serve an increasing number of customers without incurring a burdensome level of variable costs.
- *Strong free cash flow* from steady tuition payments and broad operating margins, which supports debt-free growth and scalability through the opening of new campuses or learning centers.
- *Pricing protection* behind the aegis of traditional schools that enable higher education businesses to raise prices roughly 7 percent annually.
- An *acyclical nature,* for people will go to school in bad times to improve their standing in the lengthening labor queue and in good times supported by generous employer sponsorship or their own financial strength.

Predictability is a final characteristic for which investors will pay a premium. Investors have an easier time projecting what many education companies will earn over the next year than they would projecting the earnings of a restaurant chain, for example. The University of Virginia has a clearer vision than Taco Bell of how many customers it will have in six months.

Because of this "known" quantity, and because the school's tuition is also known, investors can forecast, with a reasonably high degree of accuracy, how much money the education provider will receive over the next year (number of enrollments times tuition per enrollment). And because historical costs are a good indicator of future costs, investors can also forecast with reasonable accuracy how much profit the school will generate.

Thus, to investors, the business looks predictable and "visible"—they can "see" the business's future and gauge its profitability. These characteristics reduce the uncertainty associated with the business, which in turn drives investors to favor the stocks and to assign a relatively high valuation.

A BUSINESS THAT MAKES SENSE

Presenting a solution before a compelling problem has been identified is premature and financially destructive. Thus, Apollo Group is a good investment value only if problems are to be solved.

Apollo Group (University of Phoenix [UOP]) built a business to meet the education needs of working adults. It thus is positioned as a key beneficiary of the first two growth drivers stated earlier: the increasing popularity of lifelong learning and the expectation that labor-force growth will slow between 1999 and 2006. Its recipe for success includes the following:

- *Convenient access of UOP learning sites.* Campuses and learning centers offer easy access to the freeway and sit in business corridors, thereby facilitating easy job-to-school transition. Alternative delivery is offered at many employer-provided facilities or by electronic media (online, fax, voice, video).
- *Manageable workload of UOP programs.* Students take one class at a time for six consecutive weeks, whereas most traditional institutions require concurrent enrollment in three to four classes. UOP helps students co-manage the demands of home, work, and study.
- *Convenient time of UOP classes.* Classes are offered in the evening (except for some weekend offerings), beginning at 6:00 PM and running until 10:00 PM.
- *Relevance of the UOP assignments.* UOP's outcome-based curricula are designed to build skills in an academic setting that will provide results in a business setting. Curricula are delivered by professionals who can draw from their own workplace experiences, offering exceptionally valuable points of reference to working adult learners who want to know how to apply their lessons now.

A more subtle ingredient in its recipe for success is *frequent enrollment periods.* Classes are offered almost daily throughout the year, and each class runs for five to seven weeks. This constant learning cycle is vital because it (1) engenders a permanence in the students' (working adults') schedules so that going to school is not viewed as seasonal, but constant ("I go to school once a week, every week, all year."); and (2) facilitates enrollment so that students need not wait long for the next semester.

This constant opportunity is critical because it mitigates the risk of losing fickle education consumers to changing sentiments. For example, if an education consumer decides today that she wants to go back to school, what happens if she just missed the October enrollment period and cannot enroll until January? (Would Starbucks risk asking a coffee drinker to come back for coffee in three months?)

All in all, Apollo Group appealed to investors because its business model seemed a logical, appealing alternative to the traditional university model that will not work with customers carrying the same objectives and learning proclivities as those served by the University of Phoenix. UOP is a unique education model. It masterfully blends the credibility of the academic world with the cost effectiveness of the business world.

VALUATION: HOW MUCH TO PAY

Valuation is at the core of any investment treatise. Decisions about capital allocation are based on valuation. Clearly, the decision is more complicated with a private company (where there is no "readily available market" for the investment) than with a public company (where the investment is priced to market daily). That is why private investments are considered riskier and why private investors expect a bigger return for their invested dollars.

Whether the company is public or private, investors often will defer to comparable companies—the "comp group"—to assist in valuation. The "comp group" methodology is not unlike that commonly used in real estate.

To compile a list of comparable public companies, an investor would consider the following questions, each of which has two parts:

- In what industry (or sub-sector of an industry) does the company operate? Which companies operate in that sector or sub-sector?
- What are the growth drivers for that sector? Which companies stand to benefit from those drivers?

If someone asked, "What is the appropriate comp group for Apollo Group?" the answer likely would result in a list of companies that included ITT Education, Education Management, and Strayer Education. All provide higher education and are publicly traded equities.

Yet there is tremendous variation in the valuation of the companies on that short list. For example, Strayer Education's stock (STRA) is trading at $23, a valuation of roughly 15 times its earnings estimates for 2000 ($1.55). Apollo's stock (APOL) is trading at $24, a valuation of roughly 24 times its earnings estimates for 2000 ($1.00). Why would investors be willing to pay 60 percent more (24 times versus 15 times) for Apollo as for Strayer if they are in the same industry, enjoying the same growth drivers, and sharing similar business models?

Several reasons for Apollo's premium valuation can be identified.

Reasons Related to the Business Model

- *Less reliance on Title IV revenue* than any members of its comp group. Many of the comparable companies enroll younger students who are less advanced in their careers and are more likely to default on loans. Furthermore, none matches Apollo's levels of employer tuition reimbursement for its students. Thus, Apollo's revenue stream has less risk exposure.

- *Easier scalability* than its peers because the minimal capital needed to open a learning center makes it less expensive for Apollo to gain market share.
- *More diverse product offerings* than its peers, as well as expanding Internet-enabled offerings, insulates Apollo from changes in the workplace.
- *High levels of geographic diversity* resulting from a presence in 31 states and more than 100 learning sites reduces Apollo's risk from competitive as well as localized economic pressures.
- Apollo has one of the *longest operating histories* as a public company, with nearly 20 reported quarters without a disappointment.

Reasons Related to the Stock

Market capitalization and liquidity usually go hand-in-hand because companies with large capitalization (shares outstanding times price/share) are by definition more liquid.

Investors prefer stocks that are liquid. (Liquidity refers to the trading volume in a stock; stocks that trade well offer some assurance to investors that they will be able to sell their position in a hurry without creating an imbalance in the market.) A prospective investor also may be drawn by liquidity because he or she can build a position in a stock without creating a similar imbalance that would drive the price upward.

WHY APOLLO'S STOCK HAS COME CRASHING BACK TO EARTH

Many investors value a stock based on the earnings expected next year. Therefore, any disappointment (i.e., performance below expectation) can lead to a severe "correction" in the valuation (i.e., selling pressure). The severity of the selling pressure is often determined by the build-up (momentum) in expectations prior to the disappointment. If momentum had been strong, then the sell-off will be stronger.

Some stock prices have a built-in expectation that the company will beat estimates and as a result, future estimates keep growing. Stocks with lots of momentum reflect the accumulation of investors who begin to expect a certain performance against estimates of that performance. A stock with a built-in expectation of *upside surprises* will be sold off sharply *if* the upside stops—even if the company performs within expectations.

The disappearance of upside surprises is the first of several reasons for the 1998–99 demise of Apollo's stock. Its demise also was attributable to the following:

- A Department of Education review of the company's administrative practices that was sensationalized by the media for several months until the review was finalized with minimal business impact on the company.
- The resignation of the Chief Financial Officer (CFO) in early 1998 and the subsequent lapse of 10 months until a new CFO was hired. (Investors are always spooked when a CFO resigns.)
- The company's overall profitability—in relative but not absolute terms—began to stabilize after uninterrupted profitability expansion during Apollo's first four years as a public company.
- Decelerating enrollment in Apollo's mature markets (Colorado and California) toward 15 to 18 percent, contrasted sharply with the more than 20 percent annual enrollment growth in prior quarters.

WHAT'S NEXT ON THE INVESTMENT HORIZON?

Apollo's adult-friendly learning model was the learning model of the 1980s and 1990s. Its success was borne out of keen foresight of what then were oncoming growth drivers.

The momentum-driven ride that carried Apollo Group et al. to pricey valuations has slowed. There are numerous reasons for the deceleration, but the most important is the shifting sentiments of investors who are looking elsewhere—perhaps to the Internet—for the momentum once enjoyed by Apollo Group and other higher education stocks.

The education investment of the millenium will be borne not only by the drivers listed above, but also by additional growth drivers based primarily on the needs of business.

Internet-based education is the next family of investments that will draw the attention of Wall Street. Perhaps not since Henry Ford's development of the assembly line have we as a society witnessed something that has had such a dramatic impact on the way we do business. E-commerce and the Internet have allowed businesses to do things never before dreamed of. Imagine, just a few short years ago, being able to establish an entire business with nothing more than a few computers and a handful of employees—no inventory, no large sales force, just a Web site. Some of those companies, only a few years old, now have valuations greater than many of the oldest and most prestigious companies in the United States.

No one will argue that e-commerce has had a dramatic impact on the way business gets done. Ever since the proliferation of the Internet in the early 1990s, businesses have been turning to the Internet and e-commerce at an astounding rate. It has greatly simplified the way in which businesses contact potential customers. It has improved efficiencies in back offices, and, in some cases, has rendered human employees obsolete. "Internet enabled" has become a necessary way to do business.

Education companies are in an ideal position to benefit from the power of the Internet. The Internet enables education companies to remedy some of the most pressing problems for businesses dedicated to replenishing the human capital of the enterprise, including the following:

- *Cost issues.* The benevolent corporations mentioned earlier face resource constraints that prevent them from sending everyone to a classroom for learning—particularly given how frequently those needs arise. For example, the inexorable technological revolution continuously overhauls the workplace, forcing workers to treat learning as part of their job description. *Internet-enabled education can mitigate against many of the cost-based issues of education.*
- *Effectiveness issues.* There is an increasing awareness that classroom-based learning is not always effective, particularly as measured by knowledge retention. What is the learner's impact on cash flow, capacity utilization, employee turnover, customer loyalty, profitability, and economic value added? All learning companies will come under severe pressure to demonstrate their value within a new paradigm—away from inputs (classes and hours) and toward outputs (performance at individual and organizational levels). *Internet-enabled education can improve learning outputs.*
- *Serving an extended enterprise.* The business enterprise encompasses many more people than those on the payroll. Companies need several "smart" relationships—with employees, re-sellers (the channel), and customers, who are located worldwide. Businesses must ensure that learning objectives are met, *capturing the entire enterprise under one learning "web" to improve its information efficiency and productivity.*
- *Offering an individualized education plan.* Internet and related technologies empower businesses to offer customization on a scale that was inconceivable prior to the advent of the Internet. For example, the software that runs behind e-commerce sites enables vendors to pinpoint a user's exact needs based on a robust database of information collected and distilled about that user, including his or her preferences and past transactions. Mass customization and person-

alized content are at the core of Internet-centric businesses spring-
ing up daily. *Most education consumers soon will expect individualized
learning plans or learning streams.*

Individual education programs (IEPs) can be generated by combining the
records of the students' prior learning (from monitored usage) and the vast
database stored on the server. As students progress, information is delivered
based on what they learned and how they performed. For example, a student
would log onto the learning server and a customized course would be generated from the content database that "knows" which courses the learner took,
how well he or she did, what his or her job description is, and what problem is
most pressing. This dimension serves to focus the curriculum only on skill gaps,
saving organizations both time and money. A byproduct of individualized
education plans is increased motivation stemming from the self-centered
nature of the experience.

Internet-enabled education companies will continue what John Sperling
and Apollo Group began more than 20 years ago: treating students like
customers. The most successful companies will address the idiosyncrasies of
each worker's work environment. What does the customer need to perform
productively on task?

Education companies should build engines that correlate the goals of each
customer with the knowledge needed to perform productively. Successful
education companies will exercise *backward mapping* and will build learning by
looking at the customer's workplace context to determine the desirable
integration of the knowledge: less generic, customized content and more
customized learning.

THE DEATH OF "NORM"

At this early stage in the evolution of Internet-based education, the focus has
been on the following:

- The *ease* of preparing, deploying, and managing Internet-enabled
  education.
- The *cost savings* of Internet-enabled education (as opposed to the
  "bricks and mortar" option).
- The *market opportunity* of Internet-enabled education when universities consider the student population they could reach via the
  Internet.

In time, however, the focus will shift to the actual learning experience. The
learning experience available from Internet-enabled education typically is
superior to that available in classroom-based learning. Traditional classroom

instruction is about "teaching to the norm." But there is no one named "Norm." No one in the class is truly the norm, and therefore, no one stands to benefit from instructional models designed on learning for Norm.

The Internet creates a new education model where the learner is at the center. The new model is *not* about creating a classroom-based simulation; it is about creating a better learning experience.

Why were businesses trying to mimic the classroom electronically? Why are people looking at the future of learning by peering into the past? Why are vendors touting the "virtual classroom" as utopia in learning? The classroom served and will continue to serve its purpose. But the beauty of Internet-enabled education is that it allows businesses to *rethink* the classroom.

The Internet and its related technologies have the potential to empower individuals to learn in ways that are significantly more effective than traditional learning techniques. The Internet

- *allows for multisensory stimulation* via video, audio, animation, and more;
- *enables constructive learning* or the ability to approach mastery of a concept by building on one's own knowledge base and selecting additional building blocks based on one's own learning proclivities;
- *empowers learners to learn* by practicing as the environment enables learners to practice repeatedly (often by accessing a rich bank of problems, for example); and
- *facilitates collaborative learning* whereby students can think critically, analyze, communicate, make logical arguments, and work cooperatively in groups.

As contrasted with static text, Internet-enabled education has the capacity to link with other resources (simulations, other content, study groups, etc.), which can enhance the learning experience and improve upon the linear learning dictated by textbooks.

SENSE OF COMMUNITY

One of the strengths of traditional classroom-based learning is the sense of community that can develop among classmates. Regular interaction with fellow learners in a classroom can often engender camaraderie as students struggle with difficult lessons or even share laughs about the teacher. However, community can be difficult to engender without a classroom.

For that reason, many Internet-enabled education companies will strive to offer some vehicle through which students can develop a sense of community—a key to retaining learners as well as improving their outcomes. Communities encourage collaboration among learners. When communities exist, learners can play a variety of roles, such as observer, mentor, coach, expert, or administrator. A participant might be an expert in one area but a learner in another. Learners can interact with one another via e-mail, chat rooms, multi-user simulations, and expert coaching.

Pensare is a new Internet-enabled learning company that (arguably) is a pioneer in the development of learning communities. Pensare reformats and aggregates content for Internet-enabled courses that businesses can use to teach employees skills such as customer relations and management. The courses, involving content aggregated from leading business schools such as Wharton and Harvard, include interaction in the form of chats, forums, role plays, and simulations.

Irrespective of "community," brand will emerge as a key variable in determining the viability of Internet-enabled learning businesses in continuing education. Pensare has no brand at this stage of its development, but Wharton and Harvard offer Pensare lots of brand equity.

Brand is critical because it may be one of the few ways for consumers to differentiate among Internet-enabled learning products when they are choosing from a lengthy list. In IT (information technology) training, the brand is acquired from the software and hardware vendors whose products most learners are studying (Microsoft, Oracle, Cisco, SAP). In business skills, the source for brand is less obvious. Whom would you go to for Internet-enabled learning in finance, or health care?

One of the more prominent Internet-enabled learning companies is Online Learning.net, which resells UCLA courses. The courses are actually from UCLA Extension—a bricks-and-mortar program (the largest in the country) which enrolls more than 100,000 students in the Los Angeles area per year. OnlineLearning.net obviously has a great brand with UCLA, one of the most recognized higher education names in the world. OnlineLearning.net has the exclusive rights to distribute UCLA courses online. Learners can transfer credits earned through OnlineLearning.net, but they cannot receive a degree from OnlineLearning.net or UCLA.

Initially, Internet-enabled learning companies will build brand through alliances. For example, a company called Knowledge Well offers college-level business courses for university credit through a partnership with Kansas State University. The courses address the growing demand for professional and business management education and lead to a Kansas State business degree. Knowledge Well's products cover all management competencies, from sales to finance; the company also offers a complete business and management program available on a non-credit basis.

Many universities are trying to leverage their intellectual property by targeting the continuing education market and creating learning portals for continuing education. Unext.com (www.unext.com) provides Internet-enabled business education through an Internet-enabled business community called Cardean. Its goal is to provide content from leading business schools directly to corporate employees. Currently, Cardean partners include Columbia University, the University of Chicago, Stanford University, the London School of Economics and Political Science, and Carnegie-Mellon University.

INVESTMENT OPPORTUNITY IN INTERNET-ENABLED EDUCATION

This essay has disclosed a lengthy list of problems that Internet-enabled education companies can address. Nevertheless, the enormous market potential and astounding degree of hype surrounding the Internet-enabled education market has often distracted investors from some of the risks associated with this market. While the size of the industry makes it appealing, many risks attend Internet-enabled education.

The market for Internet-enabled education is in its early stages, and continued development is uncertain. The market for Internet-enabled education is new and emerging. Although Internet-enabled education solutions have been available for several years, they currently represent only a small portion of the overall education market. Thus, wannabe Internet-enabled education providers' success will depend on the adoption rates of the traditional education and workplace learning markets.

Early adopters of Internet-enabled education products and services, regardless of where they stand in the lifelong learning process, could be considered the "low-hanging fruit" of the industry and might not indicate the majority of potential customers. Some segments of the education market are prone to inaction as a result of inertia. This inertia could stifle the development of Internet-enabled education as a truly widespread application.

The sales cycle is lengthy and can vary widely. The sales cycle between initial customer contact and the signing of a contract varies widely, reflecting differences in decision-making processes and budget cycles. As a result, forecasting the timing and amount of sales and actual revenue can be difficult.

Educators and Internet-enabled education buyers typically conduct extensive and lengthy evaluations before committing to any product or service. Delays in the sales cycle can result from changes in a district's, university's, or corporation's budget, the need for approval from the customer's administration and faculty (in the case of a school), or the need to educate the buyer.

Providers without substantial resources may not be able to successfully navigate the treacherous waters of the lengthy sales cycle. Providers typically have little control over these factors, particularly if the product is being introduced into the "traditional" education market, where Internet-enabled education may be viewed as questionable.

Internet-enabled education may not be broadly accepted by academics and educators. Specific to the college market, some academics and educators are and will continue to be opposed to Internet-enabled education in principle. Academics and educators have expressed concerns regarding the perceived loss of control over the education process that can result from the outsourcing of Internet-enabled education campuses and courses, as well as the possibility of lower-quality learning outcomes. Some of these critics—particularly college and university professors—have the capacity to influence the market for Internet-enabled education services.

Intellectual property is another concern: Who owns the content of an Internet-enabled education course: the teacher or the school? While the issue will continue to be hotly debated in the coming years, the crux of the argument will continue to center around simple issues of control and economics: Can the teacher take the course elsewhere without restriction? Who gets paid when the course attracts students? It is conceivable that the issue eventually could be decided by the courts, which likely would only increase the complexity and ambiguity of the issue.

The Internet-enabled education market is characterized by rapid technological change. The market for hardware, software, and services (the core components of Internet-enabled education) is characterized by rapid technological change, changes in customer demands, and evolving industry standards (or the lack thereof). The introduction of services embodying new technologies and the emergence of new industry standards can render existing services obsolete and unmarketable, often in a short period of time.

An increasing number of laws and regulations pertain to the Internet; these relate to the liability for information received from or transmitted over the Internet, Internet-enabled education content regulation, user privacy, taxation, and quality of products and services. Moreover, the applicability to the Internet of many existing laws governing intellectual property ownership and other issues is uncertain and developing.

Numerous laws and regulations pertaining to the Internet may yet be adopted; these may relate to characteristics and quality of products and services, as well as content, copyrights, distribution, pricing, and user privacy.

Identifying and meeting the needs of the Internet-enabled education buyer are not easy. Given the wide variation in customers' needs, accurately determining the features and functionality required by buyers and then designing and implementing services and products that meet those requirements is not easy. The task becomes more complex by virtue of the fact that many Internet-enabled education buyers do not know what they want. Internet-enabled education providers thus must describe the options available and how those options could contribute to the buyer's Internet-enabled education initiative.

This burden can further exacerbate the sales cycle issues mentioned above, jeopardizing the ability of undercapitalized providers to complete the project.

Large competitors loom on the horizon. The Internet-enabled education market is evolving quickly and is subject to rapid technological change. The market is highly fragmented, with no single competitor accounting for a dominant market share. Participants vary in size and in the scope and breadth of the products and services they offer. Competitors vary in the different segments of the lifelong learning world, as well as in the Internet-enabled education world (content, services, access, support), and the ability to successfully execute competitive strategies can depend on the market in which the company competes.

Many Internet-enabled education start-ups are blurring the line between being a product and a business. Companies that derive substantially all of their revenues from single products are at risk, particularly if those products are dependent upon cutting-edge technology, or are vulnerable to new products, larger competitors, or companies with the ability to provide products and services.

The list of potential competitors is extensive, but in general, the following types of companies should be considered:

- systems integrators
- publishers
- software developers
- telecommunications companies
- training/performance improvement providers

The level of competition will continue to increase as current competitors' offerings become more sophisticated, as new participants enter the market, and as larger players begin to use their substantial financial and marketing resources to corner market share.

CONCLUSION

As with its predecessor (the education industry), the Internet-enabled education industry is highly fragmented and nascent. It lacks industry leadership; it is primed for consolidation; and it is fraught with risk. Answers to the following questions will determine whether investors will buy into an Internet-enabled education company:

- Are market trends positive or negative?
- Are revenues recurring or reversing?
- Is the management team talented or temperamental?

- Are the customers blue chips or brown fodder?
- Does the potential exist for operating leverage or operating hemorrhage?
- Is the revenue stream predictable or invisible?
- Is the company in a defensible niche or a defenseless valley?

If the answers are positive, investors will buy the stock.

CHAPTER 4

The Knowledge Supply Chain: The Logical Extension to Success

Stephen M. Mitchell, James D. Van Erden, and Kenneth P. Voytek

> *"As the economy changes, as competition becomes more global, it's no longer company vs. company, but supply chain vs. supply chain."*
> Harold Sirkin, Boston Consulting Group

INTRODUCTION

The most significant feature of the economic environment of the 1990s is how the combination of globalization, technological advances, and shifting labor market dynamics have radically altered the foundations for a company's competitive advantage in the United States and in the world economy. These changes have shifted the basis of a firm's competitive advantage from static price competition based on economies of scale and cheap resources toward dynamic improvements in products and services. This change favors firms that are able to create knowledge faster than their competitors. More and more, it is the workforce that enables a company to improve productivity and create value in the marketplace and that serves as the foundation of competitive advantage. As knowledge and skills become the

Stephen M. Mitchell is director, Workforce Connections, Pennsylvania Economy League, Western Division.

James D. Van Erden is director, Workforce Development, Goodwill Industries International, Inc.

Kenneth P. Voytek is chief economist, Manufacturing Extension Partnership, National Institute of Standards and Technology. (This essay was written prior to his taking this position.)

core drivers of business success, companies are developing and implementing new ways to plan, manage, and deliver them to the workplace.

The criteria for success in the marketplace, the organizational structures and management practices of businesses, and the skills required for individuals to secure and sustain employment are also changing. Moreover, change continues at an accelerating pace. Effective organizations undergo constant transformation to fit within their changing environment, while workers must constantly alter their skill sets to meet emerging requirements for successful performance.

Until now, little attention has been focused on the impact and implication of these changes on the education and training industry. Much has been written about how changes will increase company and individual training investments and expand the aggregate demand for training and education, but this is only half the story. This chapter explores the "other half" of the story: how these transformations will drive change in the underlying structure of education and training. Specifically, we examine the implications of businesses' efforts to manage their knowledge supply chains—efforts that promise to fundamentally change businesses' relationships and interactions with postsecondary and postbaccalaureate education and training providers.

CHANGES IN THE BUSINESS ENVIRONMENT

It is important to recognize the environmental pressures that ultimately will change the relationship between business and postsecondary education and training providers. The following primary forces characterize the economic environment confronting business:

- *The interconnected world economy.* Economies, companies, and employees exist in an increasingly interconnected world. The share of world output represented by the United States has decreased by half since the end of World War II. In 1950, the United States accounted for nearly 40 percent of all output in the world; today it accounts for less than 22 percent.

  The increased exposure of economies, companies, and products to competitors from around the world is one of the key drivers of the new economy. Companies are taking advantage of the expanding global marketplace to increase market access and market share. As a result, U.S. workers compete with workers from all over the world.

- *The pervasive impact of technology and information.* Technology is changing how we work, where we work, and with what we work. These changes also have important implications for the business landscape of the future. As Evans and Wurster wrote, "The new economics of information will precipitate changes in the structure of entire industries and in the ways companies compete."[1]

A recent study by Human Resources Development Canada[2] found that technology helped eliminate more semi-skilled occupations and helped create more professional/managerial jobs. The study provides a picture of how technology cuts both ways, simultaneously creating and destroying jobs and altering the skills required.

Technology also is changing how business interacts with customers and suppliers. For example, Forrester Research estimates that business-to-business e-commerce will increase to $1.3 trillion by 2003. Others forecast that online retail sales will range from between $40 billion and $80 billion by 2002. Business-to-business e-commerce benefits from many of the same advantages as retail e-commerce. For example, e-commerce can enable businesses to expand the services they offer. By opening immediate and convenient channels for communicating, exchanging, and selecting information, e-commerce is enabling firms to determine which functions they should perform "in house" and which are best provided by others. This technology already has helped to create new relationships and to streamline and augment supply chain processes. As these changes occur, logistic and financial intermediaries' roles expand.

- *Escalating levels of education and training needed for jobs.* Over the past several years, changes in the business environment have increased the knowledge and skill levels required for successful job performance. The fastest growing jobs in the coming decade will be those that require increased levels of education and training. Between 1983 and 1996, employment in occupations requiring an associate's degree or postsecondary vocational training grew 3.1 percent annually, compared to 2 percent for all employment. By 2006, more than 42 percent of the net new jobs created will require education beyond a high school diploma.

Recent surveys by the American Management Association provide further insight into how the demand for skills and knowledge in the workplace is increasing. In 1998, nearly 40 percent of applicants tested lacked the skills necessary to perform on the job, compared to just over 25 percent of applicants in 1989.

The skills gap is affecting companies' ability to grow. According to PricewaterhouseCoopers's "TrendSetter Barometer Survey," the percentage of companies reporting that skill shortages were a barrier to growth more than doubled between 1993 and 1998. In 1993, just over one in four companies reported that skill shortage was a barrier to growth; by 1998, the figure was nearly seven out of ten.

A skilled workforce is a critical source of competitive advantage for companies. Skilled workers enhance a company's ability to increase market value, sustain competitive advantage, employ new technologies, overcome knowledge and skills depreciation, and recruit new talent.

- New labor market dynamics. Companies are finding that previously successful workforce strategies are not suited to the new economic environment; change is too rapid and too constant.[3] For example, the inflexibility of the internal labor market has been overcome by greater reliance on external labor markets for new employees. Similarly, long-term tenure and opportunities for wage and career advancement through internal career ladders have been altered by the flattening of job hierarchies that has resulted from restructuring and increased outsourcing of non-critical functions. As a consequence, employment relationships are more tenuous, individual mobility is greater, and career ladders are less obvious.

Recent research suggests that a new worker is emerging in the United States today—one who has redefined traditional concepts of loyalty, job satisfaction, and career advancement. Whether or not a given individual has lost a job, the downsizing of the 1980s and 1990s created a paradigm shift in how people view their work life and manage their careers. The "emerging" worker spans all age groups, industries, and regions and is expected to represent the majority of the American workforce in the near future.[4] Driven by a unique set of values (see Table 1),[5] the emerging workforce is creating new career opportunities and presenting traditional companies with significant human resources challenges.

TABLE 1		
EMERGENT EMPLOYEES	VALUES	TRADITIONAL EMPLOYEES
Defined as contribution	Loyalty	Defined as tenure
Vehicle for growth	Job Change	Damaging to one's career
Employee's responsibility to pursue	Career Path	Company's responsibility to provide
Based on level of performance	Advancement	Based on length of service
Unrelated to commitment	Job Security	Prerequisite to commitment

In a world in which the old social contract and commitment to a single company is gone, in which an individual expects to change jobs more often, as well as to constantly require skill upgrades and knowledge building, the company of choice increasingly will be the one that offers a pathway for workers to do this. In the past, an individual would think of a career as being with the same company and as requiring a knowledge base acquired primarily before employment. Now companies look for individuals who have a broad-based work ethic and, more important, the ability to learn.

The mantra from employers is, "Give us someone who has the ability and the basic skills, and we can teach the rest." They add, "We need to do this because we don't know what new skills will be required in the future." Thus the company of choice increasingly will be one that provides its workers with the skills and knowledge necessary for the current job but that also helps prepare them for the next job, whether it is with the same or a different company.

Changes in workforce demographics and labor market dynamics are coming together to radically alter the size, shape, and nature of the labor market. In particular, a slowdown in labor supply growth and significant changes in the composition of the labor force have profound implications for companies. In the long run, growth in the U.S. economy depends on growth in labor productivity and labor supply. As a result, many companies and communities are examining ways in which they can respond to the need to increase labor supply and provide workers with the skills needed to match workplace demands.

KNOWLEDGE MANAGEMENT: THE BASIS FOR BUSINESS SUCCESS

The trends described in the preceding section are contributing to increased awareness of how workers' knowledge and skills affect companies' success. Companies are facing changes that are constantly increasing in volume (number), momentum (pace and time to respond), and complexity (interrelatedness).

In this fast-paced world, a degree of continuous learning is necessary just to stay in place. Some major technology companies number the half-life of their engineers in months (e.g., 18 months or less); with Internet time counted in weeks, one can only imagine how quickly and comprehensively learning can and must take place.

If organizations are to prosper, the skills and knowledge embedded therein will have to undergo rapid expansion and growth, using the most efficient means possible. Education and training in and for companies will be transformed; this will involve moving to flexible training systems focused on consumers' specific needs, with explicit goals and measurable outcomes. Merely sitting in a classroom or becoming involved in an inefficient learning experience will not work. "Mass customization," a major concept in the production of goods and services, will need to be translated into the way we develop new skills and training. (See Table 2.)

TABLE 2		
THE CHANGING STRUCTURE OF EDUCATION AND TRAINING IN AND FOR COMPANIES		
	Old	*New*
Focus	Job Training	Core Competencies and Performance
Target Population	Professionals	All Employees and Customer/Supplier Chain
Driver	Training Program	Learner and Workplace
Responsibility	Training Department	Learners and Work Unit Leaders
Delivery System	Mass Scheduling and Production	Mass Customization and Just-in-Time
Delivery Structure	Off Site	Workplace Centered
Style	Lecture	Teach-Do Loop
Concepts	Job Specific	Systems
Evaluation	Smile Test	Business Results and Job Performance

Increasingly, as the following examples show, companies are turning to technology and outside suppliers to help meet these demands.

- *A virtual human resource function is emerging.* Companies increasingly are using Web-based technology to complement their traditional human resource departments as well as work that was performed manually in the past. Between 1997 and 1998, the percentage of companies using Web technology to deliver human resources services nearly doubled, from 27 percent to 47 percent. (*Source:* Watson Wyatt)
- *Training—both design and delivery—is being done by outside suppliers.* A 1997 survey shows that nearly four in ten companies use outside suppliers to design training, and nearly one in three uses outside suppliers to deliver training. (*Source: Training Magazine*)
- *Companies that use outside vendors to deliver training use a wide variety of suppliers.* Half of the companies report using equipment vendors as a training provider, more than one-third use private consultants, approximately one-third use technical/vocational institutions, less than one-third use community colleges, one-fifth use four-year colleges and universities, and just over one in ten

report using government-funded training programs. (*Source:* National Center for the Educational Quality of the Workforce)

Ample opportunity exists for postsecondary and postbaccalaureate institutions to work with companies, but they must be prepared to change how and what they deliver to meet emerging business requirements. Suppliers that are successful will become part of the firm's "knowledge supply chain."

KNOWLEDGE SUPPLY CHAINS: THE MODEL

Supply Chains: The Experience

The primary issue is how to understand, track, and manage knowledge in our global, knowledge-based society. Companies are increasingly concerned about the stock of knowledge in their organizations—how to improve it and deliver it to the right place at the right time, in the most efficient manner. U.S. firms had to solve this problem in the late 1980s, in terms of products, as they faced a growing global economy and tremendous pressure from more efficient foreign firms, especially in Germany and Japan. Many delegations were sent to these countries to learn how they did it; quality systems, just-in-time inventory control systems, and numerous other modern business systems were adopted as a result.

Imbedded in these new practices was a growing awareness that a company needed to focus on its core strengths; that to increase efficiency, it was desirable to outsource functions and services to those who could perform them more efficiently and at less cost.

U.S. firms began to look carefully at their "supply chain" or "supplier network" to see how it might be improved. One of the seminal works describing this concept and how it will work in the next century came from the Agility Forum's work with leading firms and organizations. *The Next Generation Manufacturing Project* was initiated in 1995 to develop a framework for action that U.S. manufacturers could use as a guide in an increasingly competitive global marketplace.[6]

This and other work documented U.S. manufacturing and service firms' movement to highly effective supply chains. A supply chain is a network of facilities and distribution options that performs the functions of procuring materials, transforming them into intermediate and finished products, and distributing the finished products to consumers.

Companies are now working closely with suppliers to reduce production and delivery lead times and greatly increase quality. A recent survey found that to improve productivity and product quality, more companies are providing their suppliers with a breakdown of their production process to ensure that the supplier's component designs are compatible with company processes. In

1984, 40 percent of companies in the study did so; by 1993, 80 percent said they did.[7]

As the supply chain management system has matured, the concept has broadened beyond that of a single producer and a small set of suppliers. Today, it is thought of as a wide network involving multiple partners and collaborators, multiple sets of suppliers at different levels, and the primary customers of the organization and its partners.

In their article "Synchronized Supply Chains: The New Frontier," Drs. David Anderson and Hau Lee pointed out that

> The supply chain as a concept and a reality is moving far beyond the confines of an individual organization. It has become a dynamic process that involves the simultaneous acquisition and continuous re-evaluation of partners, technologies, and organizational structures. The building blocks of successful supply chains are numerous and their interactions are complex, but businesses have no choice but to embark on such an initiative: the supply chain has evolved from corporate necessity to enhancing competitive advantage for savvy industry leaders.[8]

A supply chain has the following four basic characteristics:

- It shifts the focus from a "push" system driven by the visions and needs of individual elements to a "pull" system integrated by a larger end objective.
- It reduces total system costs and cycle times, improves quality, and increases product or service functionality.
- It creates effective/timely communications, shares a common vision, focuses on outcomes, increases expectations, increases quality, and reduces rework.
- It eliminates ineffective and inefficient suppliers.

The Analogue: Knowledge Supply Chains

Thinking about how to acquire knowledge workers is not so different from discussing acquisition of component parts or critical services. According to the concept of a "Knowledge Supply Chain" (KSC), companies would get the right people (those with the appropriate knowledge and skills) at the right time (just-in-time availability) and in the right place (where they are needed for innovation, improved productivity, and competitive advantage).

In the KSC, we build on the basics of the supply chain model to

- treat the knowledge process as an integrated system where all partners are identified and included;

- *Changes in competitive standards.* As people become a source of competitive advantage and as companies become knowledge-based businesses and learning organizations, new customer requirements and competitive standards are being passed on to the education and training industry. There is an increased emphasis on graduates' demonstrated competencies rather than on credits earned. There is also an emerging focus on continuous improvement processes as a measure of institutional quality (in contrast to the input-driven measures of traditional accreditation).
- *Emergence of an industry.* Investment advisors are issuing prospectuses on education and training companies and significant investments. According to a recent Merrill Lynch & Company report, education and training companies have raised more than $3.4 billion of equity capital in the last five years. This emerging market will raise customer (and shareholder) expectations, increase competition, and drive further change in the industry.
- *Technology.* By 2001, more than half of the training services delivered in the United States will be technology based (as opposed to instructor led). Dell Corporation University holds 60 to 70 percent of its classes online. We are witnessing the advent of "virtual learning mega-universities." The UK's Open University currently enrolls more than 200,000 students in 25 countries—including 30,000 postbaccalaureate students; University of Phoenix currently serves 50,000 students at 65 U.S. learning centers. Technology is also changing how traditional college courses are delivered. For example, data from the annual Campus Computing Survey indicate that in 1998 nearly four in ten classes used e-mail, and more than a third of all courses made use of the Internet—a fivefold increase in e-mail use from 1994 and a sixfold increase in use of the Internet.

Postsecondary and postbaccalaureate institutions that want to take advantage of opportunities inherent in KSCs must prepare to manage the change that will be required to become a preferred supplier. They need to look at education and training as a business and apply the principles of supply chain management to their own operations. Education leaders must decide who their customers are and how best to meet their needs and expectations, what their own distinctive competencies are or should be, and what that means for service delivery.

- identify the knowledge need, specifications for transfer, t mate customer, and when the knowledge is needed;
- facilitate communication and information sharing among a ners to maximize the value added of each to the process;
- provide quick feedback between supplier and users regard efficiency and effectiveness of the knowledge exchange; ar
- enable each partner to be involved in the benefits of th system and in defining the role they play in the system.

The KSC integrates the entire knowledge acquisition and process. Companies forge powerful alliances with suppliers, distr retailers—all the way to the customer. A company's "extended may include temporary staffing services, community colleges, proprietary training providers, local one-stop centers, vendors videos and software, etc.

The formation and operation of a KSC are grounded in a thoro and understanding of the knowledge needed, specifications for tr where and when the knowledge is needed. As a result, companies knowledge-related processes and will shift functions to the busin best suited to perform each function. Constant analysis helps to r system costs and cycle times, improve quality, and increase produc functionality.

Effective KSCs require that companies create new relationship ferred suppliers. The companies then create systems to ensure eff timely communication within the supplier network. This open flow nication and information among all partners helps to maximize added to the process by each supplier. It also ensures that the partn common vision and maintain a focus on outcomes while increasin tions and quality and reducing rework.

IMPLICATIONS OF THE KSC FOR POSTSECONDA EDUCATION

Given the increasing importance of workforce skills, it is not surpr companies are developing new strategies to plan, manage, and deliv edge and skills to the workplace. Companies will work with preferre ers—education and training providers capable of providing consister customized service, and a rapid response while demonstrating a r investment.

The education and training industry is often characterized as change, but there are signs of restructuring in response to business d This restructuring is exemplified by the following:

Market Segments

Education and training services are delivered to targeted customer groups. One principle of supply chain management is to organize business units around market segments and to develop differentiated strategies and operations for each segment.[9] Thus, customer targeting is a strategic choice that influences most subsequent decisions and operations.

In terms of KSCs, the primary question of market segments revolves around company relationships. At least three possibilities exist.

- *Focal company.* Interest in the emergence of KSCs has been driven in large part by the relationships individual companies have established with particular colleges, universities, or other education providers. The concept of KSCs has been refined as a result of examination of how a Motorola or an Intel partners with postsecondary institutions. Such individual company partnerships are available to postsecondary institutions that are fortunate enough to be located near a major corporation or to have a reputation likely to attract a focal company.

  Partnerships with focal companies have a lot to offer. Because sourcing simplification is contingent upon working more closely with fewer suppliers, a postsecondary institution capable of establishing a strong relationship with a company can achieve leverage in the marketplace. The ideal relationship would include concurrent procurement, in which the early involvement of college staff would help reduce design or service delivery cycle times. College staff may be located on the company site or vice versa. The goal is to create a symbiotic relationship and to be in a position to respond ever more quickly to company market shifts and demands.

- *Company consortia.* Most postsecondary institutions are not able to rely on a single customer. The challenge is how to extend and apply company partnerships to small and mid-sized firms, i.e., how to expand the customer base. One approach is to focus on company consortia, of which many types exist.[10] One type, which draws on a changing view of what constitutes the business enterprise, includes the suppliers and customers of a focal company. The Consortia for Supplier Development, a partnership between several leading corporations and community colleges, is based on this supply chain approach. An alternative approach involves contacting companies to identify a common need and then developing an initiative to address that need.

- *Industry clusters.* Another possibility involves linking local economic development activities to workforce development, e.g., developing programs to address the needs of key local industry clusters.[11] This approach may be particularly appealing to colleges that see themselves as regional/local institutions. The attraction, retention, and growth of talent become key strategies in economic development; workforce development becomes part of economic development. Rather than working for a focal company, postsecondary institutions in the industry cluster scenario work toward the economic development of a region, i.e., a regional KSC.

It could be argued that occupations constitute a fourth market segment. Many postsecondary and postbaccalaureate programs are directed toward education and training for specific occupations. If the content and delivery of an occupation-based education and training program emerge from interactions with and needs analysis of a company, consortia, or industry cluster, then they are by definition part of a KSC. The program is designed to address company needs. However, if occupation programs are targeted to individual professionals, independent of company requirements, they are not part of a KSC (though they certainly may be of value).

A postsecondary institution that wants to participate in a KSC should be concerned primarily with which companies to work with, but at least one other critical decision is worth noting: What type of students or labor market segment will the institution educate or train? Answering this question requires that educators shift their focus to a demand-driven system where business and the skill needs of labor markets are the ultimate customers whose requirements must be met. Students are important clients, but educators must determine and use the best methods of instilling the knowledge, skills, and competencies students will need to be successful in existing and emerging labor markets.

At least three distinct labor market segments are worth noting. Each of these has a different base of knowledge, skills, and abilities, as well as different learning goals, and each requires different content and pedagogy to achieve the desired knowledge and skill sets. The segments are as follows:

- *disadvantaged/at-risk.* The traditional target of JTPA and now the Workforce Reinvestment Act, this labor segment has gained attention in recent years with the passage of welfare-to-work legislation. While it is served more often by community-based providers, this labor market is also served by some postsecondary institutions. Individuals in this segment need employability and job readiness skills to qualify for entry-level positions. Few postsecondary and postbaccalaureate institutions may believe this is their target labor market segment, but the rapid increase of remedial programs at the postsecondary level may spur reconsideration of this viewpoint.

- *technical.* This labor segment includes individuals who already are employed but seek to attain the technical knowledge and skills needed either to advance in their chosen careers or to move to a new career. Proprietary schools and community colleges are traditional postsecondary institutions targeting this labor market segment.
- *professional/managerial.* This labor segment consists of individuals who already are employed or have identified professional/managerial occupations as their career goals. This is the labor market segment typically targeted by colleges and universities. The desired outcomes focus on advanced conceptual and technical knowledge and skills.

Client grouping can be approached at multiple levels. For example, one could choose to deliver services to technical workers in a focal company or to professional staff in an industry cluster. Institutions may also—indeed are likely to—have several customer targets. But these groups are not equal. A single approach rarely optimizes performance by every customer segment. Where appropriate, education institutions should emphasize logistically separate operations based on service and market characteristics.

Having a clear target market is prerequisite to achieving a customer focus. The primary target or customer group creates an imperative for service delivery. It is the requirement that follows the phrase, "Deliver services to. . . . " It helps define the program's "primacy of purpose." That purpose should be the ultimate guide in the development and evaluation of alternative products and services.

Service

Being customer focused requires an ongoing process for identifying customer segments, determining customer expectations, and delivering programs and services that meet these expectations.

Postsecondary institutions that want to participate in KSCs must recognize the transformation that is taking place inside companies. The pace of competitive and technological change requires that organizations develop their employees' competencies. Training becomes a part of the job process; it involves more than an event or a course. Technology, work processes, and jobs change. A continuous learning process must be implemented so human potential can be developed as quickly as technological potential. The focus must shift from training to workforce development and knowledge management.

Alan Todd, CEO of KnowledgeSoft, a skills management software program, states, "Companies need to quit thinking in terms of training and start thinking about knowledge creation and knowledge transfer as distinct and important business processes. The question is not, How do we deliver training to x number of people? It is, How do you make sure you have the right people in the right place with the right knowledge to execute your business plan?" Sue Hayden, SAP's director of solutions marketing, adds, "Human resources management is no longer about keeping personnel records. The name of the game is to make sure you have the right talent on the right initiatives at the right time."[12] This is the business context that KSCs are attempting to address.

Successful providers work hard to develop customer loyalty. They collaborate with business to determine its needs and objectives. Preferred suppliers know that their service activities have to *benefit*—not simply satisfy—their customers. Business involvement ensures the relevance of the education and training provided.

Customer involvement strategies can be arrayed on a continuum. One end of the continuum is product centered. In the past, companies have focused on wrapping a training program around a single box at the intersection of training and content. It is here that they choose vendors for instructor-led, computer-based, and Web-based instruction, as well as distance learning and seminars. Institutions that represent this block are concerned with selling content, and they operate from a product-driven perspective. Product-centered strategies risk selling services that the provider has the capacity to deliver but that may not respond to market demand.

Demand-centered strategies occupy the other end of the continuum. These bring together the people and organizations to whom and to which services will be delivered, i.e., they define the market needs and seek out service providers capable of addressing those needs. KSCs require a shift to a demand-centered strategy.

The middle portion of the continuum includes providers that deliver service packages developed in response to customer input. The degree to which services are designed in response to customer needs and on the basis of customer input—as well as the ability to customize the offerings to meet the needs of individual clients—determines a program's relative position.

Postsecondary institutions participating in KSCs should address business customer needs and satisfy customer requirements. A customer focus should be evident in both program content and delivery.

- *Content.* Program content should be tailored to each business; providers should not try to fit company needs into their "off-the-shelf" service package.

    The idea that all education and training services need to be demand driven is misplaced. A fully demand-driven system "implies that supplies are highly flexible and virtually unlimited, and there are no costs (or premiums) tied to discontinuity, and that demand must be satisfied absolutely."[13] Services within a KSC should be demand driven and supply aware. Providers in a KSC should concentrate on answering real-time demand and cutting cycle times (e.g., curriculum development times, course update cycles). The quicker the cycle time, the easier it is to respond to changing demand patterns for specific types of education and training services.

Postsecondary institutions need to be aware of their ability to respond to demand. Institutions that have long cycle times should focus on foundation courses that do not require significant updating. Institutions with quick response capability may elect to provide more customized training services.

The diminishing half-life of skill and knowledge also has implications for program content. Content can be differentiated according to whether it is designed for beginning students or advanced practitioners or whether it is meant to be a refresher or update.

"Demonstrated competencies" are one other aspect of the transformation in business that deserves attention. Certifications of competency are not the traditional outcome measure of many postsecondary institutions. Thus, the emphasis on competence has implications for program design, as well as assessment. Competency-based programs lend themselves more than traditional "seat-time" courses to modular presentation.

- *Delivery.* Knowledge can be obtained in a variety of ways: electronically or orally, individually or in a mass forum, at the precise moment of need or over a length of time. The following list identifies some activities that are valid learning events:[14]

    Public seminars
    Computer-based training (CBT)
    Books and periodicals
    Videotapes
    Instructor-led training
    Conferences
    University degree programs
    On-the-job training (OJT)
    Self-paced training
    Certificate programs
    Journal and trade articles
    Company-specific training activities
    Communities of practice

A KSC, in its entirety, must facilitate this variety of media and business preferences. The task for the individual postsecondary institution is to determine which activities best meet customers' individual requirements (e.g., operating structures and schedules) and which it is capable of delivering. Many institutions have opened satellite campuses and/or have invested in video-teleconferencing and Internet capability as a means of better meeting customer requirements. Others have the capacity to deliver programs on site at company locations.

- *Service bundles.* The most effective KSC partners develop service bundles: packages of services that add value and benefit the customer company. One way to look at service bundles is to consider the steps that go into the development and delivery of successful education and training initiatives in the new work environment. These steps include the following:[15]

1. *Identification of necessary skills.* Business objectives determine which skills are necessary for the organization to achieve success. A formal system may set up a skill dictionary or database. (A dictionary is a map of the ideal skills for a company's employees.)

2. *Skills assessment.* An initial assessment determines which skills are already available and which are not.

3. *"Gaps analysis."* Gaps analysis quantifies the difference between current skill levels and those the company's employees need now, next year, or 10 years hence. This analysis helps the company decide where to put its training dollars now and in the future.

4. *Curriculum development and delivery.* The resulting skill gap yields a training curriculum. Curriculum is an aggregation of learning events taken in a logical progression to fill in the gaps defined by the current competence level (skills inventory) and the desired competence level (needs analysis).

5. *Post-course assessment.* Such assessment determines if a new skill has been achieved. If it has not, the learner completes remedial training, followed by a new post-course assessment.

6. *Job roles.* As business objectives change, new skill requirements are filtered into job roles. These are reflected immediately in the learner's curriculum plan, so that the training program remains relevant despite changing objectives.

Organizations need total solutions, not ones limited by the content type or format a provider chooses to use. Institutions that want to participate in KSCs would do well to develop service bundles that provide a total solution that encompasses the entire skill development process. In so doing, they can create differentiation by adding value along three dimensions: product, information, and function/process (e.g., creating a product/service bundle and taking over the customer's processes).

Capacity

Identifying and implementing the element(s) that should be included in a service bundle means aligning each business customer's principal need(s) with the expertise an institution possesses (or can build) to address those needs. Postsecondary institutions that choose to participate as leaders in KSCs will respond with specific value bundles encompassing tailored, value-added services, customized programs, and high levels of understanding about the business customer. Some will be able deliver services to a highly fragmented market, serving multiple customers, multiple market types, and multiple geographies; others will focus on narrower market niches. Both will require operational structures—e.g., account management, consumer direct marketing, customer councils—to strategize and execute consistently.

Postsecondary institutions must decide what they will and will not do to take best advantage of the opportunities afforded by KSCs. An institution's strategy will be influenced by its capacity—its "breadth, depth, and reach."[16]

- *Breadth* refers to the extent to which the institutional staff's technical skills are sufficient to meet the market's technical needs. Certain institutions have national reputations in particular fields and would do well to work with companies from those industries. Most schools have an array of expertise across the campus but rarely tap into that diversity to develop a service bundle.
- *Depth* refers to the institution's ability to innovate and tailor services to fit the needs of a particular environment. Postsecondary institutions with "low depth" may deliver packaged services while institutions with "high depth" have the capacity to adapt existing services and invent new services to meet the needs of individual businesses.
- *Reach* refers to the number of clients an institution can serve at the same time. Reach typically increases as an organization becomes larger. However, small institutions can expand their reach by adopting certain service delivery strategies (e.g., consortium of firms versus single company, classroom versus the Internet).

Flexibility is a critical characteristic of an effective supply chain, as well as its individual participants. Simplicity and speed are two components of flexibility that deserve attention.[17]

- *Simplicity* refers to actions taken to reduce complexity and increase commonality in operations. Lack of a common product language is one of the most subtle and stubborn barriers to improved supply chain performance. Industry skill standards are one basis for building a common set of standards to enhance communication and simplify operations within KSCs. Postsecondary institutions should identify existing industry skill standards for the companies with which they work and should integrate these standards into their curriculum. The development of skill standards also can contribute to an often overlooked aspect of simplification: reducing uniqueness and variety. Course descriptions based on specific skills and competencies obtained would help delineate the overlap between courses and would begin to promote modularization and reduce apparent variety. The development of programs that provide foundation competencies that contribute to a number of areas would also enhance an institution's capacity to provide customized services. The enhanced services would be based on skill modules built off of the foundation competencies and developed to meet the needs of specific business customers.

- *Speed.* Increasing speed means reducing cycle times for course design and delivery. It also means managing program delivery so that individuals get through the learning and apply their acquired skills and competencies on the job as quickly as possible. For a new employee, this may mean reducing the time from graduation to job entry. For an incumbent worker, it may mean Internet-based training available at the job site, electronic performance support systems, or on-the job learning assignments.

Information is the glue that links a KSC. Many postsecondary institutions have used formal business advisory boards as a means of maintaining contact with companies. But KSCs require more. Project task forces—teams that combine college and business staff to address a business training need—are better. Shared staff or college staff located at company facilities are better still. The ultimate in integration is to have the information technology capacity to participate in a KSC online, in as close to real time as possible. The technology must support both the planning and the execution of the supply chain activities within the institution and must link the institution to the larger company KSC. For example, students within Next Step, a college partnership providing training to members of the Communication Workers of America union within Bell Atlantic, use laptops with Lotus Notes to track the application of course concepts and learning on the job. Instructors at participating colleges review these notes and meet quarterly to revise the curriculum accordingly.

Partners

Leading companies recognize that competitive advantage is becoming less closely tied to their own innate capabilities; increasingly, their success is defined by relationships and linkages forged with organizations outside their immediate sphere of influence. The same is true of postsecondary institutions: alliances and partnerships are a good way to participate in KSCs.

Most postsecondary institutions focus on relatively few specialty areas; consequently, few could meet all the needs of their business clients. For many institutions, focusing on a single competency is a sound business strategy. It is not surprising, therefore, that many colleges have elected to "sell" their programs through other organizations. For example, Cardean, an Internet consortium that is a part of Unext.com, features classes from several universities, including Carnegie-Mellon, Chicago, Columbia, Stanford, and the London School of Economics. Cardean sells the programs to companies to include in their employee education programs.

Because the market is likely to respond more favorably to an institution that can meet a range of needs, some postsecondary institutions may find it necessary to increase their capacity by forming alliances with other providers. By leveraging focused core competencies, networks of service providers offer a stronger suite of capabilities than any could individually.[18]

Institutions that elect to address an array of business needs are confronted with the classic "make" or "buy" decision. In this case, "make" refers to those services that will be delivered through in-house people, while "buy" refers to those services that will be delivered through affiliations with partners. The two ends of the continuum are

- *full service provider.* A full service provider provides a full range of services using in-house staff. As noted earlier, colleges and universities often have diverse talent and expertise on campus. The challenge is to "package" this diverse talent in a manageable service bundle.
- *full service broker.* A full service broker provides a full range of services through alliances with external providers. (Alliances may take the form of referrals or contracted services.) In terms of KSCs, more opportunities to innovate exist among institutions than within institutions. For example, creating articulation agreements between institutions adds value to the labor pipeline. The development of service bundles across institutions holds unlimited promise for meeting business needs.

  The broker, as an information rather than a transaction manager, is a critical participant in the KSC, guiding both the formation and implementation of longer-term relationships and inter-firm

KSC networks. The broker is in an ideal position to serve as a joint problem solver and provider of intelligence about the knowledge marketplace. Savvy companies seek this insight in a prospective outsource provider.[19,20]

Partnerships can be difficult. Organizations developing strategic alliances or partnerships must understand each other's products and services sufficiently to know when to call the other and how to integrate services. Incongruent expectations and turf battles are some of the types of issues that, if not addressed up front, can doom a partnership. The critical question is how to effectively manage and leverage the skills and talents of supply chain partners.

Research on material supply chains suggests that the supply chain organization or partnership goes through a natural progression.[21] Traditionally, it starts out *disconnected* (a condition probably reflective of the status of most postsecondary institutions vis-á-vis KSCs). *Cooperation*, whereby institutions exchange bits of essential information and engage some business customers in longer-term contracts, is the threshold level of interaction for a KSC. Cooperation is a necessary though not sufficient condition. The next level of intensity is *coordination*, whereby information is exchanged in a manner that permits quick response systems, electronic transfer and exchange of data, and other mechanisms that attempt to make seamless many of the traditional linkages between and among trading parties. The final stage of evolution of a KSC is the creation of a *virtual "knowledge supply web"* which provides key business customers with access to communities of suppliers, as well as the ability to collaboratively plan, forecast, and replenish knowledge on as much of a real-time basis as possible.

The optimal KSC is just that: a chain; interconnected links that work together. The challenge for postsecondary institutions that want to participate in KSCs is to work collaboratively with business customers, individual clients, partners, institutional staff, and others to manage knowledge across the institution on behalf of the business customer.

Execution

With the emergence of KSCs, business will demand more from knowledge-related services. It will place increased emphasis on alignment with business goals, viewing learning as a continuous process, tracking skill achievements from varied learning events, ROI measurement, and new strategies to achieve quantum improvements in cost, speed, and quality of knowledge acquisition. To meet these requirements, postsecondary and postbaccalaureate institutions will need to demonstrate operational excellence in management of the knowledge supply chain.[22]

One of the best ways to demonstrate the changes required for postsecondary institutions to participate in a KSC as well as the difference between KSCs and many existing business/education partnerships is to describe barriers to operational excellence. Three barriers deserve attention:

- *Model of education.* The traditional postsecondary and postbaccalaureate model of education involves sequenced courses, a focus on foundation/academic knowledge, scheduling on an academic calendar, presentation in lecture format, academic credit for completed courses, and degrees awarded on the basis of the accumulation of specific course credits.

  This is in marked contrast to the KSC model, which involves modular units, a focus on competencies, scheduling on a just-in-time basis, presentation in a variety of formats (each using contextual learning), "credit" based on demonstration of competency, and possible certification awarded on the basis of acquisition of a specific set of competencies.

- *Provider collaboration.* The institutional structures and processes that reinforce and support the traditional model of education may pose an even more significant barrier than the model of education. KSCs include a network of providers. For this network to function, the provider partners must be able to recognize and accept course credits and certified competencies from the other partners. Despite the increasing number of articulation agreements among institutions, many colleges and universities still strictly limit the acceptance of credits earned at other institutions. The KSC model shifts the debate from course credits to recognition of competencies certified by another provider. The ultimate solution to this bureaucratic roadblock may be a degree or certification awarded through a third-party broker that combines courses or training from a variety of providers. (This is the model that Cardean hopes to pursue.)

  A related and greater challenge for many postsecondary institutions is the granting of credit for company training programs or life experience. Credentialling—granting credit for on-the-job learning—poses the least problem. Many institutions are willing to grant credit (primarily at the undergraduate level) for prior training, provided there has been an evaluation component. Yet few company training programs have an evaluation component, e.g., test or practicum, by which to assess whether a student should be awarded credit. Some institutions, such as University of Phoenix, rely on a comparison of the content of the company training to the university's course content when deciding whether to grant credit.

Evaluating life experience is a bigger challenge. While Empire State University in New York and the Council for Experiential Learning have track records in providing credit for life experience, most institutions do not have the systems required to assess and evaluate an individual's life experience. Practices at institutions such as Western Governors University, where students may "test out" of courses in a certificate program, may be one solution to this dilemma, but experience to date is limited, and the economics are uncertain.[23]

KSCs support an approach to learning that acknowledges and builds upon an individual's current competencies, however they were acquired. At the postsecondary level, rigid course sequences, academic calendars, degree requirements, and other requirements are institutional impediments to participation in KSCs. Phoenix, Sylvan, and other for-profit education and training organizations have developed models for working with companies that reduce or eliminate these impediments. The competition postsecondary in-stitutions face from these for-profit organizations is likely to erode many of the institutional barriers to participation in KSCs. But so long as these traditional institutions also strive to meet bureau-cratic university requirements to the detriment of other educa-tional purposes, such as those represented by KSCs, they will not become preferred suppliers.[24]

- *Business partners.* A KSC begins and ends with a business partner. An analysis and thorough understanding of business partner needs is a fundamental requirement of participation in a KSC. Many education institutions have taken off-the-shelf courses and "re-purposed" them for presentation to a business audience through the Internet or videoconference format. Lacking analysis that would indicate that this program meets particular business needs, this is not an example of participation in a KSC.

  Many colleges and universities make their courses available to corporate employees as part of the company's education benefit program. While the relationships established through such ar-rangements can be the foundation for a discussion on participation in a KSC, they are not, per se, examples of participation in a KSC. One of the shifts in thinking that a business undergoes in creating a KSC is from "education as a benefit" to "education as an invest-ment." This new viewpoint requires that investments in education and training contribute to achieving the business's strategic objec-tives. Simply offering courses to employees does not do that. (However, courses could contribute to strategic objectives if the company had a workforce plan to use the employees' newly acquired knowledge and skills. Assisting the company in the development of a workforce plan would be part of a value-added service bundle.)

The fundamental shift required to participate in a KSC is from "make to stock" to "make to demand." Service offerings must be tailored to the needs of the business customer. This is one of the reasons for this chapter's extensive attention to the issue of cycle time or speed of development. The ability to respond to and address business needs is what participation in KSCs is all about. Many institutions have found that creating a separate business unit focused on business partnerships and independent of the education bureaucracy is one of the best strategies for attaining this ability.

All education institutions are not equally flexible or adept at change. Postsecondary institutions that have the ability to execute—to segment markets, create targeted product/service bundles, create responsive structures, and develop the necessary partnerships to deliver the required benefits to business customers—will be preferred suppliers within the growing web of KSCs.

CONCLUSION

The changing economic and business environment makes knowledge and skills a source of competitive advantage. Companies are placing greater importance on the skills of their workforce, making workforce development a critical component of a company's competitive edge. It is the ability of companies—as well as of local communities and regions—to learn, adapt, and change that will determine their long-run economic performance and competitiveness. KSCs represent a different way to organize and manage the way in which knowledge and skills are acquired. They shift the focus in terms of managing supplier relationships from hierarchies, to markets, and now to networks.

Postsecondary education institutions can play a part in KSCs if they are willing to change how and what they deliver to their customers. Key changes include the following:

- seeing business as the customer while using whatever is needed to ensure that individuals obtain the knowledge and skills business demands;
- working as part of a collaborative supplier network;
- adopting competency-based, modular training formats;

- developing value-added service bundles, possibly through separate operating units;
- reducing cycle time, improving quality, and demonstrating results; and
- moving from product-centered to demand-centered strategies.

NOTES

1. Philip B. Evans and Thomas S. Wurster, "Strategy and the Economics of Information," *Harvard Business Review,* September-October 1997, p. 71.
2. Phillipe Masse, et al. "The Changing Skill Structure of Employment in Canada." R-99-7E, Applied Research Branch, Human Resource Development, Novemeber 1998.
3. Petter Cappelli et al. *Change at Work.* Oxford: Oxford University Press, 1997.
4. See the Interim Corporation at http://www.interim.com and click on "Workforce Trends." See also National Alliance of Business, "The New Reality: Emerging Responsibilities in a Changing Workplace," *Workforce Economics Trends,* March 1998.
5. Ibid.
6. The NGM Workforce Issues Thrust Team, "Knowledge Supply Chains: A Next Generation Manufacturing Imperative," Agility Forum, January 1997.
7. Susan Helper and Mari Sako, "Supplier Relations in Japan and the United States: Are They Converging?" *Sloan Management Review,* Spring 1995.
8. David L. Anderson and Hau Lee, "Synchronized Supply Chains: The New Frontier," http://www.ascet.com/wp/wpAnderson.html
9. Gene Tyndall, Christopher Gopal, Wolfgang Partsch, and John Kamuff. *Supercharging Supply Chains: New Ways to Increase Value through Global Operational Excellence.* New York: John Wiley & Sons, 1998.
10. See Terri Bergman. *Approaches to Forming a Learning Consortium.* Washington, DC: National Alliance of Business, 1995.
11. Michael E. Porter, "Clusters and the New Economics of Competition," *Harvard Business Review,* November-December 1998.
12. David Stamps, "Enterprise Training: This Changes Everything," *Training,* January 1999.
13. Tyndall et al., *Supercharging Supply Chains.*
14. "Knowledge: The Priceless Corporate Asset." KnowledgeSoft White Paper, 1999.
15. Stamps, "Enterprise Training."
16. Tom Tuttle, Sarah Garretson, Stephen Mitchell, Robert Meyer and Russ Hamm. *Identifying and Targeting Market and Customer Segments.* Washington, DC: National Alliance of Business, 1997.
17. Based on Tyndall et al., *Supercharging Supply Chains.*
18. Much of this discussion draws from Stephen Mitchell. *Delivering Integrated Services: Models for Facilitating Change in Small and Mid-Sized Firms.* Washington, DC: National Alliance of Business, 1997.
19. Tyndall et al., *Supercharging Supply Chains.*
20. Electronic commerce is the next supply chain battleground—for both material and knowledge supply chains—and it will change the nature of competition. In material supply chains, some distributors and resellers are becoming "master channel managers," providing and managing electronic commerce channels for others. What institution will provide the equivalent service in KSCs?

21. Tyndall et al., *Supercharging Supply Chains.*
22. Tyndall et al. *Supercharging Supply Chains,* notes that above all else, supply chain management is about operational excellence.
23. The authors wish to thank Kay Kohl for her comments and insights on university practices related to granting credit for training and life experience.
24. Arnold Packer, "The End of Routine Work and the Need for a Career Transcript," Prepared for the Hudson Institute's Workforce 2020 Conference, 1998.

PART 2

• • • • • • • • • • •

Strategies for Extending Learning Resources in an Information Age

CHAPTER 5

Tangled Web(s): The Rise of the Absent-Networked Professor and "The Translucent University"

Michael Schrage

Frederick LePlay was that most dangerous of academics. Not only was he a French intellectual, but he was an engineer turned sociologist. Although he was one of the first quantitative sociologists, LePlay occasionally came up with pithy epigrams, my favorite of which is "The most important product of The Mines is The Miner."

This observation directly inspired my own insight into the rise of the Internet, intranets, and other digital media: "The most important product of The Network is The Networker." The kinds of networks we design depend on what kinds of networkers we really want our people to be. That's hardly self-evident, and it certainly provokes hard questions. Even the most enlightened for-profit enterprises have trouble articulating what kind of networkers they want their people to be. They quickly discover that their debates about network design are far more reflective of conflicts in their values than of technological constraints.

Designing a network is very much like designing a nervous system: Where do you want to put the intelligence? Should it be centralized or decentralized? How much goes where? What about the emotions? Is a mind necessary? How about a conscience? No? Too high level? A nervous system designed by psychologists will function differently from one designed by neurophysiologists

Michael Schrage is co-director of the E-Markets Initiative of the Media Lab at the Massachusetts Institute of Technology, and executive director of the Merrill Lynch Innovation Grants competition for doctoral students.

or a tag team of computer scientists and engineers. The more choices you have, the more your values matter. Alas, the networks to hell are wired with good intentions.

Most university departments (let alone most universities) are unable even to reach a polite consensus on what kind of scholars and teaching assistants they want their graduate students to be. The idea that the academic "establishment" (however we care to define it) can reach consensus on the role new technologies should play in shaping graduate education isn't just wishful thinking; it's delusional to the point of dysfunction.

So to hell with consensus. What are some of the misleading assumptions and miscast issues surrounding technology management that threaten to violate the Hippocratic admonition, "First, do no harm"? Serious research universities must respect the truth that the rise of digital media will force them to reevaluate precisely what kind of roles, rights, and responsibilities their graduate communities should have. My personal belief (based on painful experience in the for-profit world) is that not unlike the automobile, these technologies ultimately will hurt the quality of graduate life as much as they enhance it. The question is whether universities as institutions—or administrators as individuals—will respond to the unhappier consequences of digital innovation on campus. Or will they deny that they exist altogether?

Make no mistake: Digital media will (continue to) redefine all aspects of higher education regardless of what deans, vice chancellors, and department chairs do. Market forces as much as technological innovation ensure that traditional universities will come to see high-bandwidth networks as rivals to their own missions as much as parts of their own infrastructures.

Of course, universities are different. Of course, universities stand for a different kind of experience and community than virtually any other kind of global institution. Of course, universities are "brands" that offer a "unique selling proposition" for top-quality human capital in the increasingly competitive global marketplace.

Then again, the *virtual* amazon.com offers a different shopping experience than the *physical* Barnes&Noble. AutobyTel and CarPoint offer different shopping experiences than used car dealers. Consider how the "smart money" values those rivals. At present, the value of traditional economic institutions is being challenged, redefined, and undermined by networked counterparts. Who believes that the University of Phoenix represents just a first wave of change—rather than the coming tide—in the economics of higher education?

That said, let's quickly dispose of that dangerously misleading cliche that the Internet, intranets, and digital media are driving a new "information economy." In fact, the "information age" metaphor is a misnomer. The digital technologies restructuring enterprise and academe are far less about the creation and management of new information than they are about the creation and management of new relationships.

Talk with a Tim Berners-Lee, whose CERN team effectively created the World Wide Web protocols, and you'll hear someone talk about how important it was for the high-energy particle physics community to be able to communicate with itself in a dynamic, interactive new way. Berners-Lee intuitively appreciated that the real value of a medium lies less in the information that it carries than in the communities it creates. The first book Gutenberg published with his brand new medium was not a dictionary or an almanac chock full of data; it was the Bible. And although the Bible is "about" information, it really is about managing community and relationships.

Consider this *gedankenexperiment*: Whenever you see the word "information," substitute the word "relationship." Instead of "management information systems," you get "management relationships systems"; instead of "information technology," you get "relationships technology"; instead of "digital-driven information economy," you get "digital-driven relationships economy." The word inspires a different design sensibility and awareness.

Examining the impact of digital technologies on the university is better done through the lens of relationships than through the windows of information. This is only appropriate because, frankly, most of us would agree that the real value of the university experience comes from the "collegiality" of relationships among peers and professors and proteges. The knowledge that universities generate is a product and byproduct of these relationships. A *collection* of scholars is not a *community* of scholars.

Some relationships may be healthier than others, but the fact remains: When graduate students talk about the quality of their experiences at a university, they tend to describe the quality of the relationships they've had. They hated their advisor; they had tremendous collaborators or peer support; they learned a lot from the students they taught; they learned more going to conferences than from the grad seminars; they wished their professor didn't grab credit from them; they used the Internet to solicit comments on a draft of their thesis, etc.

So when we talk about the impact of technology on the quality of graduate education and experiences, the questions we have to ask are, What kind of impact will technology have on the future of relationships? How effective are universities at creating environments that facilitate high-quality relationships? In particular, how effective are they at using technology to manage relationships?

Unfortunately, as embarrassing experiences at the University of Michigan, NYU, Harvard, UC Berkeley, Stanford, and other universities unambiguously demonstrate, most schools can't even handle e-mail conflicts without involving their deans of discipline and university counsels. Debates about "political correctness" and poorly drawn speech codes are not the province of this chapter. However, the underlying message is that most universities do a lousy job of crafting and managing the rules of relationships on campus. New technologies guarantee new problems for universities—especially those that lack the spine, guts, and wisdom to declare what values they stand for when it comes to creating productive relationships for all their students.

Alas, digital media seem to have been invented to blur the lines between crisp categories and to create hitherto unimagined loopholes. The consequence? Networks can create unhealthy interactions even more easily than they can enable value-added relationships.

Consider the following scenarios. Decide whether they are plausible and whether they represent significant "quality of education" issues for the graduate school community.

- A Japanese graduate physics student whose spoken English is not so good tells his sophomore students that he prefers to communicate by e-mail. He sets up a class Web site with FAQs. He insists that his students register confirmation that they have read the FAQs before they e-mail him a question. If they do not, he will not respond. Otherwise, he promises to respond to all questions within 24 hours. He honors that commitment. However, he graciously declines to meet with students individually or to conduct any after-class discussion groups. Only a handful of students complain. Now two other physics TAs want to substitute e-mail/FAQs for human interaction.

- A globe-trotting professor tells his graduate students that all his seminars will be virtual. Students need to load the appropriate software onto their laptops and link into the professor's site for a real-time video-teleconference. Some of the students have their own laptop cameras so the professor can see them. In addition, the site is linked to several simulations that are constantly referred to during the seminar and that are manipulable by the students. The 90-minute sessions are lively.

    The professor happens to be an adjunct at an elite Indian university. Typically, five graduate students from the university also participate in these Internet seminars. Sometimes they ask questions in English, other times in Hindi. The Indian students receive credit for the seminar; the professor receives a stipend. He never formally notified his department chair of his seminar's double duty or of his own double dipping; he is the department chair.

- Three professors at three different institutions decide to make their "invisible" college "translucent." They decide to create a virtual department around their collaborative research initiative.

Two of the three are widely acknowledged as the best in their field. The three receive both university and private funding to support their research as well as the site. There are constant debates about how the federal funding should be split. Site maintenance involves sophisticated search and simulation algorithms. All of the graduate students are required to support and update the Web site. All of their own research must be posted on the site. Their contributions are acknowledged on a separate page on the site; the three professors are listed as the main authors.

The professors are rigorous about maintaining a constant flow of upgrades and enhancements from their graduate students. The professors "audit" their contributions every week. The students are told that research that gets "clicked" and downloaded the most will receive additional funding. Two of the students have friends at other universities create "knowbots" that make it appear that their contributions are more popular than they really are. Another student sends out hundreds of e-mails to user groups in an effort to publicize her contributions to the site. Yet another student writes an applette that attaches his name to the portions of the research for which he is responsible whenever it's downloaded. The three professors, one of whom is the recipient of the largest NSF and ONR grants in the school's history, want the three institutions to contribute funds for the purchase of another server. They also want to be able to grant joint graduate degrees to two of their favorite students.

- A quintet of graduate students from four different universities discover each other over the Web. They are all working on related dissertations. They meet at a conference and determine that they should create a virtual research community. For all intents and purposes, they form a collaborative that endures for three critical years. Their work is regarded as excellent. However, one of the thesis advisers is unhappy about the level of collaboration and says a thesis requires more individual than collaborative research. The student clearly and definitively documents which aspects of his research are unique. The adviser is adamant. The vice chancellor of research ultimately intervenes in favor of the student. Each of the other students comes to the university to support his colleague.

- A survey of graduate students reveals a disturbing statistic: Women and minorities are more than 30 percent less likely to actively contribute to interactive Internet seminars and user groups than their white male counterparts. Even worse, their contributions are 20 percent less likely to evoke further comments than contributions from white males. Both the contribution level and response rates increase dramatically when comments are made anonymously. However, many schools and graduate departments forbid anonymous contributions, arguing that they contradict the spirit of open academic inquiry and discussion.

- When their accrediting agency assures them they face no risk in doing so, two universities decide to consolidate their anthropology departments and create a single degree-granting virtual anthropology department. Not coincidentally, the state governor tells her university regents that she wants to use the Internet as a medium to consolidate under-enrolled university departments throughout the state to cut costs. Twenty faculty members in their sixties sue the state on the grounds that forcing them to adopt digital technologies is a form of age discrimination.

- A private company offers major universities $50 million over seven years to provide branded international Internet/Telecon graduate credit programs to Asian universities. All the universities have to do is provide their name and any five professors of their choosing for a mere 90 minutes per week.

To be sure, some of these scenarios are more fanciful than others. Yet all are within the realm of possibility, and two are true almost in their entirety. (Perhaps a more science fiction-like approach would prove more compelling.)

I strongly believe that 25 years of technological revolution do not trump three million years of biological evolution. These vignettes are all about technology-enabled transformations in academic relationships. (Please note that I barely touched on intellectual property and research conflicts of interest, for which technology-driven scenarios are easy enough to imagine.) Nevertheless, every major university, public and private, will have difficult challenges to address regarding where they should draw the line between education as a for-profit business and education as a calling. It is increasingly difficult to tell graduate students that they are not consumers when their universities are most assuredly acting like IPO-conscious entrepreneurs.

The preceding scenarios were selected because each in its own way strikes at the heart of how universities perceive themselves and at the quality of experiences they provide. Do we use technology to make life easier for the graduate students at the expense of the undergraduate? Do we use technology to make life easier for the hotshot professor at the expense of the graduate student? Do we use these technologies to make life easier for the university at the expense of the professor (or vice versa)? Are we using networks to automate academic relationships or to augment them? What are our criteria for those choices? It is not clear whether faculty councils, deans, vice chancellors, presidents, or trustees are in the best position to frame these questions for productive debate. After all, a high-quality university is not just a "system"; it is an "environment." And managing environments poses different challenges than managing systems.

So where do universities as institutions stand on these issues? Or do universities decide that these questions are best delegated to departments? Perhaps they should be delegated to the professors. After all, the professoriate is in the best position to determine what kinds of relationships should prove most beneficial for their students. As technology continues to obliterate academic, administrative, and economic distinctions that once mattered a great deal, chaos can fill the void just as easily as fundamental values. By chaos I do not mean mindless anarchy; I mean harsh conflicts driven by egos and opportunism rather than by respect for what the institution stands for. It has been said that the reason academic battles are so vicious is that the stakes are so small. Tomorrow's stakes are not "so small," and the battles may become ever more vicious.

So there are no happy conclusions for this chapter. Some universities will conclude that technology absolutely should be permitted—indeed, encouraged—to substitute for human interaction. Other institutions, by dint of policy, culture, or an iron chancellor, will create "affirmative action" plans requiring that professors and graduate students meet their charges face to face. Ultimately, the issue is not which path is better; rather, it is whether these choices are being made by default or by design. Is technology being embraced as an excuse or as a reason; to create interactions or to avoid them; to facilitate communication and collaboration or simply to exchange information and free up time?

My concern is not that universities will fail to come up with good answers to these questions; it's that universities prefer to avoid these kinds of questions altogether. My fear is that universities consistently will choose the path of least resistance rather than the path of maximum advantage. What is the path of maximum advantage? I don't know. But I do know that it doesn't begin with a networked computer on every desk or in every dorm. It begins with graduate students, professors, administrators, and yes, even accreditors asking what kinds of relationships networks and digital technologies should enable. In the final analysis, do the networks mirror the extent to which universities stand for community, creativity, and scholarship?

CHAPTER 6

Financing Postbaccalaureate Education in an Age of Telecommunicated Learning

Michael B. Goldstein

The financial management of any enterprise is primarily an effort to predict the future in the context of the present as informed by the past. Higher education is no different. Factors ranging from new program requests and faculty salary adjustments to the probable price of fuel oil drive the expense side, and estimates of student enrollment and the proportion of institutional scholarships necessary to meet enrollment goals are among the many variables on the income side. Historically, higher education has been a relatively stable sector; institutions have been able to plan from year to year with a reasonable expectation of ending up within a comfortable distance of their estimates. Most important, capital needs could be anticipated over a relatively long time period, and the methods of financing capital costs, such as capital campaigns and bond issues, likewise could abide a longer time frame.

For an increasing number of institutions, changes in the needs and nature of learner populations and, perhaps most significant, the implications of the telecommunications revolution for teaching and learning are making reliable modeling more difficult. Predictions of the future of postsecondary education in the telecommunications age range from the utopian "everything for everyone" to Peter Drucker's "fate of the dinosaurs." Education beyond the undergraduate level is particularly volatile, for a number of reasons.

Michael B. Goldstein is a member of the law firm of Dow, Lohnes and Albertson, PLLC, where he is in charge of the firm's educational institutions practice.

- The learner population is at once more mobile and sophisticated and yet less able to accommodate to the time-and-place restrictions of traditional campus-based programs.
- Demand for instructional content is becoming increasingly narrow and situation-specific.
- Reliance is increasingly on employer-paid or subsidized tuition and less on traditional student-centered financial aid.
- Purveyors of postbaccalaureate education are less likely to be traditional institutions.
- Content-specific certification, as opposed to a traditional graduate degree, is more likely to be the desired outcome, resulting in greater reliance on third-party specialized certification in lieu of institutional accreditation.
- State regulation is becoming increasingly important as the uniqueness of conventionally accredited credentials decreases.
- Time to completion, cost, and convenience increasingly rival institutional prestige as marketing advantages; new brand names, such as Novell, are gaining value over traditional institutional brands.

Some of these premises can be challenged, but collectively they cannot be ignored. *"Just in case"* education, defined as obtaining a degree or other credential to prepare for a relatively distant future (characteristic of "traditional" higher education sought prior to entering the workforce), has given way to *"just in time"* education, where the learner seeks education for an immediate need, notably to retain or to advance in his or her position (characteristic of the much-touted "new learners" of the past two decades); this, in turn, has given way to *"just for me"* education, embodying the shift from a few models of fixed-place institution/faculty-centered education to a multifaceted learner-centered environment where time and place become insignificant and control over the choices of "how and what" shift toward the learner (characteristic, perhaps, of postsecondary education in the new millennium).[1] This shift changes the institution-centered model so significantly as to make historic precedent unreliable. The financial future of postbaccalaureate education must be planned in the midst of this pedagogically charged and technologically unstable environment.

Discussion of how market forces and technology relate to issues of postbaccalaureate teaching and learning and to the role of faculty in a learner-centered environment increasingly shifts the focus to how institutions will compete in an environment where their principal capital assets are a collection of ivy-covered buildings (or the 1960s equivalent: reinforced concrete) surrounding a graceful quadrangle (or parking structure) when the assets that are needed now relate to acquiring new technologies and the ability to apply those assets to access new markets. How can institutions founded on the premise of "come to us" learning characterized by bricks-and-mortar class-rooms *afford* to adapt to an environment where, in effect, the institution must go to the learner? And how can an institution marshal the economic resources to compete effectively in an environment where competition not only from its peers but also from "outsiders" is increasingly the norm, protection of the perceived high cost of entry has been eroded, and the very significance—and certainly the hegemony—of the traditional academic credential is in doubt? How institutions secure and commit resources to enable them to adapt to these changes and how they choose their partners in an environment that is making partnering a virtual necessity will not only determine the success of individual schools but also will shape the nature of the universe of postbaccalaureate education.

Discussions of the forces shaping graduate education and of the decisions institutional leaders are being expected to make among sharply competing forces and influences appear elsewhere in this book. But once the policy decisions are made, how does an institution meet the costs these changes entail, particularly in light of conflicting demands for the same (often scarce) institutional resources? And how is the policy debate to be informed by what is economically within an institution's reach? This chapter considers the changed environment of postbaccalaureate education—and of the postsecondary mar-ketplace as a whole—that is transforming the resource equation. Particular emphasis is placed on the decision-making process required in the context of the particular marketplace and the partnerships that might derive from or even drive those choices.

The term *marketplace* is often disquieting to academic administrators and faculty, but it is an honest and inescapable definition of the environment in which higher education—and particularly postbaccalaureate education—must compete. An institution's first and most important task in determining how to make "prudent choices" is to define its market. The dream (some would say chimera) of Clark Kerr's "multiversity"[2] is rapidly being replaced by agile niche players which identify and occupy distinct corners of the postsecondary universe. The idea of a university becoming "all things to all people" is not passé because it is wrong but because it is largely unattainable. Just as each institution must identify its market, so each market identifies its institution. In identifying its market, an institution must identify not only the other occu-pants, but also its defining characteristics, including how—in that market space—capital can be found.

Institutions have secured capital in several ways. For a fortunate few, earned revenue creates reserves that can be used for capital purposes. Most commonly, institutions beg. That is, they seek gifts and grants, which of course are the most attractive option, since the capital comes relatively free of cost.[3]

Alternatively, institutions have turned to "renting" capital through the use of a variety of debt instruments, ranging from conventional mortgages to bonded debt. In recent years, a third approach has gained favor. Following first the model of the business community and then that of the largest nonprofit sector, health care, institutions have turned toward "outsourcing." Generally seen as a way to cut costs and increase productivity, outsourcing is in fact a way to rent the use of another entity's capital. Some of the approaches to outsourcing have indeed been ingenious: Starting with such mundane areas as security, food service, and maintenance, colleges and universities have contracted out everything from student recruitment and courseware development to the offering of instruction itself. What is left in some cases is an institutional entity that carries on a set of core functions surrounded by a galaxy of supporting (and supported) organizations. Most often, these supporting organizations are *for*-profit entities, precisely because they can create capital in ways that institutions cannot. Thus, when institutions contract out their marketing operations (euphemistically called "enrollment management") to private companies, they are using the latter's working capital in lieu of laying out institutional funds in advance of revenues. It is even becoming common for nonprofit and public institutions to contract with for-profit schools to provide instruction in highly capital-intensive areas, such as information technology.

By outsourcing, capital-intensive services are financed by "renting" someone else's capital. This makes eminent sense for institutions that operate on a cash basis, like a corner grocery store (sell one can of peas, use the cash to buy another can—the traditional style of thinking in the nonprofit and public communities). But does it make sense from a business perspective? Are institutions giving away the opportunity to "grow" value by using—but not owning—other entities' capital? As discussed below, alternatives do exist to enable institutions to capture the value that traditionally has been the province of the for-profit sector.

Another important difference exists between conventional (campus-based, face-to-face) learning and that which is technology mediated. The capital cost of a campus involves its construction and, over time, its improvement and the replacement of obsolete facilities. But the major capital cost—the creation of the campus—does not usually recur. On the other hand, the cost of creating new programs is primarily an operating expense: a faculty member may be given released time to create a new course, but typically there is no associated capital cost.

Telecommunicated learning, on the other hand, requires cyclical capital investment to create, market, and deliver courseware. Development of an effective technology-mediated course can run into seven figures, requiring the involvement of an entire cast of instructional developers and technicians, as well as expensive (and quickly obsolescent) equipment; the capital demands are both large and uniquely recurrent. "Courseware" is a capital asset, yet the traditional institutional economic model treats it the same as a set of lecture notes. Existing capital formation structures simply are not adequate for this task.

Of course, there is another way to secure capital: Sell a piece of the enterprise in exchange for cash (or something else of value). That is how the business world functions; we call it "capitalism." Companies "create" capital by selling a share of their entity. Investors pay for a share of a company in the hope that the company's overall value will increase, and with it the value of their share. However, since selling a share of the academic enterprise itself has not been seen as a realistic option for nonprofit and public institutions,[4] for those institutions for whom competing in the postbaccalaureate market means a substantial capital investment—either for facilities and equipment or the working capital costs attendant upon acquiring and marketing courses—the capital market represents an almost entirely untapped resource.

An essential premise of the capital marketplace is *return on investment*. This is fundamentally different from the premises of traditional higher education capital financing (gifts, grants, and debt). In the case of gifts and grants, the value proposition is intrinsic in the concept of "doing good" (although it is not uncommon for a grantor to have its own economic interests). In the case of debt, the economic premise is based on the ability of the borrower (the institution) to pay back the principal of the loan plus reasonable interest. The funds are not expected to make the institution more "profitable," but rather to enhance its *capacity* to pay (and, if that fails, the lender typically has a security interest sufficient to reasonably protect the debt). In the case of the capital marketplace, however, the basic assumption is that the value of the investment will be multiplied by the increased value of the enterprise. Lenders think in terms of a return of a few percent; investors, particularly in start-up enterprises, contemplate returns on the order of integer multiples of their investment. The abiding assumption is that the enterprise will be worth far more as a result of the investment (and after a reasonable passage of time) than before. So if an investor acquires one-third of an enterprise for $15 million (creating the value proposition that the enterprise as a whole is worth $45 million), it is assuming that at some point, the enterprise will be worth perhaps $150 million (at least in the eyes of the investor community), making its investment worth $50 million, or more than tripling the value of the investment. If that can be accomplished in a year or two, the investor will have done very well indeed.

The concept of return on investment tends to resonate badly in academic circles. After all, the purpose of the university is not to make money for shareholders; it is to create and disseminate knowledge. But are these concepts mutually exclusive? Is there a fundamental and inexorable reason that an institution cannot remain true to its academic purposes *and* generate a "profit?" Is there anything inherently wrong with benefiting those who make resources available to the institution? That is done now. Bondholders and lenders "profit" from the interest earned on the money they provide for use by the institution; vendors "profit" from the difference between the cost of providing services to the institution and the price paid. Is there really a good reason that the institution cannot retain some of that profit?

Although nonprofit (and public) entities cannot have shareholders (and therefore no one to whom they can sell a share of the institution), institutions can *separate their functions* to create entities that *can* be capitalized. (The preceding discussion of outsourcing demonstrates the extent to which institutions have moved substantial parts of their programs outside of the nonprofit or public entity.) Postbaccalaureate education certainly is amenable to such a scenario. All that is needed is a plan to develop a program (i.e., an educational service) that, with adequate capital (including working capital to develop, market, and deliver product), can demonstrate significant market penetration and the prospect of a substantial return over a discrete period of time. The economic forces of the capital marketplace take over from there. The real question is how to identify the programmatic areas that can achieve this growth and assemble the structure that will provide for its financing, all the while preserving the institution's fundamental values.

Indeed, these values properly drive constraints. Chief among these is the premise that the institution must retain an appropriate level of academic control; the capitalization (i.e., for-profit) entity must not exercise control over the institution. Likewise, the structure should be transparent to accreditors, regulators, and learners. Finally, use of a capitalization entity should *support* the overall institution rather than siphon support and resources from that which the institution defines as its "core." Use of a properly designed structure can ensure that each of these needs is met.

A precondition of capitalization in the for-profit community is understanding the marketplace. In discussing the financing of postbaccalaureate education, it is important to know the potential players so an institution can both determine opportunities for partnerships and identify competitors for the same resource. (A fundamental premise in the analysis of partnerships is that any likely partner is also a potential competitor, either because it could compete directly or because it could apply its resources to partner with a competing institution.) The nature of potential partners varies according to what is being financed. It is therefore useful to review the general types and characteristics of partner entities, particularly because an entity could fall simultaneously into several categories; for example, a *contractor* could also be a *lender* (to finance equipment), as well as a *passive investor* or *strategic partner*.

- A *lender* is a temporary source of funds, usually (though not always) for a *security interest* either in the subject of the loan (building, equipment), in a defined revenue stream (income from a specific program), or in the borrower's general revenues (tuition, auxiliary fees). The loan could be made to the institution itself or to a for- or nonprofit entity controlled by the institution. A lender expects to benefit from the interest earned on the loan and ceases to participate when the loan has been repaid. A lender rarely becomes directly involved in operations but may require varying levels of reporting. Lenders may be banks (or other kinds of financial institutions), public financing authorities (in which case the debt is usually in the form of bonds), or high-value individuals. (In many respects, an investor who holds "preferred" shares of stock is more like a lender than a shareholder.)

- A *contractor* provides services to the institution or to a for- or nonprofit entity controlled by the institution. A contractor benefits from the difference between the cost of providing the service and the price paid and has no interest in ownership or management of the institution or its entities. Nor does a contractor benefit from appreciation in the value of the entity with which it contracts (except that the price set for services could be pegged to indicators, such as volume, which in turn relate indirectly to increases in value). The scope of a contracting relationship is unlimited, from providing a discrete service to undertaking a major component of institutional operations.

- A *strategic lender* is a variant of the pure financial lender and makes the loan not only to benefit from the interest earned but also to support an activity that benefits its own business. An example would be an entity which provides telecommunications services and supplies financing so an institution can acquire facilities that will enable it to better use the company's services. Interest rates may be below market, in return for an obligation to use the lender's facilities or services.

- A *passive investor* provides funds in return for a share in the ownership of a *for-profit* entity created or controlled by the institution. A passive investor usually participates in the governance of the entity in proportion to its ownership interest; it expects to benefit from the appreciation in the value of the entity in which the investment is made and typically seeks an "exit strategy" allowing for the sale of the investment at a profit, often in the form of an initial public offering of stock in the entity in the capital market (i.e., stock exchange). It sometimes provides technical assistance (usually in the form of financial expertise) and may require involvement in financial management, often by playing a role in the selection of the chief financial officer of the entity.

- A *strategic partner/investor* provides funds and other resources (e.g., access to a network) in return for a share in the ownership of a for-profit entity created or controlled by the institution. Typically, a strategic partner/investor has a common business interest with the entity in which it has invested and participates in the governance of the entity in proportion to its ownership interest. A strategic investor expects to benefit from the *appreciation* in the value of the entity in which the investment is made but does not necessarily seek an "exit strategy" requiring sale of the investment; instead, it may consider participation in the entity a long-term commitment supportive of its business strategy.

- The *strategic partner/joint venturer* is a variation on the strategic partner/investor model but involves the creation of a *new* for-profit entity owned jointly by the strategic partner(s) and either the institution or another entity controlled by the institution. The new entity may be a corporation or partnership and is typified by common control.

- A *competitor partner* pools resources with the institution to create an entity which benefits both and is beyond the reach of either. Typically, it seeks to benefit from economies of scale, broadened market access, co-branding, and reduced duplication of effort. It often combines with structures such as spin-out entities and various financing strategies—passive investment or strategic partners in particular.

Institutions in their current (nonprofit or public) form have long used some of these financing alternatives, such as relationships with lenders and contractors. Other financing alternatives—notably passive investor, strategic partner, and (usually) competitor investor—require the creation of a separate, for-profit entity because they embrace the concept of shared ownership and the ability to extract value from that ownership interest.[5] The future of postbaccalaureate education requires that institutions carefully consider each alternative to identify the one(s) that best suits their needs, priorities, and culture.

Choosing a financing mechanism begins with identifying what needs to be financed. The sources and indeed the nature of financing tangible things (e.g., equipment and facilities) differ significantly from obtaining working capital to launch or advance a new program or service. Material differences exist even within the financing of tangibles. With capital financing, a key initial issue is the difference between paying for something with a long, useful life, like a building, and paying for things with very short life spans, such as the facilities and equipment required for information technology. Historically, colleges and universities have paid for new or improved buildings either by soliciting contributions (capital campaigns) or by borrowing (usually with bonded debt). While the impermanence of equipment—particularly information technology equipment—makes such campaigns somewhat more difficult, debt financing is considerably more so because as a general principle, the term of the debt is tied to the useful life of the subject of the financing. While institutions may borrow over a 10-year term for a piece of equipment that will have to be replaced in two years, they need to consider the implications of paying for an item long after it has been replaced. Moreover, if a lender cannot obtain a useful security interest in the subject of the loan (that is, if the value is gone long before the loan is paid off), it usually will require that the loan be secured by general institutional revenues, which in turn results in a cap on borrowing capacity.

Obtaining funds for working capital is more complex. Donors are least likely to contribute to "general support," and borrowing to meet current expenses is extremely costly (in addition to being questionable as a financial management tool). In a traditional setting, that leaves current revenues or dipping into reserves as means of funding new initiatives. Historically, that is exactly how institutions have funded expansion into new arenas.

There is nothing wrong with this approach, so long as a consensus exists within the institution to divert current funds (or reserves) to the new activity. But to the extent that activity is removed from the institutional "core" (as defined by various campus constituencies) and there is an actual or perceived scarcity of resources, obtaining such a consensus can be difficult. Because competing in the postbaccalaureate field often requires just such a departure from the institutional core (particularly when it involves non-credit, non-degree instruction or the offering of programs through nontraditional means, at nontraditional locations, and to nontraditional learners), alternative financing strategies can enable institutions to compete without having to risk being seen as savaging other parts of the academic enterprise. What is needed is a vehicle that allows higher education institutions to mine the same vein that fuels the for-profit sector: the capital marketplace.

A number of mechanisms allow a nonprofit (or public) institution to access private capital. The common element is the creation of a for-profit entity to carry out a certain part of the postbaccalaureate enterprise. A portion of the ownership of that entity (i.e., its equity) is sold to one or more investors in return for cash. When the value of the enterprise increases, the investor can sell its interest at a profit. The fundamental prerequisite is that the activity being financed can demonstrate what is referred to as a "value proposition":

investors must be satisfied that over some discrete period of time, the value of their investment will increase. The higher the potential earnings and the lower the risk that the enterprise will *not* succeed, the easier and less costly the capital. Ultimate value and risk are factored into what the investment community will pay for a share of the entity created to support the program. The economic impact is straightforward: The higher the risk and the lower the potential earnings, the more equity required for the same level of investment. Thus, a key question for the institution is how much of its ownership interest in the new enterprise it is willing to sell in return for the desired investment.[6]

The predicate to creating and obtaining financing for a for-profit entity is defining what it will do. Simply announcing the establishment of "University Corporation" will not attract investors. Likewise, transferring the institution's academic functions into a for-profit entity, though perhaps attractive from an investment perspective, is really transforming the institution rather than creating a parallel financing mechanism. Outright conversion to for-profit form is simply not an option for the vast majority of institutions.

Certain types of postbaccalaureate programs are particularly appropriate to this hybrid type of structure. Many such programs are non-credit and non-degree, so shifting their preparation, marketing, and delivery to a for-profit subsidiary is less likely to offend institutional sensibilities. But an institution need not stop there. Many institutional functions, such as the marketing and technological delivery of credit programs, can appropriately be shifted to the "captive" for-profit entity. Indeed, any function that could be "contracted out" can just as easily (and potentially more profitably) be carried out by the for-profit entity. The key is to maintain an appropriate level of institutional control. The institution can do so in several ways, including.

- through its ownership interest (that is, by maintaining working control of the entity's board of directors);
- through a contractual relationship between the institution and the for-profit entity for services, facilities, and other resources provided by the institution; and
- through the terms and conditions of the licenses granted to the for-profit entity for use of the institution's name, courseware, and other intellectual property.

In effect, the institution can become hybridized, with the academic core remaining in the existing nonprofit (or public) entity and all or some part of the non-academic services, as well as certain non-core academic activities, planted within one or more for-profit entities. Revenues generated by postbaccalaureate services provided by the for-profit entity flow through that entity (consistent with the goal of maximizing revenues realized by the for-profit so as to increase its market value), with an appropriate portion flowing back to the institution to pay its costs.

The simplest model calls for the establishment of a for-profit entity controlled and initially financed by the institution; capital invested in the entity is treated from an accounting standpoint like any other institutional investment. The initial working capital is used as startup money, enabling the entity to develop a financial track record. Eventually, the entity attracts passive investors who purchase a portion of its equity. The invested funds are used to further grow the enterprise (as well as pay back some portion of the original institutional investment if the entity has been particularly successful).

More commonly, the institution endows the new entity with intellectual property and other intangible rights (such as the right to market certain of the institution's courses and to use its name, known as *branding*). A passive investor simultaneously purchases a portion of the equity in the entity. The cash raised by selling a portion of the entity's equity is used as working capital to develop and market the instructional product.

An example of this approach is a private university that created a for-profit company to develop, market, and deliver telecommunications-based courses. The entity was established for several reasons, only one of which involved access to outside capital. Of greater immediate importance was the flexibility afforded by an entity that stood outside the academic structure of the institution, allowing new approaches to the engagement of faculty and instructional media developers and, at least as important, flexibility in forms of compensation, including those that would offer a direct stake in the success of the enterprise. By setting up a separate entity, the university also could venture with other partners and take on risks that would be difficult were the operation subsumed within the structure of a very large institution. Finally, the entity afforded the university the opportunity to secure capital financing by selling shares in the new entity. (See Figure 1.)

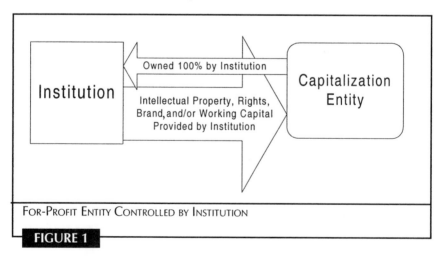

FOR-PROFIT ENTITY CONTROLLED BY INSTITUTION

FIGURE 1

The entity with the introduction of outside investors looks only slightly different from that illustrated in Figure 1. (See Figure 2.)

The entity now has a capitalization value based on the value of the share of equity purchased by the investor. That is, if the investor pays $10 million for one-third of the entity, then the value of the entity is $30 million. If the entity proves successful, it can sell a portion of its equity to the public (an Initial Public Offering, or IPO). A public offering (or a subsequent secondary private placement, which is simply a solicitation for additional investors without the complexity of a public offering) allows the initial investor to recover all or part of its investment and a profit on that investment by selling all or part of its equity in the entity. Likewise, the institution can *monetize* (i.e., sell) a portion of its interest in the entity, generating cash back to the institution itself, while still maintaining a sufficient ownership interest.[7] In addition, the institution has created capital value that is reflected on its financial statements.[8]

The institution can realize several revenue streams in addition to the appreciated value of its equity in the entity. These streams can take the following forms:

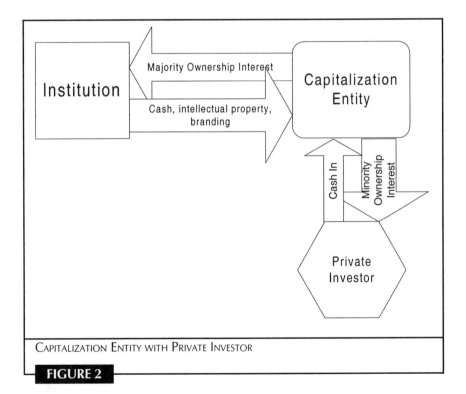

CAPITALIZATION ENTITY WITH PRIVATE INVESTOR

FIGURE 2

- *License fees and royalties* are based on the entity's use of the institution's name and courseware.
- *Fees for services* are paid to the institution for providing contract services to the entity.
- *Dividends* may be paid by the entity back to its owners (the institution and investors) as a distribution of profit.

If the institution's ownership position is less than 80 percent, license fees, royalties, and dividends should be treated as passive income and are not subject to unrelated business income tax. In any event, net income derived from fees paid for services that are within the exempt purposes of the institution should not under any circumstances be subject to taxation.

Another unique characteristic of a for-profit entity is that ownership interests can be distributed to faculty, instructional designers, and other employees, as well as to persons not already affiliated with the institution. Technology transfer entities have proven that providing key personnel with an equity interest (and therefore an opportunity to benefit from the increase in value to which they are contributing) can be a powerful incentive for the most valuable and creative contributors; they will be more likely to remain a part of the institution's effort and less likely to "defect" to the private sector, where such inducements are common.

The capitalization entity may contain as much or as little of the parent as circumstances warrant. One nonprofit graduate institution was very successful in creating a high-quality educational product, but its growth was stymied by a lack of capital; it was unable to aggressively market its services and create new learning opportunities and delivery systems. Although it was able to benefit from a public bond offering to build a state-of-the-art headquarters and operations center, in addition to obtaining a number of federal grants for its technology-based delivery system, it was wholly reliant on tuition for its operating revenue. Thus, the institution could not generate sufficient working capital to enable it to exploit the opportunities available in the marketplace.

When the institutional leadership examined the available options, they determined that seeking private capital was the most favorable approach. But rather than set up a subsidiary, the university bifurcated itself, keeping all of the primary academic functions within the existing nonprofit and spinning out virtually all other functions to a new for-profit entity. The key was to create a structure that, in effect, would be transparent to those concerned with academic integrity (particularly state regulators and accrediting agencies) but that would allow for an infusion of capital in return for equity. The resulting model was actually quite straightforward. (See Figure 3.)

The investor acquired one-third of the for-profit corporation's stock in return for an investment valued at the time at $15 million. The proceeds of that investment were used to establish the marketing and product develop-

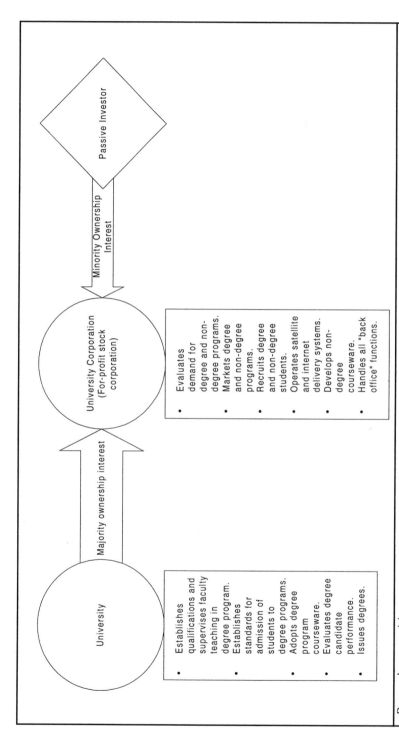

PASSIVE INVESTOR MODEL

FIGURE 3

ment capabilities of the for-profit entity. And the university's accreditor and state licensing agency saw this approach as a valid way for the institution to create needed capital without sacrificing its academic integrity.

A variation on the passive investor model involves the participation of a strategic partner. The institution creates a for-profit entity in which the strategic partner invests, or, alternatively, the institution and the strategic partner jointly create the new entity. Here, however, the strategic partner contributes more than just money; it provides specific substantive resources necessary for the success of the enterprise. Such resources include technology (e.g., a new delivery system) or a unique and already extant infrastructure (e.g., centers for testing competencies). (See Figure 4.)

The last model involves a *competitor partner*. Here, institutions competing in the same or similar markets create a joint venture, either for- or nonprofit, to enhance both of their abilities to reach their markets. If the new entity is nonprofit, then the model is like many consortia; if the new entity is for-profit, the opportunity exists to capitalize the venture to supply the resources it requires to be most competitive. Capitalization can come from passive investors or strategic partners. Multiple owners make for more complex arrangements, but the combining of institutions—their resources, capabilities, branding, and rights—can greatly enhance value. (See Figure 5.)

Given the variety of models available, the question that arises is how to choose the model that is best for a particular institution. There is no one "right" answer. Even among apparently similarly situated institutions, enough

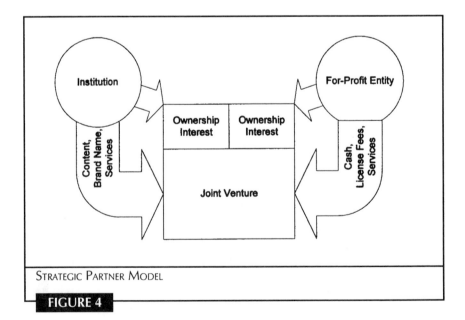

STRATEGIC PARTNER MODEL

FIGURE 4

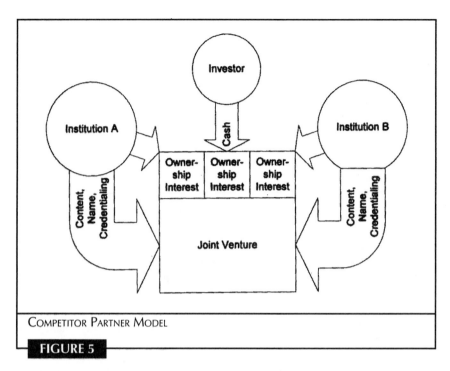

COMPETITOR PARTNER MODEL

FIGURE 5

actual differences exist to make a "me too" approach not only less than useful but even potentially damaging. Before seeking access to the capital market-place, institutional leaders need to ask whether the institution really is pre-pared to do business in this environment. Creating a for-profit venture is outside the culture of most institutions; even those that have long experience with such activities in terms of technology transfer, commercialization of discoveries, and operation of health care facilities may find it difficult to reconcile academic activities with profit motives.

Likewise, working with investors is likely to result in a clash of cultures. The investor wants to maximize the return on its investment while the institution has a variety of interests at stake in the development and delivery of its services, only one of which is economic. Investors often express concern that this is precisely why nonprofit (and public) institutions are difficult (if not impossible) partners; at critical junctures, the fear is that the institution will put other things above enhancing or protecting the value of the investment. This concern, which is neither irrational nor, in terms of institutional motives, necessarily a bad thing, reflects itself in the following questions:

- *Is the institution willing to take the steps necessary to instill investor confidence?* Some investors may simply be unwilling to enter into a transaction with a university. Because competition among investors increases value, such an attitude can diminish the value of the enterprise. Shared understanding of desired outcomes is key. The expectations of the institution and the investor need not be precisely the same, but they cannot be contradictory. An investor may enter into a transaction with the expectation that it will be bought out within a certain period of time—an expectation very different from that of the institution, which presumably intends to retain a significant stake in the enterprise. These intentions are not necessarily contradictory, but they must be understood at the outset.

- *Is the institution prepared to sacrifice immediate financial rewards for long-term value?* This critical element is an all too common deal killer. The institution, although owning a substantial portion of the equity in the enterprise, demands that it receive full cost recovery for the services it provides (such as courseware delivery). By seeking to take out the fully loaded cost of its services at the front end, the institution dramatically reduces its contribution to the value of the enterprise. Deferred gratification is an essential principle of commercial ventures.

- *Is the institution willing to give the investor protection that its investment will not be sacrificed over non-economic concerns?* Defining the reciprocal protections afforded the investor and the institution is complex but essential, often involving a series of soul-searching questions for the institution:

    1. Is the institution willing to relinquish enough elements of control to satisfy the investor that its investment will be protected?

    2. Is the investor sufficiently comfortable that the persons the institution has designated to the entity's board will fulfill their fiduciary obligations as directors to properly represent the interests of their institution as a shareholder?

    3. Is the institution willing to vest its board designees with the authority they will need to oversee the enterprise, and will the designees be willing to cede to the management of the enterprise the authority it needs to accomplish the tasks at hand?

    4. Is the institution willing to cede to the entity sufficient rights, including use of the institution's name and courseware, to enable it to carry out its purposes?

    5. Is the institution willing to allow the entity to contract with its faculty to create courseware and to be involved in other activities that are outside of the usual modes, including differential compensation that could involve receiving equity in the enterprise?

6. Is the institution willing to allow the entity to contract with non-institution instructional developers and others to create courseware that will carry the institution's name?

There is, of course, a converse to that which the institution must accept in entering the capital marketplace. The investor, be it passive or strategic, also must be willing to accommodate to working within a very different kind of structure and—perhaps more important—culture. The process of negotiating the several agreements that are necessary between and among the investor/partner, the institution, and the capitalization entity can go a long way toward providing a common level of comfort. The key is to separate the governance function from the contractual services between the institution and the capitalization entity. The former must focus its attention on the economic value of the entity, while the terms of the latter should include an appropriate focus on assuring quality and protecting both the institutional name and substantive academic integrity. By keeping these elements separate, there is a dynamic tension that is more likely to result in a useful balance between the economic and academic driving forces and constraints. It is here, as well, that the most serious effort must be expended to ensure that these series of agreements in fact properly address the needs and concerns of each of the parties, as well as their collective concern for the value and effectiveness of the capitalization entity.

One final factor needs to be considered in moving toward an enterprise which someday might be taken public. Once an entity sells its stock to the public, it thrusts at least a portion of its operations into a glare of oversight and publicity that is foreign to most institutions. Not only are stock transactions closely regulated, but extensive and complex reporting requirements must be met. The marketplace thrives on information, so that an unwillingness to share information can significantly depress the value of an entity's shares. An institution entering this arena must be willing to act in accordance with the rules of the capital marketplace—rules that are very different from those of the academy.

The legal issues pertaining to the creation of for-profit analogues of nonprofit institutions are neither unique nor insuperable. The law clearly allows nonprofit institutions to have a substantial—indeed, a controlling—interest in for-profit entities; if it is done properly, there should not even be any tax liability.[9] Shared governance in a corporate setting is an established fact, almost always reflecting relative ownership interests. An institution's rights and integrity can be protected through a variety of means, including the shareholders' agreement (limiting certain actions or requiring a supermajority for some), licensing agreements (controlling use of the institution's name and intellectual property), and one or more service agreements (defining who is responsible for what activities and what performance standards will apply). While these instruments can be complex, the models exist to enable an institution to enter into such a relationship with reasonable confidence that its interests will be protected.

The future of postbaccalaureate education is not at risk, but the identity of the providers is in flux. Economics will be a determining factor in whether the current purveyors—"traditional" institutions—will continue to play a major role. Mechanisms to creatively finance some types of institutional efforts are available. The marketplace is ready to receive them. It is the ability to look beyond traditional methods of financing—earning, borrowing, begging—that is likely to distinguish those institutions that succeed in the new era of telecommunicated learning.

NOTES

1. Richard N. Katz, ed., *Dancing with the Devil: Information Technology and the New Competition in Higher Education.* San Francisco: Jossey-Bass, 1999.
2. Clark Kerr. *The Uses of the University,* 4th ed. Cambridge: Harvard University Press, 1995.
3. Even contributed capital may not be free. Many an institution has learned to its sorrow the recurring costs of operating a new building. This can be even more true when dealing with technology-mediated learning.
4. One notable exception is the use of for-profit "spin-offs" to enable institutions to commercialize discoveries. But there are significant differences in this use. The capital obtained is intended for an *external* function, i.e., support for bringing discoveries to the marketplace, rather than creating capital resources for the institution itself. And the goal is for a new technology enterprise to ultimately detach itself entirely from the institution—quite the opposite of the purpose of an entity created to support a continuing instructional function.
5. A fundamental legal premise of nonprofit entities is that no "ownership interest" exists, with the result that no one can share the appreciated value.
6. A potential crossover point is where the cost of necessary capital requires the institution to sell a majority interest in the for-profit entity—a difficult proposition for many. However, even this is not an insuperable barrier, since the institution's rights still can be protected by shareholder agreements and the terms of licenses and contracts for services entered into between the institution and the entity. It is a premise of outsourcing that the institution does not have a controlling interest in the contracting company. Yet outsourcing seems to work without loss of institutional integrity.
7. The proportion of equity owned by a shareholder does not necessarily dictate relative voting rights; indeed, in most cases, equity investors are accepting of a minority role in governance and often accept *non*-voting stock, and shareholder agreements can give the institution "supermajority" rights in areas that affect academic integrity. As discussed below, by dividing the necessary protective controls between the governance and contractual services components, it is easier to keep the roles of the governing body of the capitalization entity separate from the contractual relationship between that entity and the institution.

8. If the entity were worth $30 million at the time of the initial investment and were valued at $150 million at the IPO, then the institution's two-thirds interest would be worth $100 million. Whatever of its ownership interest the institution sells (i.e., monetizes) as part of the IPO is a liquid asset of the institution.

9. Because unrelated business income tax is based on the net income (i.e., profit) from an unrelated activity, even if an institution were to have to pay the tax, it would simply be put on an equal economic footing with commercial enterprises. However, if the purposes of the capitalization entity were deemed "related" to the exempt (i.e., educational) purposes of the institution, no tax liability would accrue.

CHAPTER 7

Risk, Tribe, and Lore: Envisioning Digital Libraries for Postbaccalaureate Learning

Peter Lyman

What must a digital library be and do if it is to support postbaccalaureate learning in the future? Digital libraries as such do not exist in fully realized form; thus, the design of the library of the future might yet be influenced by a statement of the needs of postbaccalaureate learning. The purpose of this paper is to begin to explore the social, pedagogical, and technical dimensions such a vision might encompass.

Clearly, the basic function of a digital library must be to provide access to information—the raw material of knowledge—along with appropriate reference tools for identifying and evaluating the possible sources and types of information. Thus, the many kinds of information that constitute the intellectual capital of postbaccalaureate learning first must be digitized, then organized in a manner that can be searched intelligently and reliably, ideally using technologies that would not require extensive technical training. Perhaps most difficult of all, a sustainable business model to support the digital library must be identified.

Today, three very different models of digital libraries are emerging, reflecting parallel approaches to intellectual property, for it is intellectual property law that will shape the future of postbaccalaureate teaching and learning more than technology itself. Each of these models suggests new possibilities for postbaccalaureate learning, yet each also poses new problems.

Peter Lyman is professor and associate dean in the School of Information Management & Systems (SIMS) at the University of California, Berkeley.

- *Digital archives.* Research libraries are placing collections on the Internet by digitizing print collections and developing online catalogs, often in support of faculty innovations that make use of the Internet for teaching and learning. Online collections are a necessity if academic programs are to reach beyond traditional institutional boundaries, for learning is enhanced by independently exploring a field's literature and research materials. Such innovations are widespread and include online collaborative research, nonprofit electronic journals, listservs, and Web pages. But these new forms of publication are more often considered part of the informal research and teaching process than formally recognized academic publications.
- *The Web.* The World Wide Web allows writers to place their own intellectual property directly into a new, global public domain. In 1998, information accessible on the public portion of the Web was estimated to be the equivalent in size, if not quality, of a library of a million volumes. The public portion of the Web includes information ranging from government documents to electronic journals, but most distinctively includes the information created and placed in the public domain by seven million authors from around the world.
- *Electronic commerce.* Print publishers are creating an e-commerce library, providing digitized journals and texts online for a fee on the private part of the Internet (that in which intellectual property is protected by password and encryption technologies). In the next few years, it is estimated that the 5,000 most important print journals in the sciences, technology, medicine, and industry will be available online, anywhere in the world, for a fee.

Because digital publishing is still a relatively new innovation, we can expect these three models to evolve rapidly. But they will not converge, for the economic models underlying them are based on three distinct kinds of intellectual property: copyright, gift exchange, and contract. The models are distinct, but they may not be mutually exclusive. For example, William Mitchell's *City of Bits* was published online for free by MIT Press, but it has sold far more print copies than projected.[1] This suggests that market and gift exchange may be complementary or symbiotic—not opposite—intellectual property regimes. Discovering the relative value for higher education of each of these kinds of intellectual property regimes is one of the most interesting challenges of our time.

Although these dimensions of information access are necessary, they are not a sufficient definition of the digital library if it is to be a place of learning, for the essence of learning is turning information into knowledge, and knowledge into practice. From the perspective of information access, digital libraries may be described as inventories of information (collections) and information management tools (online catalogs, search engines). From the perspective of administration, the digital library requires new levels of budgetary support for information and infrastructure, as well as operations. The challenge will be to find a sustainable business model for the digital library, if, as it now appears, it supplements rather than replaces the print library. This decision will require consideration of whether to subsidize the use of library information or to charge for it.

And yet, this choice is not solely about information access, for libraries are also social institutions that support a sense of academic community within disciplines and professions and among students.[2] Can digital libraries support these social dimensions of learning?

For digital library design, this second dimension of libraries suggests that we should ask how we can design a library that *directly* enhances the quality and productivity of the academic enterprise. Digital libraries have not yet been designed to support the social dimensions of the library, linking information resources to the learning communities that create and use information. And yet, users of digital libraries tend to be geographically dispersed, lacking a shared sense of place. Digital libraries must fulfill this function if postbaccalaureate learning is to reach beyond the campus; they will become indispensable as the Internet makes scholarship ever more collaborative and international. But where is the appropriate technology?

Today, no discussion of education or information policy would fail to mention the World Wide Web, though as recently as 1994, it was not mentioned in the federal information policy vision, *An Agenda for Action*. The Internet could be searched for promising technologies for digital libraries that could support learning communities in the future. In fact, the elementary forms of three modes of learning can be found on the Internet; in time, these might develop into interesting models for the social dimension of digital libraries serving postbaccalaureate learning; they might be called "risk, tribe, and lore."

- *Risk—the uses of simulations.* "Risk" might describe the modes of learning that seem to be possible within computer simulations of social life, through role playing, or by participating in online environments such as Internet Relay Chats (IRC), Multi-User Domains (MUDs), and Muds-Object Oriented (MOOs). Can simulations provide or support mentoring or role playing so students can participate in educational experiences not otherwise accessible? Can anonymous role playing complement classroom-based learning, encouraging participation in learning by those traditionally silenced by the hidden currents of power and authority in the classroom?

- *Tribe—the experience of virtual community.* "Tribe" describes the sense of community that participants often experience on the Internet, which in fact may not be any more "virtual" than the other kinds of community available in modern urban life. Can the digital library be designed to overcome the geographic isolation of distant learners and to foster a sense of participation in collaborative cultures of learning? Can a new kind of "imagined community" be sustained online?

- *Lore—online communities of practice.* "Lore" might describe the online knowledge practices that characterize professions, enabling independent practitioners, perhaps geographically distant, to feel themselves to be members of a community that collectively practices the crafts of knowledge. Print literatures have been created by scholarly communities and in turn have sustained their sense of being members of the scientific community.[3] How can these knowledge communities be created—or sustained—across time and space on the Internet?

Collectively, these social dimensions of information technology are now often called "knowledge management," meaning that technology must be designed to enhance the intellectual performance of individuals and the creativity of groups, not just to manage information inventories. Although very new, the technologies supporting what I have called risk, tribe, and lore already are the focus of innovative teaching and learning experiments across the country. Evaluating these experimental practices might enable us to shift the priority for technological development away from the design of commercial training software (often focused on drill and practice) to the design of more open environments for learning.

How might these two dimensions of the digital library—information access and knowledge management—be combined into a comprehensive strategy for postbaccalaureate futures, providing every learner from every location the opportunity to participate in academic communities as they practice the arts of teaching, learning, and research? This kind of digital library will not evolve by accident; it must be part of a collective vision of postbaccalaureate learning sufficiently powerful to command new resources.

Finally, even if such a digital library were to be built, it would not necessarily be sufficient for postbaccalaureate learning. Technology-mediated learning is disembodied, lacking the tacit dimensions of teacher/student mentoring and communication. The communal feeling of networked groups is far stronger when the groups are also able to meet face to face. And yet, the existence of such a digital library might fundamentally change the way postbaccalaureate learning is organized by extending its scope and reach in dramatic ways, and perhaps by encouraging the development of more learner-centered pedagogies.

INTELLECTUAL PROPERTY AND THE FUTURE OF DIGITAL LIBRARIES

For all of the promise of information technology for postbaccalaureate learning, the future of education will be determined more by intellectual property policy than by technology. It is not access to information *per se* that is educational, but rather the modes in which individuals and groups are allowed to use information in the learning process; these factors are controlled by intellectual property law. The digital library is not yet a social institution, for we do not know how information will be managed and used within networked information spaces. Today, three kinds of digital libraries are evolving in parallel, reflecting three modes of intellectual property management: the subsidized research library, based on copyright law; the public domain information of the Web, based on gift exchange; and the market economy of commercial electronic publishing, based on contract law.

Copyright and the Library

Libraries, archives, and museums are now digitizing collections and placing them on the Internet, their ownership protected by a copyright notice. Generally, blanket permission for educational uses is granted. To digitize and publish a document, the institution must own the copyright, not just the copy; for that reason, digital collections typically include unique archival documents or published works for which the copyright has expired.

In many cases, digital collections are designed to meet the needs of academic disciplines for which information access is very difficult, either because the discipline is small and geographically dispersed or because research materials are rare. Several projects to publish archival materials in specialized fields are underway, e.g., the study of papyri (see http://sunsite.berkeley.edu/APIS) and medieval history (http://sunsite.berkeley.edu/OMACL/). The Sloan Foundation has funded a series of projects called "Science and Technology in the Making," a pilot project using the Web to investigate and document contemporary events in the history of science and technology (http://sloan.stanford.edu/). In science, both competitive pressures and collaborative research have encouraged the development and use of digital library software. Most famous in this category is the preprint server at Los Alamos, in the Library without Walls project (http://lib-www.lanl.gov), on which can be found most of the important electronic preprints in physics. Internet2 planners are working on technologies to support collaborative research spaces and scientific digital libraries (http://www.internet2.edu). There are literally thousands more examples.

These projects share the same business model as the print research library in that the consumption of information is subsidized; thus, each faces the dilemma that research library budgets are growing far more slowly than the price, volume, and technological formats of information.[4] Unfortunately, digital research collections do not seem to be less expensive than print collections, nor do they usually replace the need for print collections. Thus, a business model supporting the subsidized digital library has not yet been established.

Nevertheless, libraries have long experience in controlling costs through interinstitutional cooperation. For example, cataloging has been organized through national cooperatives such as the Research Libraries Group (http://www.rlg.org/) and OCLC (http://www.oclc.org/), institutions that are creating digital collections paid for by membership dues or subscriptions. New kinds of consortia are also being created. The research library members of the Digital Library Federation (DLF) are building an American history archive called "The Making of America" (see http://www.clir.org/diglib/dlfhomepage.htm). An alternative mode of cooperation is illustrated by the Mellon Foundation's startup funding for the Journal Storage Project (JSTOR), intended to grow into a nonprofit but self-supporting business to digitize and provide access to back runs of rarely used but essential scholarly journals (at http://www.jstor.org). JSTOR is funded by subscription, and if it can attain fiscal self-sufficiency, it will bring the last century of journal publications to every networked desktop licensed to use the database.

These are important beginnings, but what is still lacking is national coordination, in the form of both common technical standards and collection policies and priorities. Moreover, the need for institutional cooperation may be subsumed by competition among institutions for grants and faculty, in which the prestige of the library may be an element.

These models do not include current research journals, for which publishers have been given the copyright. Some argue that the digital library might require rebuilding the system of scholarly communication created a century ago; founded as a system of nonprofit university presses, it has since been commercialized by publishers. Digital library collections could be built directly from the copyrighted publications of faculty if colleges and universities claimed a share of the ownership of copyright (as is often done with patents). This claim could be limited to educational rights, leaving faculty authors all commercial rights. Such a step, however, requires rethinking faculty-university relations, and the relationship between tenure and publication in particular.[5]

The Web as a Gift-Exchange Society

If print libraries serve as the model for digital libraries, using librarians' traditional modes of professional quality control through bibliographic records and collection building, then the World Wide Web is being built directly by authors, without structure or quality control other than that implicit in software standards.

Information on the Web is usually "born digital"; it is not digital by conversion. Information born digital carries all of the new kinds of value of digital documents. Copying digital documents is inexpensive, and global access is implicit. Storing digital documents is inexpensive and compact in comparison to traditional library storage (though methods and standards for the preservation of digital information are still early in their evolution). Information access is easier because digital documents can be searched and reorganized in seconds. The most unique consequence of this is that the concept of authorship is changing, for people all over the world can collaborate in writing new digital works.

The Web is an original new medium for cultural expression, one that transforms both writing and reading. The Web began as a medium for publishing, using a rhetorical structure based on hypertext (HTML), which allows the reader to organize the sequence (and therefore the context) of information. It is a multimedia text including mostly words and numbers, some fixed and some dynamic, and images equivalent in size to a library of about one million volumes. As of late 1998, seven million writers were on the public portion of the Web, each creating and giving away intellectual property in the largest gift exchange community ever created.[6] In abolishing the distinction between writing and publishing, a new culture of information is being created; often, Web publications are written collectively—at times by groups of participants who do not know one another personally.

On the Web, there are writers but no authors or authorities; everything is published; and value is determined by readers (or "users"). This raises questions about the quality of information online. Unlike a book, every "reading" is a unique performance in which the user links information together in a pattern. These links are the trails through an information wilderness, one in which the quality of information is defined by its utility to readers, individually and collectively, not its provenance. This poses a distinctive problem vis á vis the education of independent learners.

This problem of information quality is being addressed in different ways by the variants of the digital library. Collections are vetted by librarians, and digital publishers use traditional editorial authorities. Amazon.com's Web site demonstrates a third possibility: collaborative filtering. When I recently ordered the CD of Arvo Part's *Kanon Pokajanen*, my computer screen informed me that others who had ordered the *Kanon* were likely to have also ordered Piazzola's *Maria de Buenos Aires*. Rather like evaluating a scholarly work by tallying the number of other works' citations of it, "collaborative filtering" defines a sense of social collectivity by using link analysis technology to allow people with common interests in one area to become aware of how they collectively evaluate information in other areas. In focusing on information use, this method perhaps resembles the measurement of faculty research quality by the use of citation indices.

Some argue that this sort of access to information will shift market power from the producer to the consumer, and that the key to business success in the information age therefore will be the creation of customer loyalty by establishing such communities of users. One business text puts it this way:

> As virtual communities tip the balance of power in commercial transactions toward the customer, they'll provide a powerful vehicle for vendors to deepen and broaden their relationships with customers. This is likely to affect the way traditional businesses are run in "physical space" as well as in the virtual world . . . . In fact, ownership of customer relationships as a whole is likely to be thrown up for grabs by the emergence of virtual communities.[7]

These themes—the evolution of authorship toward collaborative writing, and from individual to collective learning in virtual communities—are the subject of the second part of this chapter, on knowledge management. In retrospect, it should not be surprising that a discussion of information quality leads back to the problem of learning—on the Web or elsewhere.

The E-commerce Library

Commercial publishers are creating online libraries that will sell digital versions of peer-reviewed print journals. This is not simply a change in format, but a new kind of business model. Unlike print collections, which are governed by copyright, publishers do not *sell* digital books or journals to libraries; rather, they use contracts to *license the use* of their "information content." These licenses are very new, and contract terms are changing rapidly as publishers and consumers learn to use the new format. The copyright doctrines of first sale (which allows interlibrary loan) and fair use (which allows copying for educational purposes) are not part of the new contract regime. Indeed, the term "information content" was invented by the publishing industry to signify its emerging role as merchant bankers in intellectual property; the business of publishing now concerns licensing the use of information. Publishers' contracts generally forbid the use of digital documents in the manner permitted by copyright, such as fair use, although in practice it is difficult to prevent illegal copying.

The use of contracts formalizes the transition from a national information policy based upon public libraries to a market system of online distribution based upon licenses for fee for service payments. These revenues will fund the development of online libraries with editorial quality comparable to today's print journals and will provide far greater access to scholarly information from any geographic location. But this system will also create new inequalities of information access, which a Commerce Department report recently called "Falling through the Net: Defining the Digital Divide" (http://www.ntia.doc.gov/ntiahome/fttn99/introduction.html).

The primary unsolved problem in this scenario is the preservation of digital documents. In the past, libraries have preserved and stored printed information as an archive of the history of knowledge. As information loses its commercial value, it is unlikely that commercial rights-holders will subsidize its continued existence. And unlike print collections, licenses may not allow libraries to archive the originals.

In practice, then, access to library information may be governed either by individual ability to pay or by a license subsidizing use by a given user population. Given the commercialization of scientific publishing, the price of journals will continue to increase at double-digit annual rates, and library budgets will not increase proportionally simply to subsidize free access to information. Subsidized library collections likely will represent increasingly smaller proportions of published information, which will be complemented by on-demand, fee-based document delivery services.

In sum, digital libraries are likely to include three kinds of relationships between readers and information, corresponding to three kinds of intellectual property regimes: (1) free access public domain information, including government information, Web access, and archival collections that are out of copyright; (2) fee-for-service models, which will govern access to commercial scholarly information, including subscriptions, document delivery, and new forms of publication (such as disciplinary article databases); and (3) copyright, which will apply to some collections (print and digital), including those created by faculty and published on the Web for educational purposes.

The action agenda for postbaccalaureate education is twofold. First, within the commercial model, can licenses be developed that serve the needs of learners wherever they are located, rather than only for institutional venues? Considering the growth in the market for education outside traditional higher education institutions, it may be possible to aggregate users into a powerful buying cooperative that could demand and receive substantial discounts. Or, second, is it possible to develop a new kind of digital university press, nonprofit but self-sustaining, to copyright and publish educational and scholarly texts?[8] Either of these models might require higher education to work cooperatively across institutional boundaries.

NEW PATHWAYS TO LEARNING

The traditional assumption that information and knowledge are scarce resources that must be concentrated within colleges and universities—geographic locales to which learners must travel and where they must live—is no longer valid. Information is no longer scarce, and knowledge can be delivered to learners. If higher education controlled the social context of learning in the past, postbaccalaureate learning now must enter the social world of the learner. When the learner is distant from the traditional social world of the university, new modes of postbaccalaureate learning might well have to be collaborative to create and sustain an educational culture inherently in competition with the worlds of family and work. For this reason, a brief exploration of the social worlds of the Internet (primitive as they may be at this point) may be helpful in thinking about how to design and use a digital library to support distance learning.

The second part of this chapter is "experimental," then, in two senses. It provides examples of network technologies that might be described as experiments in learning to solve the problem of remote learning, and beyond, to enable distant institutions to share scarce faculty expertise. Second, it suggests that the pedagogy of postbaccalaureate learning might go beyond a basic "classroom model" by taking advantage of new forms of collaborative learning using new technologies. Like the Web, many of these technologies were developed to facilitate scientists' collaborative work and are now being adapted to the needs of corporate training and development. What role might they play in postbaccalaureate learning?

Risk: The Virtues of Anonymity and Role Playing

The screen is a window on a simulated world, though this world is still constructed largely of words. Simulations of social relationships—e-mail, chat groups, games, MUDs, and MOOs—derive their power from digital speech, which combines the facticity of the printed word with the spontaneity of conversation.[9] The relationship of words on the screen to emotion—and perhaps cognition—is new, and the global reach and scale of the social relations built upon digital speech on the Internet is certainly new.

In one sense, the power of digital speech to create a sense of community is only a new form of political community based upon media, such as those which Benedict Anderson called "imagined communities," or the power of newspapers to create a shared sense of political community.[10]

What is interesting about some of the "cities in speech" on the Internet is that invented names (or "avatars") disguise the real identities of participants, creating a dramaturgical space that frees people from their ordinary identities and everyday life contexts. In *Life on the Screen*, Sherry Turkle describes how software and network communications are transforming the psychology of personality formation.[11] She argues that a more deconstructed sense of self might better explain the way we balance many selves in many social contexts; if identity is an experiment in progress, then risk-free play on the screen might be a place for growth.[12] A psychoanalyst, Turkle is sensitive to how life on the screen consists of emotional and intellectual experiments, taking advantage of anonymity and invented personae to take risks, "working through" emotional knots. Turkle as sociologist concludes that "virtual life" is emotionally and intellectually part of "real life," but virtual life contains a possibility of emotional play that can promote learning and healing. Turkle does not argue that computer simulations always promote learning; indeed, she is skeptical that is the case; she only remains open to the possibility that they can. The possibility of a link between play and learning on screen and the use of online simulation for learning is intriguing.

Nevertheless, Internet communication thus far has been more successful as a tool for games than for learning; indeed, investment in computer games is far greater than investment in computer learning. But the spontaneous development of learning technologies on the Web, in parallel with far more sophisticated MOO technologies using multimedia representations of information, have led to increased investment in these technologies for business training and development (see, http://www.pensare.com/). MOO learning technologies include video mentoring by experts, business simulations, and links to online discussion groups.

One possibility is that risk-free learning environments may encourage participation and experimentation that leads to learning. (We do not yet know when and how simulations lead to learning as opposed to entertainment.) The remaining unanswered question is whether skills learned in simulated environments will prove transferable to real world social contexts.

Tribe: Membership in Virtual Communities

The term *virtual community* describes the feelings of emotional solidarity among individual users when participating in a group activity using interactive network software. The strong case for virtual community is made by journalists Howard Rheingold, describing "The Well," a San Francisco Bay area-based chat group, and Julian Dibble, describing Lambda Moo, an experimental virtual rooming house at Xerox PARC.[13] Social scientists Barry Wellman and Milena Gulia make the moderate case for the existence of virtual communities, arguing that social networks on the Web are not very different from social networks experienced anywhere else in modern urban society. They argue that deep feelings of community are rare in modern life, and virtual communities are more like the relationships most people have with casual acquaintances (as opposed to those they have with intimate friends).[14] Critics argue that media are designed to simulate feelings of community, masking the social isolation and anonymity of a human/machine relationship.[15]

Virnoche and Marx point out that "virtual communities" and "real life" are not opposites and that indeed, the most durable sense of community develops when people engage in both network and face-to-face meetings.[16] Thus, they differentiate three kinds of virtual communities, each with its own quality as a meeting place: community networks, virtual extensions, and virtual communities.

- *Community networks.* Community networks are founded upon traditional communities built around shared place and work, but participation in a sense of place and community is extended by network communications, such as e-mail, Internet relay chat, bulletin boards, and Web pages. Examples of community networks include municipal governments using the network to involve citizens in political deliberation, corporations using e-mail and teleconferencing, and students using Web pages and e-mail for discussion outside of classroom hours. Clearly, a traditional sense of community is dependent upon frequent personal interaction, but community networks reinforce a sense of membership by making information or communication more accessible.
- *Virtual extensions.* Virtual extensions sustain a sense of community among a group of geographically distant people who have intermittent personal contact. Virtual extensions typically foster a sense of place through collaborative work on a shared problem, requiring occasional face-to-face meetings, but sustained by a sense of shared culture and expertise. Professions are good examples of virtual extensions; consider, for example, physicists who communicate by e-mail, Web pages, and the Los Alamos preprint server and also frequently meet at conferences.
- *Virtual communities.* Virtual communities in the strictest sense are groups of geographically distant strangers who share a common interest expressed through ongoing participation in computer-mediated communication. Such communities typically are unstable over time and involve relatively more listeners than speakers. Yet they are of interest because they stimulate participation. In essence, they are a sustained conversation based on a topic or problem of mutual interest rather than physical proximity. Thus, many of the most successful sites provide otherwise scarce information and advice about very specialized topics, such as political movements or the treatment of rare diseases; they may simply be a place to talk about a controversial topic with minimal risk.

How, then, do network communications create and sustain a sense of community? According to Wellman and Gulia, communal relations in cyberspace tend to be built upon specialized topics or issues; social structure is based upon a sense of reciprocity derived from the immediacy of interaction itself, and those who contribute information seek the social status gained by giving good answers; finally, anonymity fosters communication among a wider diversity of people than most face-to-face communities.

Like other communities, virtual communities are built upon the exchange of gifts; unlike traditional communities, the exchanges do not persist over a long time period, they do not require frequent contact, and they do not address a wide variety of concerns or pursue topics in depth.

Each of these models of virtual community might be useful for postbaccalaureate learning, whether at a distance or not. We do not understand the architecture of virtual communities very well, those variables that help to construct and sustain a sense of community and participation, but there is little question that important new kinds of social relationships are possible on the Internet.

Lore: Communities of Practice

Describing how people learn by doing while working collaboratively, Jean Lave and Etienne Wenger coined the term *communities of practice*, pointing out that much of our learning comes from apprenticeship within the social contexts we find at hand.[17] One review of the literature describes various kinds of communities of practice, ranging

> from the effectiveness of the invisible colleges in the progress of the scientific enterprise, to the roles of cliques in the functioning of bureaucracies. In between, they run the gamut from informal networks of cooperation among chemists working for competitive pharmaceutical industries, to back channel exchanges between members of the foreign offices of adversary countries and the appearance of gangs in schools and prisons.[18]

Because computer networks enable such communication on an unprecedented scale and depth, the idea of communities of practice is rapidly becoming the theoretical foundation of new theories of economic and social organization in cyberspace, particularly in literature on the corporation of the future. In the new management literature, "communities of practice" are about the use of networked information in the *practice of knowledge;* this topic has become important in discussions of intellectual property and innovation in the digital economy. Here again there are interesting parallels between corporate training and development literatures and work on the use of digital libraries in education.

In this literature there is a particularly striking passage that describes leading-edge scientific research, which has profound implications for how we think about the relationship among information, communities of practice, and knowledge production. Describing authorship in biotechnology, Don Cohen says that

> the complexity and rapid pace of research means that advances are necessarily made by large teams connected by their interlocking areas of expertise rather than by employment at the same institution or location. Thus . . . a recently published paper on the DNA sequence of yeast chromosomes listed 133 authors from 85 institutions. In the biotech industry, collaborative networks are becoming the places where important intellectual activity occurs; belonging to them is essential to success in an industry that exists on the frontier of developing knowledge. . . . These virtual teams point to the future shape of knowledge work in general, which some predict will be accomplished by widely dispersed groups and individuals woven into communities of practice by networks, groupware, and a complex common task.[19]

While biotechnology may be an unusual field in terms of the degree of collaborative research across both corporate and national boundaries, it raises profound questions about our concept of authorship and the role of groups in the creation of knowledge.[20] As a consequence of the role of groups in industry and the sciences, computer science has created a field called "computer supported collaborative work" (CSCW); new software products are called "groupware."

Professions and academic disciplines are also communities of practice— ones that operate on a global scale (although as much by shared literatures and travel to professional conventions as by computer networks). These are also the traditional domains of postbaccalaureate learning and are relevant to its new audiences as well.

CONCLUSION

This chapter is intended to stimulate conversation to envision a digital library capable of serving the needs of postbaccalaureate learning in an information society. Three kinds of change have been described: changes in intellectual property, information technology, and in social relationships in organizations. All represent opportunities for innovation in the form and process of postbaccalaureate education.

- *Intellectual property.* American intellectual property policy is currently focused on the rights of property owners, with far less attention to the rights of learners and education (rights represented in the past by the copyright doctrine of fair use). If higher education does not participate more effectively in intellectual property debates, it is likely that the cost of supporting research libraries will increase even more rapidly, even as the scope of the libraries diminishes relative to the amount of information published. Unless subsidized by higher education, commercial digital libraries will shift library and information costs to the learner. On the other hand, they will provide independent or geographically remote learners with far more access to scientific and scholarly information than in the past.

- *Technology development.* Commercial software development is focused on the infrastructure of the digital economy, which will support far more effective transactions with consumers on the network, including more individualized transactions, faster network speeds, and multimedia. This infrastructure might be highly useful for education on the network as well. However, the success of the business training and development market is likely to lead to more competition with the nonprofit higher education sector, particularly for new markets, and possibly for traditional markets as well. Educational software will emerge from federal funding for science (such as NSF funding for digital library software development and for science education) and from business markets for training and development (which tend to be more structured than traditional academic pedagogies).

- *Organizational development.* Research on virtual communities and communities of practice on the Internet, partial as it is, suggests that new organizational and institutional practices may emerge from this new medium of communication and coordination. This possibility is described as the emergence of the "virtual enterprise," a global organization that is highly flexible and innovative.[21] Educational pedagogies traditionally have been organized around a sense of place, in part because of the scarcity of information, faculty, and facilities. The significance of extension and educational uses of the Web (and other technologies) now might go beyond "outreach" to experiments in virtual place and new kinds of organizational strategies to support learning.

NOTES

1. See http://mitpress.edu for several important experiments in electronic publishing.
2. See Christine L. Borgman, "What Are Digital Libraries? Competing Visions," in *Information Processing & Management* 35 (1999): 227-43; Peter Lyman, "Designing

Libraries to Be Learning Communities," *Information Landscapes for a Learning Society*. London: Library Publishing Association, 1999, 75-87.

3. John Seeley Brown and Paul Duguid, "The Social Life of Documents," *Release 1.0: Esther Dyson's Monthly Report*. New York: Edventure Holding Inc., 11 October 1995.

4. Brian Hawkins, "The Unsustainability of the Traditional Library and the Threat to Higher Education," in Brian Hawkins and Patricia Battin, eds., *The Mirage of Continuity: Reconfiguring Academic Information Resources for the 21st Century*. Washington, DC: Association of American Universities and Council on Library & Information Resources, 1998, 129-53.

5. See Stanley Chodorow and Peter Lyman, "The Responsibilities of Universities in the New Information Environment," in Hawkins and Battin, *The Mirage of Continuity*, 61-78.

6. This statistic is from Internet Archive research, http://archive.org/

7. John Hagel III and Arthur G. Armstrong, *NetGain: Expanding Markets through Virtual Communities*. Cambridge: Harvard University Press, 1997, 187.

8. See the Mellon Foundation-funded Project Muse at Johns Hopkins University Press, which now offers more than 40 online scholarly journals at http://www.press.jhu.edu/muse.html.

9. A directory of MUD sites is located at http://mudconnector.com/. MUD sites worth exploring are http://www.pennmush.org/, http://www.anguish.org/, and http://www.imaginary.com/.

10. See Benedict Anderson, *Imagined Communities*. London: Verso Press, 1998. On newspapers, see Richard R. John, *Spreading the News*. Cambridge: Harvard University Press, 1995.

11. See Sherry Turkle, *Life on the Screen: Identity in the Age of the Internet*. New York: Simon and Schuster, 1995. See also Sherry Turkle, *The Second Self*. New York: Simon & Schuster, 1984.

12. Sherry Turkle, "Artificial Intelligence and Psychoanalysis: A New Alliance," *Daedalus* 117(1): 241-68.

13. See Howard Rheingold, *The Virtual Community: Homesteading on the Electronic Frontier*. New York: HarperCollins Books, 1994; and Julian Dibble, "A Rape in Cyberspace: How an Evil Clown, A Haitian Trikster Spirit, Two Wizards, and a Cast of Dozens Turned a Database into a Society," in Mark Stefik, *Internet Dreams: Archetypes, Myths, and Metaphors*. Cambridge: The MIT Press, 1996, 293-316. Lambda Moo may be explored at telnet: lambda.moo.mud.org.

14. Barry Wellman and Milena Gulia, "Net Surfers Don't Ride Alone: Virtual Communities as Communities," *Networks in the Global Village*. Boulder, CO: Westview Press, 1999, 331-66.

15. A critique of the notion is James R. Beniger, "Personalization of Mass Media and the Growth of Pseudo-Community," *Communication Research* 14:3, June 1987, 352-71. See also Sherry Turkle, "Virtuality and Its Discontents: Searching for Community in Cyberspace," *The American Prospect* 24, Winter 1996, 50-57.

16. Mary E. Virnoche and Gary T. Marx, "Only Connect"—E. M. Forster in an Age of Electronic Communication: Computer-Mediated Association and Community Networks," *Sociological Inquiry* 67:1 (1997): 85-100.

17. See Jean Lave and Etienne Wenger, *Situated Learning: Legitimate Peripheral Participation*. Cambridge: Cambridge University Press, 1991. See also Seth Chaiklin and Jean Lave, eds., *Understanding Practice*. Cambridge: Cambridge University Press, 1993.

18. Bernardo A. Huberman and Tad Hogg, "Communities of Practice: Performance and Evolution," *Computational and Mathematical Organization Theory* 1:1 (1995): 73.
19. Don Cohen, "Toward a Knowledge Context: Report on the First Annual U.C. Berkeley Forum on Knowledge and the Firm," *California Management Review* 40:3 (1998) 23, italics added.
20. On the end of authorship, see Mario Biagioli, "The Instability of Authorship: Credit and Responsibility in Contemporary Biomedicine," *The FASEB Journal* 12 (January 1998): 3-16; Walter W. Powell, "Learning from Collaboration: Knowledge and Networks in the Biotechnology and Pharmaceutical Industries," *California Management Review* 40:3 (1998): 228-40.
21. See Manuel Castells, *The Rise of the Network Society.* London: Blackwells, 1996, 168-72.

PART 3

· · · · · · · · · · ·

Creating and Credentialing High-Quality Learning

CHAPTER

Recasting Postbaccalaureate Programs as Learning Systems

Alan R. Bassindale and Sir John Daniel

INTRODUCTION

Postbaccalaureate education is undergoing a transformation, and the United Kingdom-based Open University (OU) is a prime example of how new learning systems are developing and evolving. Comparisons are also sometimes made with worldwide "virtual" and "distance" universities and other providers of high-volume, high-quality graduate education programs, and we therefore provide a brief description of the new United States Open University. We believe that taught postgraduate programs have a more lasting impact if study is combined with employment so that students can develop the habit of reflective practice; we explore the implications of this for higher education institutions.

CHANGES IN POSTBACCALAUREATE EDUCATION

The changes in postbaccalaureate education that we describe are related to the rapid pace of change in many fields of industry and business, combined with startling developments in communications technologies. The past five to ten years have witnessed fundamental changes in both the curriculum and the

Alan R. Bassindale is the pro-vice chancellor (Research & Staff) at the Open University in the United Kingdom.

Sir John Daniel is the vice chancellor at the Open University.

delivery mechanisms of postbaccalaureate education programs. These changes have been in response to transformations in patterns of demand, in methods available for delivery, and in the nature of higher education institutions and providers.

Changes in Patterns of Demand

Throughout the higher education sector, there is a growing emphasis on learning rather than teaching. Students are becoming more concerned with learning how to learn than with receiving preselected, prepackaged information. Users of higher education also are making greater demands for flexibility in modes of study—particularly at the postbaccalaureate level, where there is a strong desire (or need) to combine employment with study. At least three readily identifiable groups demand flexible study at this level. The first are recent graduates. In the United States and in the United Kingdom, the high cost of graduate programs combined with the increasingly high level of debt incurred in earning a bachelor's qualification are both potent drivers toward work-based study. In our experience, the opportunity to combine work and study is welcomed by students and employers alike. Students gain financial independence, and employers are able to ensure that their employees are acquiring skills and undergoing training that will benefit the organization.

The second category comprises those who recognize the importance of lifelong learning and already are established in employment but are unable, for career or financial reasons, to return to full-time study. Members of this group need to maintain or enhance their expertise in their professions and hence develop a competitive advantage, frequently through the medium of part-time graduate programs.

The third group is the growing number of people who need (or simply desire) to change their profession as employment needs and opportunities evolve.

These new constituencies are making different demands of higher education, and the global market economy has ever-changing demands for a multiskilled (or reskilled) workforce. Employers have fresh requirements, and where they believe the education sector is inadequate or unresponsive, they look beyond it or provide their own programs of study.

Alongside the other demands is a growing demand for flexibility in the period of study and in the program's start date. Not all students want to start studying in September or October and complete the program in one or two years. Increasingly, the demand is for programs that are flexible in time and place, skills acquisition, delivery methods, and qualifications awarded.

Changes in Methods of Delivery

New technology is liberating learning from the constraints of time and place. Until relatively recently, the style of much of higher education was based on methods that would have been familiar 2,000 years ago to students at Plato's Academy. Faculty and students at many institutions—including traditional universities—make great use of the Internet, e-mail, teleconferencing, and computer-mediated learning in its many forms. When used intelligently, these new methods can enrich the learning experience and complement face-to-face learning and written materials. The delivery options now available are much more diverse and have enabled institutions to be more responsive to individuals' learning needs.

Changes in Institutions

Perhaps the most profound change in higher education is that established universities are no longer monopoly suppliers of postbaccalaureate study programs. So-called corporate universities are almost commonplace. Partnerships between universities and business and industry are growing rapidly, as are consortia of universities delivering graduate programs.

Another phenomenon is the rise of mega-universities. A *mega-university* has been defined as a distance teaching institution with more than 100,000 active students enrolled in degree-level courses.[1] This definition is deliberately restrictive and combines three criteria: distance teaching, higher education, and size. Mega-universities provide flexible, usually home-based, learning to large numbers of students at low or very competitive cost. The economies of scale mean that the learning materials are of high quality and involve a wide variety of different media.

There are now more than a dozen mega-universities worldwide. The Open University (OU), which has provided the model for many of them, was granted its Royal Charter in 1969. The OU now has more than 200,000 students, including some 30,000 postbaccalaureate students. It operates primarily in the United Kingdom but also delivers courses to 25,000 people in more than 25 other countries. Like other successful global organizations, the OU has various well-developed partnerships, the biggest and most enduring of which is with the British Broadcasting Corporation (BBC) to produce and deliver broadcast television and other audiovisual materials. It is now extending its partnerships with a variety of universities, including California State University and commercial organizations. In 1998, it set up a sister institution, the United States Open University, to bring its methods of supported open learning and elements of its broad curriculum to the U.S.

Other mega-universities include Turkey's Anadolu University, founded in 1982, which has 578,000 students enrolled in degree programs offered at a distance. It has an annual intake of more than 100,000 students and produces

26,000 graduates per annum. Anadolu University is a dual mode institution that combines its large distance program with conventional teaching to 17,000 students at its Eskisehir campus.

An exclusively distance teaching mega-university is the Indira Gandhi National Open University of India which was established in 1985; it now has an annual intake of approximately 100,000 students and a total enrollment of 431,000 students, both undergraduate and postgraduate. The Indira Gandhi National Open University is remarkably cost effective, with 39 programs and 487 courses on offer, provided by a very small central academic staff complement of about 250 faculty and delivered by a distributed, part-time complement of almost 20,000 academic consultants.

Other mega-universities are located in Africa, China, Europe, India, and the Far and Middle East. The total undergraduate and postgraduate enrollment at these institutions was approximately 2.8 million in 1996; between them, they now produce more than 250,000 graduates each year.

There are other very large education providers in addition to the institutions we define as mega-universities. The University of Wisconsin System was established in 1971 with two doctoral universities, 11 four-year universities, 13 freshman-sophomore centers, a statewide Extension Independent Learning University, and an administration unit. This highly complex system falls outside our definition of a mega-university because it is a multi-campus institution where teaching is primarily face to face, although the campuses offer many successful distance education courses. Within the system, the Wisconsin Association of Distance Education Networks serves mainly the people of Wisconsin. Its mission is to work collaboratively to advance and improve distance education opportunities for all learners in Wisconsin. It has a sophisticated World Wide Web-based Distance Education Clearinghouse that offers more than 1,000 courses. Graduate courses are offered for credit; for example, the three-graduate-point "Strength of Materials" course, delivered by e-mail and the World Wide Web, is available from the UW-Stout campus.

The private, for-profit, University of Phoenix was accredited in 1978 and now claims to be one of the largest institutions in the United States for business and management postbaccalaureate education. It aims to serve working adults and has 65 campuses and learning centers across the United States which deliver teaching material in a variety of ways, mostly face to face but also online. The university distinguishes between younger students still deciding on a career and its target audience: adult students who have established personal and professional goals. Students can study at the time of their choosing and at their own pace. Using the CPEInternet, students can take tests and interact by e-mail with a personal tutor. The university emphasizes its flexibility.

The University of Phoenix has designed its own Academic Quality Management System (AQMS) which aims to ensure consistent, high-quality programs and student services regardless of the mode of delivery. The university enrolled approximately 60,000 students in 1999.

In addition to the accredited universities, there are also more than 1,000 non-accredited corporate or virtual-corporate universities in the United States alone. These often are located within a company and are designed to meet in-house training needs at the higher education level. Frequently, their formation has been driven by the desire to develop a learning culture within the company, which, it is believed, will help make the company more competitive and successful. Corporate universities usually employ a core staff of professional trainers, but they frequently make use of other higher education providers as well.

An interesting example of a U.K. corporate university with a mission that extends beyond the in-house training function is the New Academy of Business founded by Anita Roddick, chief executive and founder of Body Shop International. The New Academy was founded with the explicit aim of promoting the view that business practice should be guided by principles of social justice, spirituality, and human rights. Though its perspective is distinctively different from that of conventional providers, the academy does make use of courses from the traditional higher education sector. For example, it offers modules from the University of Lancaster's M.B.A. program and from the University of Bath's M.Sc. program in "Responsibility and Business Practice." Significantly, the New Academy is research active, with support from (among others) the Ford Foundation.

A new virtual-corporate university is the British Aerospace Virtual University, which was launched in May 1997. It is predicated on an integrated business strategy coordinating almost all of British Aerospace's activities and is available to its 46,000 employees. Its mission is based on four aims: to build and encourage centers of excellence by reshaping and realigning, among others, research and development partnerships, management development, and customized graduate degrees; to embed "best practice" in the organization; to become a think tank for British Aerospace; and to make lifelong learning a hallmark of British Aerospace.

Building on successful practice elsewhere, the British Aerospace University will depend on partnerships with existing providers to deliver many of its programs. The first project, which is to provide a British Aerospace Certificate in Management, is being developed in partnership with the Open University Business School and the University of Lancaster.

Motorola University is a corporate university that will customize training and development programs for other organizations and that encourages the formation of company-specific management and executive institutes tailored to reflect relevant critical business issues. Motorola University does not accredit higher education qualifications and does not appear to be involved in postgraduate programs, but it is a good example of the way in which organizations are becoming more involved in lifelong learning.

The Ford Motor Company, without having a formal corporate university structure, has 6,000 employees involved in part-time degree programs worldwide—more than any other company. In 1987, Ford in the United Kingdom launched its Employee Development and Assistance Programme (EDAP), which aims to provide all of its employees access to higher or to sub-degree education, as appropriate. Programs are run in collaboration with approximately 10 U.K. universities. Currently, almost 500 U.K. employees of the Ford Motor Company are registered for taught postgraduate degrees, and 26 are registered for Ph.D.s.

These few examples are not meant to be an exhaustive list of new kinds of postgraduate providers, but they do illustrate the range of styles and types that are available, in addition to the thousands of traditional universities that continue to offer their services.

CONSEQUENCES OF THE CHANGES IN POSTBACCALAUREATE EDUCATION

The changes in demand and the rise of new kinds of learning institutions are having an impact on all types of institutions and on the kind of provision they offer. Broadly, postgraduate education is now partitioned among three different types of institutions, differing by orders of magnitude in the numbers of students enrolled in their largest programs.

Small, local providers with maximum enrollments measured in tens of students enrolled in face-to-face, full- or part-time programs are serving a niche market frequently (but not exclusively) made up of the local industry and business workforce. These are valuable programs where demand is likely to continue to be strong as long as the local infrastructure of industry is viable. The added value of these programs is the ability to tailor provision to local needs, often in partnership with industry. This type of provision is not limited to strictly local enterprises but generally is limited to employees in a particular location. The Ford Motor Company's EDAP uses such providers and partnerships. A feature of these small-scale, local programs is that they are not usually scalable: there is neither the demand for large-scale expansion, nor is it a simple matter to replicate the teaching style on a larger scale.

Large, national universities are able to provide programs for hundreds of students usually in full-time programs. Frequently, these are prestigious and can attract students nationally and internationally. Their success depends on excellence of provision, faculty excellence, and the institution's reputation (for example, the Harvard Business School). Large, residential universities can successfully deliver specialist programs or can be more generic in their offerings. The advantages to individuals attending such institutions derive from a combination of factors, but the most potent (beyond the quality of the knowledge acquired) are the cachet associated with a first-rank institution and the quality of the personal contacts made. The disadvantages have been outlined earlier and pertain primarily to short-term financial issues and the limitations in time and place imposed by a residential course. Of course, major national universities can also present small programs to meet local or regional needs if desirable.

Large programs from excellent universities with international reputations are in such demand that the potential for modifying them (sometimes described as "versioning") for mass delivery by mega-universities is great. The global market for the best programs is potentially huge, and there is likely to be even greater activity—and competition—in adapting the learning style of such programs while maintaining their quality and content.

Mega-universities are configured to present programs to thousands of students without the limitations of time and place. The best of these universities also have an excellent reputation for quality of provision. In the United Kingdom, undergraduate teaching quality is nationally assessed, subject by subject, for each of the 100 and more universities. The OU is ranked in the top 10 percent of U.K. universities for teaching quality, despite being the largest provider by far and having no academic entry requirements to its undergraduate programs. (Postgraduate programs are not separately assessed.)

The mega-universities also are generally prepared to form partnerships with industry and other universities anywhere in the world, as long as there is mutual benefit. Because mega-universities have efficient logistics, based on strong infrastructures, they also can deliver small, highly specialized courses to meet national or international needs.

The influence of the mega-universities is most clearly evident in the philosophical shift away from universities as teaching machines toward universities as learning systems. This shift was necessary for the success of the mega-universities, which must reject many long-held assumptions about the nature of successful universities if they are to flourish. The primacy of synchronous teacher/student interactions, such as lectures and seminars, in delivering knowledge is not possible in distance teaching organizations which have, in response, developed a new learning paradigm based on self-paced, student-centered, supported, open learning. This new paradigm in turn requires the university itself to develop new, flexible, and responsive learning systems.

THE OPEN UNIVERSITY AS A LEARNING SYSTEM

The Open University was founded in 1969 and has now awarded more than 200,000 degrees, providing annually approximately 5 percent of the entire U.K. graduate output. It also has the largest graduate school in the United Kingdom, with 33,000 students (its M.B.A. program accounts for 25 percent of all M.B.A.s awarded in the United Kingdom).

As described at its inauguration, the OU mission is to be open as to people, places, methods, and ideas. The first of these means a commitment to being accessible—a word that is hard to define at the postgraduate level. It is important to define entry requirements in ways that ensure that students can benefit from their courses rather than using entry grades as a surrogate for program quality.

Initially, the second principle, of openness as to places, was interpreted as a commitment to making OU study equally available anywhere in the United Kingdom. That has now been extended to a commitment to making the programs available internationally, often in partnership with local organizations. The OU uses all available learning methods and is a leader in the use of new technology. However, technological requirements need to be evaluated in light of the principle of accessibility. The fourth principle requires a commitment to research, which is an integral part of the activities in a successful learning system.

The unique achievement of the OU is to have broken the traditional and insidious link between quality and exclusivity. Scale and quality can increase simultaneously—a revolutionary idea for postbaccalaureate education, but an enduring factor in the success of the OU. It even can be argued that large scale is *necessary* for high-quality provision of higher education programs using distance and computer-mediated delivery.

The OU has erected a learning system upon the following four pillars of practice:

- high-quality, multiple-media learning materials produced by expert teams;
- personal support to each student;
- efficient logistics; and
- faculty who conduct research.

These pillars of practice together create the powerful system that combines access, scale, quality, and knowledge.

A defining feature of the OU approach to course writing is the use of teams to produce all teaching material. The team has a variable number of members, depending on the size of the course, but always is led by an academic "course team chair"; the team also involves other faculty, editors, designers, software specialists, graphic artists, and a course manager who is responsible for project management. The team works by applying a robust critical analysis to its teaching and learning materials at the planning, design, and production stages. This time-consuming and expensive process can only work with economies of scale.

The desire for scale creates tension between quality and choice, but in a learning system such as that of the OU, more students generally means a better learning experience for each one individually. More intellectual and financial capital can be invested in large courses, and the academic support can be richer and more extensive. One consequence, however, is that programs typically offer few electives.

At the postgraduate level, students expect to have the opportunity to follow their own special interests. Defining quality at the postgraduate level has caused the OU to examine its assumptions. The key to success at the undergraduate level is the presentation of attractive, high-production value materials, which encourage a structured approach to the development of skills and knowledge. Through the course of the bachelor's degree, the student is led toward independent learner status. Many of the techniques used in the learning materials are concerned as much with how to acquire knowledge as with knowledge itself.

For postgraduate students, who are independent learners, the challenge is different: How can students construct their own knowledge? The course team approach has been maintained for postgraduate courses, but the team is more concerned with generating and identifying a wide variety of source materials and with finding ways for more effective communication between and among students and their tutors.

Fortunately, modern technology can make scale and quality synergetic. The Law of the Telecosm (Metcalfe's Law) states that the value of a network to a user is proportional to the square of the number of other users. More and more students are online from home (50,000 in the OU in 1999), and in an increasing number of postgraduate programs, this is becoming a requirement. The Internet and a local OU intranet are also finding increasing use as learning resources. The combination with e-mail and conferencing is exceptionally powerful and allows personal contacts to be made and maintained with no limitations of time or distance. Individual students can work on individual projects but still be part of a vibrant academic community. The larger the community, the greater the quality and level of interactions as there is a greater chance of a commonality of interest or approach between individuals. It is worth emphasizing that in this system, students use *one another* as primary learning sources. The role of the tutor frequently is to moderate and to mediate such interactions, as well as to oversee tuition and assessment. The emphasis in postgraduate learning is more on the quality of the interactions and the development of reflective practice than on the production values of the learning materials.

Efficient logistics are the foundation of the "value chain" of a learning system.[2] Students need materials to be delivered to them on time, to quality, and at an appropriate price. The Open University has an extensive infrastructure concerned exclusively with logistical support for course teams which is able, if necessary, to deal effectively with all stages of course materials production, delivery, tuition, and assessment. Local support is organized by 13 regional offices across the United Kingdom and Northern Ireland.

The quality of teaching materials, the innovative nature of programs, and the creative use of new technology are possible at the OU only because its academic staff are leaders in their professions. Faculty are recruited explicitly to carry out research as well as to teach. It is particularly important at the postbaccalaureate level that the teaching materials and information provided are authoritative and current, and this can only be guaranteed by hiring those who are active in their subjects at the highest level.

THE OPEN UNIVERSITY IN PRACTICE

The Open University is rapidly expanding postbaccalaureate education in a number of directions. Programs include

- very small-scale (less than 100 students) master's programs, such as the Internet-based Master of Arts in Open and Distance Learning;
- small-scale (low hundreds of students), academic, non-vocational master's programs, such as the M.A. in literature and the M.Sc. in science;
- a medium-scale (mid hundreds of students) program leading to an M.A. in education (and thence to an Ed.D. in some cases), primarily for practicing teachers; and
- large-scale business qualifications (thousands to tens of thousands of students).

The final sections of this chapter describe, through selected examples, how the OU learning system is applied.

The M.Sc. in Science

The M.Sc. in science was first presented in 1998, and the program enrolls approximately 200 students. It is a generic program that does not lead to a professionally recognized vocational qualification.

The taught M.Sc. in science is topic led, which allows students to explore broad scientific issues at the postgraduate level. The program is modular and is equivalent to one year of full-time, residential graduate study. It is organized around two main "strands": "Studies of Science" (including the courses "Science and the Public" and "Communicating Science") and "Frontiers in Medical Science" (including the courses "Imaging and Molecules in Medicine" and "Issues in Brain and Behaviour"). Students choose three courses, as current courses are a year long and are scaled to one-third of a full-time workload. Project courses also are available for those students wanting to pursue a substantial piece of independent research.

Students may elect to follow a single strand or to mix modules from both strands and to do some original project work. Each module is a discrete course taken over one OU academic year (February through October) and consists of a specially prepared study commentary, a collection of articles or a set book, and a CD-ROM. Some modules also include BBC-produced audio- or video-cassettes. Electronic tuition and conferencing is an important feature, and students are provided with online access (as necessary) to bibliographic databases, electronic journals, and relevant Web sites. Day schools as well as face-to-face and telephone tutorial support are also offered. Each group of about 25 students has, for each course, a personal, specially appointed tutor. These Associate Lecturers (ALs) may be full-time employees of the OU but are more likely to be academic staff at other institutions or otherwise highly qualified individuals who are appointed for part-time work and are fully trained in Open University teaching methods. Student contact with these ALs is via face-to-face tuition, e-mail, and telephone.

Students are assessed on the basis of a combination of assignments and projects submitted to their tutor, as well as by sitting for an examination at the end of each course.

As with other OU programs, the student becomes a part of the learning system, adding favorite articles and personal work to the database, as well as helping the course team maintain and improve the quality of support. Feedback (solicited and unsolicited) from students is collected regularly and is an integral part of the quality assurance process.

A Graduate Program in Business Studies

Since 1983, when the Open University Business School (OUBS) program began, more than 140,000 individual students have studied in the postgraduate taught courses, and more than 20,000 postgraduate qualifications have been awarded. The program consists of a structured, nested set of Professional Certificate and Professional Diploma, which increase in level and complexity and can lead finally to an M.B.A. The program is presented globally; students currently study in 23 countries, in English and in translation. The excellence of the provision has been recognized by the U.K. Higher Education Funding Council, which awarded the OUBS the highest rating of "excellent" for its teaching and support systems. The OUBS also provides the only wholly distance-taught M.B.A. to be accredited by the Association of MBAs (AMBA).

Employers seeking to develop their workforce are looking for cost-effective, practical, and flexible management development. These study programs offer all those benefits, and long-standing relationships exist with a wide range of organizations who have decided that OUBS-supported distance learning is the best, most cost-effective way of bringing management development to their employees. The OUBS has worked with more than 13,000 organizations—including many of the largest companies operating in the United Kingdom, including BT, Halifax Building Society, and IBM—to provide a range of management development opportunities. Public sector organizations, such as the police and health services, are among the corporate clients. The OUBS has tailored many of its modules to meet specific delivery and content requirements by including input from company personnel as well as tutorial support staff. Such partnerships provide a bridge between corporate provision, which is not validated or subject to external quality audit, and the university sector, with its publicly accountable quality systems.

Although the Open University is exclusively a distance teaching institution, the personal element of student support is vital to the success of its learning system. For example, within the OUBS, tutors marked more than 70,000 assignments in 1996. Face-to-face tuition accounted for more than 330,000 hours in 1996. That year, 150 two- to three-day residential schools involving 10,000 students were held at 30 locations. More than 20,000 hours of online access were logged.

Issues of access in an open system are challenging. There is no open access to the M.B.A. itself, which requires a minimum age of 27 years, an honors degree, and business experience. These entry requirements have been defined to ensure that students can benefit from the course. There is open access to the Professional Certificate, which is designed to help students develop the skills necessary for the Diploma and the M.B.A. as well as to be freestanding for those who do not wish to proceed further.

The following course illustrates how the teaching system operates:

> B800, "Foundations of Senior Management," can account for one-third of the study needed for an M.B.A. Throughout the course, computers play an important role as a learning and communications medium. They are used for online conferencing and communication with students, tutors, and the course team, and for Internet access, a business simulation game, and financial modeling and analysis.
>
> B800 is a large course for which students study for about 10 hours each week for 32 weeks. All course material is delivered to the student's home or workplace at staged intervals throughout the study period. The learning materials are multiple-media with specially written texts,

broadcast TV programs, videotapes, commissioned articles, study files, and other learning aids, such as use of the new media described above. Students must successfully complete four written assignments and pass an end-of-course examination. Each student is assigned to an OU-trained tutor (AL) who, instead of being a local academic, may be a senior member of the student's own company (if such a partnership has been formed). Regular tutorials are reinforced by a compulsory weekend residential school which brings together some of the main course themes and gives students an opportunity to examine their own experience and career development.

The advantages of the OU learning system are not confined simply to earning the qualification. The habits of reflective practice (defined by Laurillard as linking feedback on actions to topic goals),[3] at every level of activity, improve performance on a continuing basis. The familiarity with new media that is gained from the courses also adds value long after graduation. The use of new media to encourage and nurture "virtual communities" provides the graduate membership of a worldwide business and academic network with contacts that can rival those made at face-to-face institutions.

THE UNITED STATES OPEN UNIVERSITY

The Open University has established a sister institution, the United States Open University (USOU), to weave into the rich tapestry of American higher education the quality and methodology of supported open learning as practiced by the Open University. Formally, the USOU is a private, not for profit, 501(c)(3) membership corporation registered and licensed in Delaware. It was accorded candidacy status for accreditation by the Middle States Association of Colleges and Schools in 1999 and is seeking licenses in other states. A majority of the members of the board of governance are distinguished Americans from various walks of life. The founding chancellor, Richard S. Jarvis, former chancellor of the University and Community College System of Nevada, took office in September 1999.

Beginning in 2000, the USOU will develop and offer a broad curriculum at the upper-division baccalaureate and postbaccalaureate levels. The first postbaccalaureate programs will be in the areas of business/management and software engineering. These subjects, as well as liberal arts programs in European and international studies, are the foundation of the undergraduate offerings. In the first instance, most of the USOU courses will be adapted from courses already offered internationally by the Open University from the United Kingdom. As it develops, however, the USOU will develop some of its own courses and also will adopt and adapt courses from other universities.

We noted above that one reason for the acknowledged success of the Open University in the United Kingdom is the active involvement of its research-active faculty in all aspects of its operations. The USOU will operate on the same principle. It gradually will build up a high-quality faculty, with both full-time and part-time members, to ensure that the university is driven by academic values and is fully engaged in American intellectual life.

THE WAY FORWARD

In this chapter, we have only outlined the methods, characteristics, and influence of learning systems. More detailed analyses are to be found in Daniel and Laurillard. We have focused on the Open University, but there are many similarities in the strategic challenges that confront it and campus-based universities.

The first strategic challenge is to improve the effectiveness of learning and new media, or knowledge media as defined by Eisenstadt.[4] The availability of knowledge media has been crucial in helping to change the paradigm from teaching to learning. This does not mean that the role of the teacher is diminished; in fact, the importance of the teacher as guide, mediator, facilitator, and assessor is enhanced. The most successful mega-universities all have some form of local and personal academic contact with students.

The concept of the university as a learning system (in which the university rather than any one individual is the teacher) is a powerful force for improving the quality of learning. For years, the quality of university-based research has been enhanced by peer review, teamwork, multi-institutional collaboration, and links with industry; the same is now happening in teaching. At the postgraduate level, the employer-student-university triad is itself an integral part of the learning system.

Another common goal for universities is to recreate the academy as a community. This has been a particular challenge for distance teaching institutions, but community is possible when knowledge media are used intelligently.

The expansion of distance learning is only one response to the new challenges of postbaccalaureate education. However, the concept of student-centered learning freed from the constraints of time and place, new approaches to community in the academy, and the increased use of knowledge media all contribute to redefining the university as a learning system. The understanding, application, and refinement of the learning system concept will be a powerful part of the process of defining the future of postbaccalaureate education for all sectors of higher education.

NOTES

1.   J.S. Daniel, *Mega-Universities and Knowledge Media: Technology Strategies for Higher Education.* London: Kogan Page, 1996.

2. M. E. Porter, *Competitive Advantage: Creating and Sustaining Superior Performance*. New York: Free Press, 1985.
3. D. Laurillard, *Rethinking University Teaching: A Framework for the Effective Use of Educational Technology*, London: Routledge, 1993.
4. M. Eisenstadt, "Overt Strategy for Global Learning," *Times Higher Education Supplement*, Multimedia Section, 7 April 1995, vi-vii; M. Eisenstadt and T. Vincent, *The Knowledge Web*. London: Kogan Page, 1998, p. 4.

CHATER

Assessing the Quality of Postbaccalaureate Learning in the New Higher Education Marketplace

Steven D. Crow

D elivery of postbaccalaureate certificate programs is a growing business. The rapidly changing economy, the growing demand for "knowledge workers," and the transforming impact of new technologies on education, combined with the aging baby boom generation, have resulted in a massive market for the focused, job-related content of short-term programs. Moreover, development of certificate programs—or content for them—is the primary business of many new organizations that market them alone or that seek to partner with colleges and universities, which already are busy creating their own short-term programs. Accrediting organizations such as the Commission on Institutions of Higher Education of the North Central Association of Colleges and Schools are just beginning to realize the potential impact on their work on this booming new business and its poorly defined credential.

Four hundred and fifty-one of the Commission's 991 affiliated institutions offer graduate degrees. One hundred and sixty-six of those institutions reported on their most recent annual report that they provide "graduate certificates." Through the Council of Graduate Schools, we learn of the significant growth in postbaccalaureate certificates—at least as measured by the National Center for Education Statistics. But we also are warned that the numbers listed—8,369 postbaccalaureate certificates and 8,401 post-master's certificates in 1994-95—do not reflect the actual variety and volume of certificates

Steven D. Crow is the executive director of the Commission on Institutions of Higher Education of the North Central Association of Colleges and Schools.

awarded, because postbaccalaureate certificates "are often granted outside of the mainstream of institutions and therefore may not be reported in the IPEDS surveys returned to NCES."[1] Within and without our colleges and universities, postbaccalaureate certificates appear to be here to stay.

Some of these certificate programs—particularly those being developed by university departments rather than continuing education units—rely on traditional classroom delivery and thus require students to attend classes, whether on campus, at branch or satellite centers, or at the workplace. But the marketplace that is generating the demand for these programs also places a high premium on convenience, as well as quality. Location of instruction is just one of several variables now defining convenience. Programs that accommodate working adults' special needs—flexible scheduling and customization of content, to name two—seem to be particularly attractive. Use of new technologies and distance education therefore have the potential to figure prominently in many of these certificate programs.

Postbaccalaureate certificate programs not only culminate in newly defined educational credentials, but they also involve new delivery systems and new patterns of educational partnerships. Thus, any discussion of quality assurance of postbaccalaureate certificates inevitably entails consideration of several broader changes reshaping higher education.

This tangled skein defies easy unraveling, even if we could agree upon and trace its most prominent threads. Like all other regional accrediting associations, the commission thought it addressed off-campus education years ago when it developed accrediting requirements based on the "duplication/replication" model of evaluation. Essentially, institutions were expected to duplicate the curriculum in off-campus settings and replicate for off-campus students the services available on campus. But replication of a campus was never really possible, so the model eventually substituted "comparability" for replication and "effective adaptation" for duplication. But the home campus remained the benchmark for quality.

Distance education—particularly through delivery systems based on new technologies such as online education via the Internet—is at the same time both similar to and different from off-campus education. When off-campus education was primarily classroom instruction conducted at a distance, accrediting agencies demanded replication of home campus faculty, sometimes even requiring instruction by full-time faculty rather than comparably credentialed site-based adjuncts. Home campus faculty were expected to have strong control over the curriculum, even if that meant prepackaging almost everything used off campus by students and part-time faculty. "Acceptable library support" sometimes meant considerable investment in books at off-campus sites or, at a minimum, extensive and ready access to print materials from the home library.

Online education—even though the student is distant from campus—
might well be designed, delivered, and evaluated by campus-based full-time
faculty. But that faculty member, who typically required little assistance for
the classroom-based course, now is likely to be supported by teams of instructional designers or computer specialists. For years, campus libraries have been
building Internet access and electronic databases into information systems
available for student use; now distance students can make use of those
resources. The asynchronous learning enabled by new technologies enhances
students' expectations of access to faculty; students also need support services
on a 24-hour basis. As the home campus, its educational processes, and its
services are being transformed by technology, its capacity to serve as a
dependable benchmark for distance education is open to question.

Most institutional accreditation agencies are on a rapid learning curve
when it comes to technology-mediated instruction and distance education.
Using the foundation laid in 1995 in the WICHE Telecommunications Project's
"Principles of Good Practice for Electronically Offered Academic Degree and
Certificate Programs,"[2] regional institutional accrediting commission staff
created a related statement of good practices in distance education.[3] Those
"Good Practices" currently inform our evaluations of online courses and
programs, whether delivered by an online institution, a community college, or
a public research university. The "Good Practices" appear to have the flexibility to apply to short-term certificate offerings as well as to degree programs.

It is time to define the next generation of good practices, for as the
commissions and their institutions gain experience with online education,
they can more effectively determine the effectiveness of a variety of ways of
structuring and implementing good practices. Experience generates useful
benchmarks. For example, not all efforts to develop "virtual libraries" are
equally effective. Even when a virtual library is impressive in its design and
accessibility, other services—such as those that provide students with access
to print resources—remain vitally important.[4]

Perhaps we are approaching this incorrectly, taking quality measures for
traditional higher education and modifying them to fit significantly different
educational environments. Perhaps we are looking for the wrong benchmarks
for quality. As the higher education enterprise makes the difficult but necessary shift from assessing quality largely by measuring a variety of invested
resources to measuring it by the achievement of goals—including those that
define expected student academic achievement—we are redefining benchmarks. Any discussion of quality assurance for postbaccalaureate certificates
must acknowledge this, for it certainly shapes the current discussion about the
role of accreditation in quality assurance in higher education.

Some argue that concern about the quality of new postbaccalaureate
certificate programs should not sidetrack us from the broader challenge of

assuring quality in graduate education in general. Graduate degrees now bear an astonishing diversity of titles and are offered by a growing number of non-traditional institutions, as well as institutions new to graduate education. Overnight, it seems, new degrees at the master's and doctoral levels are emerging in response to increasing expectations for professional competence. For some time, graduate education has been influenced by marketplace demands and new technologies. Have we simply deferred to the educational marketplace in defining acceptable quality in graduate education? Are we about to do the same with regard to postbaccalaureate certificates? Critics of contemporary higher education would say so.[5] The Commission's recent four-year effort to identify hallmarks of quality in graduate education suggests that such deferral has not occurred, but neither have new standards emerged.[6]

In this chapter, we have the opportunity to focus on a small but important aspect of change in graduate-level education. Because postbaccalaureate certification is new and the credential is not well defined, we must consider whether institutional accreditation has a meaningful role to play in the quality assurance of postbaccalaureate certificate programs. The answer must be "yes," but the complexity of the situation belies quick and easy definition of that role.

A good way to explore accreditors' potential interests in these programs is to review the variables weighed by institutions in deciding whether to offer postbaccalaureate certificates. Any institution's decision will be based on a unique variety of variables, but the following will be common to all:

1. *Financing.* Even though much of the cost of undergraduate and gradu-ate education is subsidized, institutions offering postbaccalaureate certificate programs expect that at a minimum, such programs will be self-supporting. In fact, most institutions expect the programs to result in new revenue streams. The development costs of distance education may make the programs expensive; alternatively, the costs may be borne elsewhere in the institutional budget.

2. *Students.* Certificate programs must be directed toward an increasing and potentially self-replenishing student clientele. Demographic trends favor providing service to the "baby boomers" now in mid-career. Alternatively, the market might be corporate, industrial, and service sectors of the economy slated to experience rapid changes in the foreseeable future. Gaining access to sufficient numbers of students might necessitate expansion of the institution's service area beyond regional, state, or even national boundaries.

3. *Flexibility.* The programs must be responsive to rapidly changing eco-nomic and technological developments in the workplace. In short, program flexibility and speed of response are "musts." Decision-

making structures may need to be modified or streamlined, or decisions about certificate programs may be made apart from traditional
governance practices.

4.　*Mission and service.* Many institutions that exist to serve public needs
will feel pressure to develop and deliver new programs. For institutions
with strong ties to the professions, the changes in those professions—
particularly those tied to licensing requirements for protection of the
public welfare and safety—also demand responsiveness from the educational community that provided entry to the profession. As mentioned above, the search for an appropriate student clientele may
significantly expand the geographical parameters of an institution's
mission.

5.　*Impact on accreditation.* While colleges and universities have several
options in formulating their responses to new educational opportunities, this chapter highlights a fifth variable that has not always figured
very prominently in institutional decision making, though it should:
Accredited institutions should review the potential relationship of
their postbaccalaureate certificate programming to the external quality assurance traditionally provided through accreditation.

Fundamental to this discussion is the understanding that accrediting associations, both institutional and programmatic, though external to institutions
of higher education, are also shaped by and through the institutions and
programs they accredit. Thus, institutions and programs should not think of
themselves simply as passive recipients of any accrediting process. Rather, they
must take advantage of every opportunity to ensure that the external evaluations they seek support institutional missions and goals as well as internal
quality assurance programs. Institutions and programs also need to appreciate
the fact that overall, the higher education community is remarkably ambiva-
lent about some of the broad changes affecting it. New postbaccalaureate
certificate programs represent one facet of those changes. So we explore the
future like a group of cats; herding is difficult, and leading sometimes appears
fortuitous rather than intentional.

USING ALTERNATIVE FORMS OF VALIDATION

Institutions should not underestimate the value of quality assurance programs
that might be provided by organizations other than accrediting agencies.
Rigorous external validation by bodies other than current institutional and
program agencies should be respected by regional accrediting agencies. This is
particularly true if those bodies have recognized and respected standards for
postgraduate certification. Were an institution to follow this path, it should

seek assurance from its accrediting bodies that the external validation would be honored, not duplicated, by the accreditor.

Colleges and universities might seek external validation from organizations whose certification speaks to well-recognized industry and professional standards. Some of the certificate programs being offered through higher education institutions are responsive to highly specific skill requirements, particularly in the areas of safety and health. The precision with which external groups define the contents of and the competencies expected in those certificate programs almost automatically endows the external groups with the responsibility to appropriately define external quality assurance. A quick review of the variety of extension offerings at the University of California-Berkeley provides a good example. The Asbestos Management certificate program is tied directly to specific training and accreditation for individuals doing asbestos inspections and related work in schools. Doubtless, the university's primary concern is to meet Asbestos Hazard Emergency Response Act (AHERA) requirements, not the Western Association of Schools and Colleges' accrediting standards.[7]

A college considering this approach would be well advised to weigh it against several potential problems. The proliferation of external certification agencies compounds the anxiety of institutions that already claim to be victims of too many multiple and duplicative external agencies. Moreover, things that matter to graduate deans and graduate faculties might receive little attention from external certifiers whose sole concern is that certifiable competencies result from a student's studies. Accrediting agencies tend not to defer to other organizations' judgments (particularly those organizations that are not recognized as providing institutional or program accreditation). There is no assurance that regional institutional accrediting associations will recognize other quality assurance programs/organizations valued by the higher education community, the graduate community, or the communities investing in the postbaccalaureate learning experience. Institutions may find themselves duplicating external reviews, at odds with their institutional agency, or in a state of healthy disagreement over what constitutes good quality assurance for a specific program.

MAKING ALL CERTIFICATES
GRADUATE CREDIT-BEARING OFFERINGS

At some universities, all postbaccalaureate offerings carry graduate credit either integral to or related to graduate programs offered by the institution. By and large, this decision does not present many difficulties for an accrediting association equipped with standards for graduate education. These offerings clearly fall under institutional governing structures for graduate education, and they are shaped and evaluated by those responsible for overseeing graduate instruction. This approach also seems to be sensitive to the student demand that learning—even that which takes place in certificate programs—translate readily into traditional academic degree credentials. If we are concerned more about what a student knows than where the learning takes place, the decision to grant credit for all postbaccalaureate learning will ensure the transportability of acquired learning at least within the institution.

But there are risks here, as well. From the perspective of the external reviewer, it is not clear that credit-bearing certificate programs—even those created from existing graduate courses—will be understood and appropriately evaluated by those whose definitions of graduate education are shaped by years of creating and delivering master's and doctoral programs. Many believe "modularized graduate education" is an oxymoron at best and a travesty at worst. Moreover, using existing graduate programs as the "parents" of all possible certificates might diminish institutional flexibility or, alternatively, result in the proliferation of graduate degrees. If the latter occurs, the institution's effort to adapt graduate education to fit a variety of new settings might result in questions about its understanding of graduate education. In short, if postbaccalaureate certificates bear graduate credit, then some of the current concerns about the changing nature of graduate education in general will come to play in the evaluation.

MAKING CERTIFICATES NON-CREDIT OFFERINGS

As it contemplates the offering of postbaccalaureate certificates, an institution might choose to distinguish between credit-bearing graduate education and certifiable but non-credit-bearing postbaccalaureate learning experiences. Current accrediting practice actually seems to reward this approach. For the most part, accrediting agencies have turned a blind eye to institutions' non-credit activities, including programs that award continuing education units for professional certification. Rightly or wrongly, the primary focus has been on institutions' credit-bearing activities. Even if non-credit activities are conducted through contractual or collaborative relationships, they typically do not require approval or significant review by accreditors. Moreover, if students in such programs do not qualify for federal financial aid, the Department of Education shows no interest in them either. This strategy should meet with considerable institutional acceptance; several institutions preparing to develop certificate options already have adopted it, having determined that postbaccalaureate certificates should be built around non-credit-bearing courses.

The major flaw in this strategy is that it fails to provide the institution with dependable external review. If an institution wants external quality assurance of certificate offerings, this approach may not provide it (at least not from the institutional accrediting agency). Deciding that postbaccalaureate offerings will not bear credit is an invitation—perhaps even a request—that institutional accreditors look at them cursorily, if at all. Too often, the strategy also sets the non-credit programming outside of the institution's own quality assurance processes (at least those focused on basic educational offerings).

In light of the potential growth of such programs, this is at best a short-term strategy. As institutions respond to increasingly diverse demands for education and training, they challenge the claim that institutional accreditation "evaluates an entire institution and accredits it as a whole."[8] Commentators on accreditation within community colleges have drawn attention to the vital role of the non-credit "shadow college" in giving many of these colleges the capacity to fulfill their mission and purposes.[9] The chancellor of a major urban community college noted that one-sixth of his institution's $600 million budget came from non-credit customized programs; the same will become true of four-year institutions. New "shadow colleges" already are emerging within some highly entrepreneurial schools and departments; they provide the revenue stream vital to the fiscal health of graduate education. Some might argue that certain research and comprehensive universities' Schools of Continuing Education are "shadow colleges." Institutional accrediting agencies will not be able to look the other way when the well-being of an institution's credit-bearing offerings depends on other institutional activities.

SHARING IN COLLABORATIVE PROGRAMS

Some institutions interested in offering certificate programs have chosen to collaborate with other organizations in developing or delivering postbaccalaureate learning experiences. This might be particularly attractive if the institution is providing academic legitimacy to what it considers to be a highly reputable program (or large components of a program) offered by an unaccredited entity. The partner could be a courseware developer, an organization known for high-level training, or a consulting corporation. During the past decade, the commission has extended the accreditation of several institutions to include courses and programs offered largely through the services of an external provider. The Institute for Professional Development, a component of Apollo, Inc., provides a wide variety of services (including courseware) to its contracting institutions, such as Indiana Wesleyan University, Cardinal Stritch University, and Fontbonne College. Videobased courseware from Kantor and Associates is used by several institutions for graduate-level education courses and serves as a major component of the master's degrees offered by Grand Canyon University and Marygrove College.

Contracts inevitably raise the level of visibility of postbaccalaureate certificate offerings and the potential for their external review, regardless of whether the offerings bear graduate credit or not. Accreditation is not extended by contract, so nothing catches an accrediting agency's attention faster than when it appears that an institution is extending its accredited status through contract. Moreover, institutions also should consider that most accrediting agencies have yet to promulgate dependable guidelines as to what constitutes an acceptable contractual arrangement. The Commission's own guidelines are only months old.[10] Experience—not unfounded suspicion—leads some accrediting agencies (the Commission included) to question contractual arrangements. For example, when a contracting institution agrees to do more than it reasonably can, the stronger, better financed, and more efficient partner begins to dominate or even redirect the program. When institutions cannot fulfill contractual obligations, accrediting agencies tend not to be particularly sympathetic. In this highly competitive marketplace, unfortunate misunderstandings can result from the misuse of regional accreditation either to market the product to other institutions or to students. Very few accrediting agencies have the financial resources to take exploiting partners to court, so most are skeptical of contractual arrangements.

At yet another level of analysis, institutions considering collaborative arrangements with accredited or non-accredited entities should explore the impact of accrediting processes on those relationships. The current approach to accreditation is to locate control and to place all the responsibility on the "controlling" partner. While this might seem reasonable, it does not allow much room for synergy and creative collaboration. In fact, more than one institution has downplayed the actual creative interplay among partners in an effort to prove that it was the controlling party in the contract. Among relatively equal partners, ill will might well result from accrediting agencies' demands that the higher education institution be considered the "superior" partner. Programs involving more than one accredited entity have faced similar challenges.

SHAPING THE REGULATORY ENVIRONMENT

An important subtheme runs throughout the preceding discussion of institutional options: Accrediting agencies are hard at work creating new evaluative tools to respond to the changes transforming higher education, and institutions should want to aid in this work. The rapid emergence of postbaccalaureate certificate programming is almost overshadowed by the breathtaking speed of development of online education. In almost every sector of higher education, entrepreneurialism has become a new value, prompting alliances and programming inconceivable barely a decade ago.[11] The Stuart School of Business of the Illinois Institute of Technology provides a good example, for it has developed a Web site that invites businesses to collaborate in the development of customized programs. To give a sense of the range of possibilities, it proposes more than two dozen.[12]

If our institutions are going to be positioned to operate in a new, more dynamically competitive educational marketplace represented only in part by postbaccalaureate certificates, we cannot continue to hold them to accrediting standards and processes anchored to outdated assumptions about how colleges and universities should function. The emergence of new varieties of postbaccalaureate training and education underscores the need for regional accrediting associations to generate and advance standards and processes appropriate to a new age.[13]

Almost every regional institutional accrediting organization is currently engaged in revising standards and accrediting processes. Discussions among regional associations are marked by a new sense of urgency as each region explores new hallmarks of quality in higher education. The Commission typically has been perceived as "open" to the newest trends in higher education. Yet our criteria and requirements do not mention the new postbaccalaureate pathways—certificates—even though we ask institutions to report them. According to the Commission's current policies, the offering of postbaccalaureate programs does not constitute a change worthy of consideration unless such programs are an institution's only graduate-level course offerings. Many of our institutions report that they are in the certificate business—postbaccalaureate and other—but we have had little to say about it. For example, our accreditation handbook is devoid of text that speaks to entrepreneurialism evidenced by the IIT Web site mentioned above. New standards or guidelines of good practice are necessary if accrediting associations intend to incorporate the quality assurance of these endeavors into institutional accreditation.

The mandate for responsibility might be clear, but the means of carrying it out are not. If accreditation tools emphasize resource configuration over outcomes, then evaluation by accreditors might limit the flexibility colleges and universities need to compete. If accreditors attempt to provide the documentation necessary to enable prospective students and employers to make wise choices among competing processes, they might well develop a costly, staff-heavy system that lacks the support of member institutions. They also might find themselves pushed into implicit or explicit ranking or rating, something almost all member institutions do *not* want from accreditors. But we cannot defer discussion of quality in postbaccalaureate certificates until some time in the future when all of these broader matters are resolved.

At a minimum, we ought to agree:

- that postbaccalaureate certificates testify either to the completion of a clearly defined program of learning (as do credits and degrees) or to tested competencies gained through a program of study;

- that certificate definitions should be public and should follow common practices (where appropriate);
- that internal institutional quality assurance programs include these certificate programs in a meaningful way (in short, that institutional systems document institutional accountability);
- that institutions should expect external reviewers to validate the effectiveness of their implementation of quality assurance programs; and
- that regional accrediting associations should effect these agreements.

Implementing this proposal is somewhat more difficult than it might appear. It certainly requires that institutions and their accrediting agencies approach the development of quality benchmarks in a new manner.

OPENING THE DIALOGUE

In this rapidly changing educational environment, accrediting agencies first must choose to involve a variety of communities in discussions about and determination of standards for postbaccalaureate certificate programs. Though this seems an easy and popular course of action, it proposes that higher education institutions and their accrediting agencies transform their understanding of who is involved in defining and credentialing achieved learning and competence. Some professions (medicine is the most obvious) may argue that academics alone have never been responsible for providing these definitions. But for much of higher education, the operative assumption is that the academy, the community of scholars, alone makes those decisions. It will not be so simple in the new higher education marketplace. Defining the meaning, purpose, and content of market-driven postbaccalaureate certificates will require a new, inclusive dialogue.

DEFINING THE CREDENTIAL

It is likely that for many of the new certificates, no definition of the program's contents is widely shared; nor is there likely to be consensus on what constitutes quality. Other certificate programs might be closely connected to professional certification, about which considerable agreement exists; quality assurance options for some of those programs might already be available. Some certificates are tied so closely to a specific corporate need that broad agreement on their content and nomenclature is not possible; yet even within rather narrow industries, considerable agreement might exist with regard to specific certifiable competencies that cross corporate boundaries.

It seems inconceivable that any accrediting association—even a program agency—could or should attempt to develop specific curricular requirements for every possible variation of certificate offerings. At the very least, though, an institution could be expected to research the field to see what similar certificates are in the marketplace and to position its programs against benchmarks for content, length, and guaranteed competencies.

FOCUSING ON STUDENT LEARNING

It is not possible for an institution to have an acceptable quality assurance program that fails to consider achieved student learning a central measure of quality. Therefore, each certificate program—whether it includes credit-bearing courses or not—should clearly define the skills, knowledge, or competencies a student should gain and should include methods by which students can demonstrate achievement of them. For some certificates, this should be no problem; others will present the same challenge faced by universities, departments, and programs struggling to implement student assessment programs.

USING GOOD PRACTICE AND IDENTIFYING BEST PRACTICE

It seems likely that some good practices institutions can use in creating, marketing, and evaluating postbaccalaureate certificate opportunities will emerge from inclusive discussions. Only a couple are identified in the preceding paragraphs. Further collaborative study by institutions and accrediting agencies could result in identification of best practices to serve as guides for institutions.

FOCUSING ON INTERNAL INSTITUTIONAL QUALITY ASSURANCE

Increasingly, accrediting agencies are being called upon to rely on internal institutional quality assurance programs. Accreditation standards or guidelines should focus primarily on the effectiveness of an institution's internal programs for quality assurance. For example, when a university decides that its postbaccalaureate certificates will be constructed of graduate credit courses, those programs should be integrated into new or existing graduate school quality assurance programs. A review of the documents of some universities that have made this decision suggests that the measures of quality currently being used are connected closely with traditional inputs (e.g., faculty qualifications, resource support, admissions and advising services, etc.).[14] While an institutional accrediting agency might provide for a broader range of appropriate quality measures, it should be ready to honor an institution's own measures. Heavy reliance must be placed on the institution's capacity to create and implement an effective, internally consistent quality assurance program. For those who doubt the commitment of new and nontraditional institutions to quality, this expectation places at the forefront of an accrediting experience the requirement that institutions define quality and have effective programs to document its achievement.

An institution that does not currently have internal quality assurance programs soon will. Much of the focus of accreditation within the next few years will be on evaluation of an institution's internal quality assurance systems. Many universities already claim that their internal processes are of greater value than preparing for and hosting an accreditation visit. Others argue rather convincingly that if accreditation truly aims at institutional and program improvement, then it must be structured around an institution's continuous and ongoing quality improvement programs based on sound quality assurance programs, not decennial visits and myriad substantive change policies and procedures.[15]

All of this said, it will be a challenge for accrediting agencies to accept institutional quality assurance regimes rather than formulating, through the setting of standards, their own regimes. Moreover, the culture of regional accreditation has been more insular than inclusive, more prone to reinventing a wheel than to using a reasonably good one built by others. But in this new world of certification, new associations and agencies might well be involved in institutional quality assurance programs. In short, the appropriate program might involve a very different set of measures and players than are involved in traditional regional institutional accreditation. Comfort with this new arrangement will not come automatically, but the basic commitment must be to forego the duplication of evaluative efforts whenever it is possible to do so.

If the new higher education marketplace calls for more participants in the setting of standards, and if standards become less prescriptive and more related to the effectiveness of an institution's quality assurance programs, then accrediting associations must recruit and train site visitors capable of exercising professional judgment in this environment. It is clear that the need for well-prepared evaluators is not related solely or even primarily to the emergence of postbaccalaureate certificate programs. Unless site visitors appreciate the new environment and exercise informed judgment in interpreting and applying new standards or guidelines, we run the risk of placing appropriate evaluative tools in the hands of the wrong people.

Institutions that offer postbaccalaureate programs must expect the rational and helpful collaboration of accreditors in assuring quality in those programs. But institutions cannot be passive; they need to set the agenda, invite the accreditors to participate, and get on with the task. Accrediting agencies often claim that "our institutions are us," but the fact is that institutions speak with many voices; many voices can be heard even within a single institution. Creative ideas emerge from deliberative groups focused on issues related to postbaccalaureate certification. Such ideas inform both the institutions engaged in developing postbaccalaureate learning experiences and the accrediting associations charged with providing external validation of the quality of their endeavors. In many of our responses to postbaccalaureate education and training, we are learning as we go. That is never a particularly comfortable situation for accrediting associations, and it is almost intolerable for institutions anxious for clear, strong, and dependable answers.[16] Nevertheless, it is the best possible response.

NOTES

1. Stephen R. Welch and Peter D. Syverson, "Postbaccalaureate Certificates; A First Look at Graduate Certificate Programs Offered by CGS Member Institutions," *CGS Communicator*, November 1997: 10-12.
2. "Principles of Good Practice for Electronically Offered Academic Degree and Certificate Programs, June 1995, <www.wiche.edu/Telecom/projects/principles.htm>.
3. "Guidelines for Distance Education," March 1997, <www.ncacihe.org/aice/guidelines/gdistance.html>.
4. See Edward D. Garten, "Access or Exclusion to Library and Information Resources? Good Practice in Transnational and Virtual Learning Environments," Paper presented 1 October 1999 at the 5th Annual Conference of the Global Alliance for Transnational Education, Melbourne, Australia.
5. David Noble, "Digital Diploma Mills," available from <http://www.firstmonday.dk/issues/issue3_1/noble/index.html>.
6. The Commission's study included the convening of a task force and led to a new pattern of evidence for graduate education together with paragraphs of explanation and a new policy on counting prior learning for graduate credit. See Commission on Institutions of Higher Education, Handbook of Accreditation, Second Edition. Chicago: CIHE, 1997: 46-47, 50-51.
7. See the University of California-Berkeley Web site, <http://www.unex.berkeley.edu:4243/em/asb0.html>.
8. Commission on Institutions of Higher Education. *Handbook of Accreditation*, Second Edition, p. 1.
9. James Jacob and Roberta Teahen, "Shadow College and NCA Accreditation: A Conceptual Framework," *A Collection of Papers on Self-Study and Institutional Improvement, 1997*. Chicago: North Central Association of Colleges and Schools, 1997, 13-19, reprinted in *NCA Quarterly* 71 (Spring 1997): 472-78.
10. "Good Practices Regarding Contractual Arrangements Involving Courses and Programs," <www.ncacihe.org/aice/guidelines/contracts.html>.
11. The best discussion of this change is found in Donald Hanna and Associates, *Higher Education in an Era of Digital Competition: Choices and Challenges*. Madison, WI: Atwood Publishing, 1999.
12. See the Web site for the business school at Illinois Institute of Technology at <www.stuart.iit.edu/BusEd>.

13. My sense of the new thinking marking regional accreditation can be found in Western Association of Colleges and Schools, "An Invitation to Dialogue," April 1998, and Commission on Institutions of Higher Education, "Effective Collaboration for the Twenty-first Century: The Commission and Its Stakeholders," February 1998.
14. Wayne Patterson, "Certificates: A Survey of Our Status and Review of Successful Programs in the U.S. and Canada, Background Readings, Part I." Washington, DC: Postbaccalaureate Futures Project, 1998.
15. On 1 July 1999, the Commission began the three-year "Academic Quality Improvement Project" funded by a grant from the Pew Charitable Trusts. The goal of the project is to develop an alternative accreditation program structured around quality improvement principles. See <www.ncacihe.org/AQIP/index.html>.
16. I have also discussed this challenge in "Making Collaboration Work: A Challenge for the Commission," NCA *Quarterly* 72 (Spring 1998): 463-64.

CHAPTER 10

Certification for Employability: What's New?

Alice J. Irby

Certificates have been awarded to individuals and posted on the walls of their homes and offices for years. Similarly, individuals have been studying off campus for years, through correspondence courses, video-tapes, and TV. Universities have awarded certificates in teacher education, agriculture, and other continuing education programs throughout much of the century.

What's new is that certification, in both university and non-university settings, is taking on new definitions, carrying new meanings, and becoming pervasive as a means of earning educational credit and demonstrating competence for jobs and roles in the workplace. The U.S. Department of Education has recorded more than 2,000 certificate programs at the postbaccalaureate level in its IPEDS database. In the university, in the professions, and in the corporate sector, the nature and dimensions of certificate programs are very different than in the past. These new credentialing programs are at the vortex of societal changes reflecting new demands of the workplace and global markets, the explosion of knowledge in existing and new fields, and ever-new technologies in education, training, and work.

Alice J. Irby is president emeritus of the Chauncey Group International.
Author's Note: For much of the early research undertaken for this chapter, the author is indebted to Karen McQuillen in Brigham Library and Kent Ashworth in Communications Services at Educational Testing Service.

The growth in certificate programs and the desire to demonstrate competence comes not from people suddenly becoming more enlightened and interested in lifelong learning for the sake of learning. As industries change and diminish and as new ones emerge, people recognize the need to change careers. Employers no longer hold out the promise of tenure and job security that comforted employees in the past. Yet companies realize that employees are their most important assets. Competition and profitability are driving the push for continual learning. Skill and knowledge acquisition can lead to significant performance differences among divisions within an organization and companies. Research at Arthur Andersen suggests that variances in learning and best practices can lead to performance differences of 100 to 300 percent among divisions within an organization.[1]

Someone has compared the learning paradigm of the past to that of a once-in-a-lifetime vaccine that protects forever and wards off disease (i.e., unemployment). In fact, what we need are daily megavitamins to keep us current in our fields and able to move in and out of roles and jobs. That calls for education in different doses at different times and the ability to demonstrate and certify continued competence on an ongoing basis. The contract between company and employer is contingent upon corporate financial success and relevant competence on the part of the worker.[2]

The transformed U.S. economy is more dependent than ever on well-educated managers and office workers. The report *Education for What? The New Office Economy* credits the 52.6 million well-educated workers for making the economy go.[3] The skills needed in these office and managerial roles are increasingly ecumenical, e.g., they involve the ability to function globally and to operate in multiple cultural contexts. Multinational companies are training their managerial employees in foreign languages, international business management, and cultural awareness in addition to company-specific products.[4] Certification at the postbaccalaureate level is being driven by both demand and supply. The demand for educated workers is growing even faster than the supply, which is also increasing rapidly.[5] Workers with college degrees earn higher wages than those with associate degrees or lower. Advanced degree holders have the highest real hourly wages, and the gap seems to be increasing.[6] Clearly, the word is out among workers and employers that education pays off.

The expanding market for education and training is shaping educational and professional development programs in several ways.

- The traditional credentials of the academy—baccalaureate and graduate degrees—no longer suffice. Additional specialization, demonstrated knowledge, and job-relevant know-how have increasing currency in the workplace. Degrees traditionally have represented a beginning: qualification for entry into a field or profession. Now, skills and competencies must be up-to-date, increasingly job relevant, and, in some professions, provide evidence of competence for continued practice.[7] The certificate—whether offered by graduate schools, professional associations, or companies—has emerged to fill this gap.

- While a number of university-sponsored certificate programs use time-honored methods of classroom instruction in campus settings, some universities and almost all of the programs in the private for-profit sector are taking advantage of technology solutions to deliver education and assessment directly to students.

- The size of the emerging market is attracting new players; some estimates suggest the market numbers between 40 and 45 million people.[8] For the past few years, the continuing education market has been estimated to be worth about $50 billion. Companies alone spend that on employee training, which puts the market at close to $100 billion today; the amount increases further when professional associations' certification programs are included. One estimate is that the amount spent on distance learning alone totals $300 billion a year.[9]

While universities are designing and offering both terminal degree and certificate programs to focus on employment opportunities in the workplace,[10] other players—some new to education—are emerging to serve the same audiences.

THE PLAYERS

Ted Marchese's survey of new service providers in the May 1998 *AAHE Bulletin* catalogs a number of distance learning companies and other entities which are becoming competitors to the usual offerings of the university. While these new providers account for approximately 2 percent of the postsecondary market,[11] they may reach larger proportions of the adult graduate and professional markets in the near future. What characteristics mark the companies and organizations active in these graduate and professional markets? Some are for-profit companies, with funding from large equity markets (a relatively recent development for Wall Street), while others try to be niche players in narrow industry segments. Others are professional associations, boards, not-for-profit industry groups, accrediting organizations, and government-sponsored or regulatory boards.

A sampling of some of the key players in the for-profit category demonstrates their variety:

- The Apollo Group, Inc. operates not only the University of Phoenix, but also an Institute for Professional Development and a

College for Financial Planning. It offers both classroom courses and courses via the Internet.

- The Chauncey Group International (The Chauncey Group), a subsidiary of the not-for-profit Educational Testing Service, whose mission is psychometric consulting and the development and delivery of assessments and examinations in the workplace, the professions, and the governmental sectors.
- Galton Technologies, Inc., a test development and certification resource company specializing in the information technology industry. Taking its name from Sir Francis Galton, it adds value through innovation, customization, and standard setting.
- Gartner Group, a well-known company in the information technology industry that provides research, advisory, and best practices data to technology companies. It has moved into the learning field through the acquisition of companies such as Knowledge Soft (Gartner since has sold a majority interest to Harcourt Brace) and is announcing a new company to enter the certification field.
- Harcourt Brace, a large publishing company expanded by a testing company, Assessment Systems Inc., and, more recently, a training company, National Education Training Group (NETG). Harcourt can play on several educational courts, from the publication of materials and correspondence courses, to examination development and delivery and off-the-shelf training products.
- Jones Education Companies, part of a communications empire that includes Knowledge TV and offers degree and certificate programs through its non-profit affiliate, The International University.
- PBS The Business Channel, a joint venture of PBS and The Williams Companies, which provides professional development courses for the corporate sector. It is beginning to partner with universities to offer certificates. It identifies the demand and need, contracts with a university to develop the content, and pays for and produces the broadcast program.
- Sylvan Learning Systems, a company offering test delivery services through Sylvan Prometric and delivery of educational services through its Caliber unit.

Some of these companies provide the educational content of the graduate degree or certificate program while others primarily operate delivery networks. Some focus on the credentialing/examination function, and a few are fully integrated, providing multiple functions.

The non-profit sector has players as well, in addition to universities. The following sampling reveals similar variety in focus and core function:

- Industry associations such as the Computing Technology Industry Association (CompTIA), an association of hardware resellers that has entered into examination development for certification in several technical jobs.[12]
- The Northwest Center for Emerging Technologies, underwritten by the Boeing Company and Microsoft, develops standards for certification.
- The Society of the Plastics Industry, Inc. is a newcomer to certification. Starting with a job analysis of managers and executives to identify test specifications and gaps in training, it eventually will provide guidance on training needs and an examination with a certificate.
- The Joint Commission on Accreditation of Healthcare Organizations (Joint Commission) is a well-known accrediting body in the health industry. It is developing an academy with a curriculum and a certification program.
- The National Board for Professional Teaching Standards is an organization dedicated to developing professional standards for early childhood, elementary, and high school teaching.
- The National Skills Standards Board is a federal government-initiated effort to encourage industry participation in setting standards for jobs and performance in the workplace.
- Professional associations such as The Educational Society for Resource Management (APICS), the Certified Financial Planners Board of Standards, and the National Association of Securities Dealers (NASD) offer educational seminars and provide educational materials and programs toward the award of one or more certificates at the managerial/executive level.
- Regulatory boards such as the National Council of Architectural Registration Boards (NCARB) and the National Council of State Boards of Nursing (NCSBN) offer database, educational, and/or certification services that go beyond licensing examinations. Their examinations are among the most psychometrically and technologically advanced in the field of computer-based testing.

What stands out is not only the variety of players but also the fact that although some of them are competing with one another and with universities, they also are collaborating with universities, individual faculty, and one another. Some of them are operating in their specialty areas in a complementary fashion to universities. MIT is collaborating with PBS The Business Channel; John Hopkins is working with Caliber; the Joint Commission has five university partners; The Chauncey Group is aligned with Sylvan Prometric for exams such as the NCARB and NCSBN.

A fundamental change signaled by the emergence of these new providers is a splintering of functions critical to the learning process—functions that were thought to be the exclusive prerogative of faculties. The component parts can be and have been disaggregated.

- What is taught? And by whom?
- How is education/instruction delivered?
- What outcome (achievement/competency) is certified?
- Who awards the credential or gives the stamp of approval?

Distinct terms are used in the market to describe these components.

- *Content:* What is taught? *Content* is the word frequently used to refer to subject matter, discipline, and field of study. *Content* is something one can place somewhere, e.g., on the Internet, in a testing center, on a satellite
- *Delivery:* How and in what way is the content distributed or promulgated? Our mental image has been that of a faculty member in front of a class, in a specific geographical location, engaged in lecture and dialogue, e.g., the community of scholars. Now that modality is called *ILT*, or *instructor-led training*, to contrast it with other forms of delivery, e.g., Internet, TV, video.
- *Competency:* Grades, based on project papers, class discussion, and end-of-course exams (if any) once were sufficient evidence of achievement. With greater focus on employability, evidence of competence and performance—not just grades—becomes increasingly relevant and important. With students scattered and engaged in learning at different times and at multiple institutions, the dispersion of the learning environment raises questions about the efficacy of regular methods of evaluating academic achievement. For instance, who's really at the computer at the other end of the electronic connection? What kind of evidence demonstrates performance in the workplace?
- *Credential:* Who posts the stamp of approval? Historically, faculty determine the requirements for the degree, give grades, and award degrees. But now, they are not the only ones. New kinds of credentials are being awarded and sponsored by organizations that are not tied to the well-established institutions. And, in an educational company or consortium with instructors spread among institutions and countries, who or what is the engine behind the awarding of the degree or certificate? In examining the promotional materials for some of the newer universities, it is sometimes difficult to ascertain who the faculty are.

OPPORTUNITIES AND THREATS

Anyone in the field of education, training, and assessment recognizes the winds of change. No one can foresee with precision the outlines of the future, but some of the movements and shapes toward that future can be delineated. One is the blurring of lines among the players. Courses, certificates, and graduate degrees awarded by established universities and the newcomers are, to the consumer, often indistinguishable. Product differentiation is increasingly difficult. Moreover, to the learner, the distinction between certificates offered by graduate schools, professional associations, and companies is relatively unimportant if the content fits the need. There is also a blurring of government's role in funding and sponsoring certification programs and that of the boards created to design and administer them.

From these overlapping functions and activities emerges a new cadre of standard setters: professional societies, regulatory agencies, industry groups, companies with brand recognition, and professional accrediting organizations. The growth of adult learning at the postbaccalaureate level, coupled with the growth of technologically based distance learning and testing, raises questions of quality. Revolution has hit healthcare, financial services, manufacturing, and communications; why not education?

The winds of change have beneficial effects as well. The variety of players and learning options is exciting. Technology supports innovation and imagination; it makes possible training models heretofore limited to the research lab. Computer-based examinations, using major advances in psychometrics, offer simulations of performance and measure not just cognitive knowledge but also skills, judgment, problem-solving abilities, and "how-to." What can be assessed is broader and richer. And the tests, like the courses, can reach the learner anywhere. These forces may lead to the ultimate *democratization of access* to education and training.

Investment from the private sector constitutes a major source of funding and equity capital. For-profit companies engage in aggressive marketing, which can stimulate awareness among the public and greater demand for all programs. As volumes flowing through the delivery pipelines increase, enterprises can support the up-front costs in course and examination development and equipment. The new environment offers options to students and workers that accommodate their personal needs and learning styles. The new paradigm may greatly expand learning in society. As faculties adapt, graduate and continuing education programs can benefit from the larger total market.

But there are risks[13]—some obvious and some not so obvious. The very advantages brought by the private corporate sector can lead to a preoccupation with technology; a push for large volumes of students and tests to ensure profitability; pretentious or aggressive advertising to attract students who have little recourse to remedy should the certificate earned hold little currency in the labor market; and an unhealthy focus on courseware *delivery* rather than *substance*. The pizzazz of technology can overshadow three other key elements: the quality of the subject matter, the focus on competence, and the validity of the outcome credential With the entry of powerful, bottom line-oriented companies into the market, individual universities and collegiate faculties (except for mega-universities or consortia) may find they have little leverage. Easy access to technology can make a lot of junk look good.[14]

There is also the matter of the learning environment. While some adults are disciplined and trained to make full use of the online medium, many continue to learn most easily and fully in traditional classroom or seminar settings. The technology may be advancing more rapidly than the population's ability to make good use of it.

Developing high-quality courses and examinations is expensive. Faculties' willingness and ability to make full use of the technology and to participate in the design of courseware affects both the rate of entry into the market and the quality of academic offerings. Lead times can amount to years, not months. Scripting authoring, packaging, and production are time consuming and costly; cost curves shift forward to cover high levels of new development. Without new and different kinds of incentives for faculty—financial, release time, modified criteria for promotion and tenure—will the easy route of simply replicating what is in existence dominate the learning models of university certificate programs?

DETERMINING THE AUTHENTICITY OF AUTHORITY

The forces of change bring to the fore issues of authenticity, validity, and standards. What faculty—and if not faculty, who—determines what is taught? Who determines competence at the point of certification? On what authentic assessment model is the certificate based? Who determines the criteria for competency? Who, for example, are the faculty in the Western Governor's University and other distance learning institutions?[15] When all the functions enumerated above—including delivery—are no longer controlled by an educational enterprise that holds the public trust, information can masquerade as expertise, invalid credentials can disguise incompetence, and the distinction between gold and garbage is lost. For the public as well as the consumer, the question pertains to the *authenticity of authority.*

In an unstructured, evolving, fragmented industry, companies usually move to branding and consolidation based on high-quality product differentiation, excellent service to the customer, or least expensive or lowest price. Graduate education and professional certification are no different. According to Vice Provost Louis Fox of the University of Washington, this area of higher education is the fastest growing, and "branding" is the biggest issue facing the institutions and organizations active in this market.[16] The fact that some Ivy League universities are moving to establish online programs may focus greater attention on the standards issue.[17]

COMPETENCY MODELS

How are education providers addressing some of the issues? What models of educational programming and outcomes assessment are being used or created? How are standards set and insured? Examples from several professions—from industry segments and from established higher education institutions—reveal very different approaches.

Health Care

Nowhere has there been greater upheaval than in the healthcare industry: technology has modified practice; the economics of managed care has altered historical relationships and created new positions and roles; the Pew Commission report awakened the regulatory community with 10 recommendations for overhauling agencies;[18] telemedicine and distance learning technologies have raised questions about educational programs and regulatory boards.

Among the issues faced by healthcare regulatory, certifying, and accrediting agencies are the following:

- definition of new roles and redefinition of existing jobs;
- continued competence of practitioners;
- multi-state licensing;
- certification of specialties and licensing for advanced practice; and
- use of technology not only in the delivery of care but also in the education and professional development of practitioners.

Organizations are addressing these issues in different ways. The National Council of State Boards of Nursing is developing a multi-state licensing system. Another example is an initiative of the Joint Commission on the Accreditation of Healthcare Organizations. Recognizing the need for both a curriculum and certification examination for leaders, executives, and managers in healthcare delivery settings, the Joint Commission has designed and initiated an Academy for Health Care Quality. The academy is described as a "corporate university without walls."[19] It will offer graduate-level training in four modules with survey courses focusing on core competencies.[20] Approximately 180 hours of self-paced study will be required in addition to a five-day concluding seminar. Faculty from the five participating universities, the Joint Commission staff, and experts in the field will offer the curriculum electronically via the Internet and peer group chat sessions. An examination testing the core skills required in these multiple roles (one that tests both knowledge and performance) will lead to the credential "Diplomate of the Academy."

Nancy Deal Chandler, vice president for education, and her colleagues have addressed the following issues in their planning:

- *Governing structure:* A governing board, separate from the Joint Commission, and involving university partners, will ensure independence.
- *Job-related skills definition:* Focus groups and expert judges will determine the essential skills critical to executives and managers in a number of roles, e.g., medical administrator in managed care, hospital administrative personnel, third-party payers. Job relatedness is fundamental to a competency model and can aid in the design of curricula.
- *Curriculum:* A "GAP" analysis will determine gaps between job requirements and curricula. Existing curricula, both in university graduate schools and non-university bodies (such as the American Board of Medical Quality) will be surveyed. New courses or components stemming from the job analysis will be added.
- *Independent examination:* An independent certification program council, separate from the curriculum advisory panel and with different expertise, will develop specifications for and design the examination. Examination development and psychometrics will involve professional testing consultants such as The Chauncey Group. Delivery will be at secure testing sites.
- *Database services:* A registry will maintain student progress and Diplomates' records.

Not only is the involvement of multiple players (universities, testing consultants, and accreditation specialists) "new," but so is the thoroughness of the research and curriculum development, the care in establishing the independence of the certification, and the elegance of the curriculum and testing design.

Information Technology (IT)

Certification for IT technicians and professional workers is voluntary. Its development has been driven by software and hardware manufacturers, largely in support of their sales channels. Novell led the way with its examination for network engineers; the examination was based on educational materials Novell developed and distributed through training companies (Novell-authorized training centers). Network engineers knowledgeable about Novell software not only reduced the volume and cost of network technical support to the manufacturer but also enhanced the market for its software. Microsoft became the second big player. Now, more than 50 vendor-sponsored programs are in operation.[21]

Unlike the health professions and others such as architecture, engineering, and law, there have not been universally recognized associations of stature to address issues of quality and standards. Examinations based solely on products that are soon obsolete cannot simultaneously address the underlying job skills required for roles broader than executing and troubleshooting specific kinds of software. The short shelf life of IT products already rushes test development and leads to shortcuts in item development and analysis. Terms such as "psychometrically sound and legally defensible"—the anchors of good licensing and certification examinations—are seldom heard among IT vendors.[22]

All of this notwithstanding, advances are being made on several fronts.

- Two testing companies, The Chauncey Group and Galton Technologies, are becoming significant players. Both uphold high standards of quality and examination development. Yet according to David Foster, president of Galton, corporate clients still need much assistance in understanding the components of a good certification program, in developing the business plan for one, and in promoting and marketing it to participants.

  Both the Chauncey Group and Galton Technologies have repositioned themselves in the last six months. Galton assumed some of the test development and client specific programs of Chauncey. Chauncey has announced the development of a new suite of examinations for IT professionals: the Associate Technology Specialist certification. These examinations, which are neither vendor nor software specific, became available in September 1999. They are geared specifically toward supporting much of the training conducted at community colleges and are being pilot tested in partnership with the League for Innovation.

- Some emerging associations are sponsoring certification examinations based on jobs or job families and aimed at individual workers and consultants in the workplace. The Information Technology Training Association (ITTA) and the Computer Education Management Association (CEDMA) sponsor an examination and certificate awarded by The Chauncey Group which is called the Certified Technical Trainer program.

- CompTIA has developed an examination for service technicians called A+ and has announced a second one, Network+.

- Microsoft, Novell, and CompTIA are becoming involved in the discussion of standards in the Association of Test Publishers.

- The Northwest Center for Emerging Technology (Northwest Center) has conducted job analyses for seven job domains in the IT industry, though they are not yet widely used. That will change, however, as a result of a partnership with The Chauncey Group. The IT skill standards developed by the Northwest Center are serving as the basis for the new Associate Technology Specialist exams of The Chauncey Group. One of the main purposes of this collaboration is to close the qualification gap by linking industry expectations and the education being provided to students.

Despite its shortcomings, the IT industry has been a leader in its use of technology to deliver computer-based certification examinations. Almost all vendor and association certificates are based on computer-delivered exams. Along with the National Council of Architectural Registration Boards (NCARB), these groups, with the assistance of testing companies, are pushing the use of technology in developing practice simulations, in using video stimuli, and in designing hands-on tasks to measure performance.

To date, these examinations have been administered through secure test centers such as Sylvan and VUE, a technology exam-delivery company. Both Galton and The Chauncey Group are exploring Internet delivery. Already, the Internet can be used for registration, billing, accounting, and administration of low-stakes exams. Two barriers have to be overcome to deliver high-stakes examinations: secure methods for protecting the pool of questions that must be reused and validation of each examinee's identity.

A new player, well known in IT circles, is launching a major certificate program for corporate executives who manage information systems within companies. The Gartner Group,[23] known for its research and advisory services and its measurement of best practices and benchmarking, is establishing The Gartner Institute, to be headed by President & CEO Tony Abena. Gartner sold its majority position in its learning companies to Harcourt Brace and now is putting a major effort into the certification field.

The Gartner Institute will sponsor certificates for IT managers and CIOs. Targeted markets are IT managers within corporations and agencies, IT executives in IT companies, and individual consultants to corporations. According to Abena, the primary issues in certificate development in the IT industry are perceptions versus reality in job requirements and functions (he estimates that 50 percent of the traditional MIS departments in corporations will be gone by 2002); vendor independent examinations that are based on competency models of job families and job requirements; and balancing the emphasis on product, e.g., software, with what is required of a manager.

More than any other industry, the information technology industry has made certification more readily available by using rapid development techniques and hundreds of testing centers worldwide. What have lagged behind and are just now getting attention are the hallmarks of good certification: job relatedness, high-quality psychometric development and content, and independence of the certifying agent.

The Teaching Profession

Without question, some of the most ambitious, imaginative, and costly efforts to develop rich and robust certification programs are in the field of teaching. For several years, organizations were working simultaneously but independently to develop standards of practice and examinations that measured the job of teaching—not just pedagogy relative to teaching. These included the Educational Testing Service (ETS) and the National Board for Professional Teaching Standards (National Board).[24] While this account focuses on the work of the National Board and its contractors, the research and development work of ETS dating back to the early 1980s should also be recognized. That work has resulted in a number of programs for assessment in education as well as preparing a foundation for the National Board's innovative portfolio assessments. Programs include computer-based instructional units for use in schools of education, licensing examinations used in a majority of states, a school leader's licensure assessment for principals (in collaboration with the Council of Chief State School Officers), classroom performance assessments, and professional development programs for beginning teachers. ETS provides measurement, test development, and scoring services.

More than $100 million in federal and private foundation funds have been directed toward setting standards; developing assessments at the childhood, elementary, and high-school levels; and operating the program.[25] In 1998, the federal contribution was $18.5 million, plus monies directed to states for fee subsidies. The fee for the assessment is $2,000, and more than 95 percent of the candidates have their fees paid by third-party payors.

Two challenges were equally daunting: setting standards for high levels of competence in the teaching profession and developing reliable, valid assessments (called "authentic" performance measures) that could serve as the basis for a national certificate. Unlike other professions, such as law and architecture, no nationally recognized and accepted disciplines, best practices, or definitions of skills necessary for excellent teaching existed. Even though federally sponsored regional and research labs, schools of education, and organizations like ETS had researched good teaching practices, the findings had not evolved into established standards. There was neither agreement nor even a common vocabulary pertaining to the structure of the domain or the evidence needed to demonstrate mastery. Yet from the outset, complex performance assessments were mandated.[26]

Through an elaborate deliberative process and commissioned research spanning several years, a robust and elegant assessment program has emerged which has been made operational on a national scale. To date, certificates are offered in 12 fields. The examination program uses both portfolio assessment and an assessment center. The exercises in the assessment center are computer-based and measure pedagogical content knowledge. The portfolio involves four classroom entities, two of which are videotapes of classroom interactions and two of which are collections of student work. This particular configuration is the result of much research, as well as trial and error, in fashioning the portfolio exercises to be valid (i.e., to distinguish good and excellent teachers from the not-so-good) and reliable (repeatable with equal results) and comparable for all candidates. The links between standards development, design of exercises to address the standards, and the scoring of complex and variable portfolios is challenging not only to the educators and practitioners who set standards, but to the testing and psychometric specialists as well.[27]

On the one hand, the examinations are valid with a sound research base and link to standards; on the other, the lead time required to develop and make operational, coupled with the high cost of both development and operations, raises the question of whether other professions, universities, or consortia should attempt to replicate it. The National Board and its contractors are working to reduce the operational costs. Regardless of the short-term pressure on costs, it is important to recognize the richness and power of the certification model. Assessment methodologies will be valuable in shaping examination programs for certification in other professions and the workplace.

Architecture

The National Council of Architectural Registration Boards (NCARB) is a professional organization that provides a number of services for its member boards and beginning architects. All 55 jurisdictions of the U.S. and all Canadian provinces have adopted its examination for licensure, which is probably the most advanced battery of tests of any licensing program. It uses simulations to measure architectural practice as well as computed-based examinations to measure cognitive knowledge. Before describing some of the features and issues, it should be noted that NCARB provides a certification program to registered architects in the United States and in Canadian provinces whereby the holder can acquire registration in other jurisdictions without having to retake the initial examination. This program is unique in that it allows an architect to practice with other architects or firms in jurisdictions in other than his or her home state. Approximately 60 percent of the jurisdictions will not grant a registration unless the architect's qualifications are certified by NCARB.

NCARB also conducts a professional development program, the Intern Development Program (IDP), for architects not yet registered in a jurisdiction. These architects are required to complete a practical training program. The IDP, consisting of 16 areas of practical training, provides guidance for both the intern and the professional mentor in the intern's daily activities. Nearly all U.S. jurisdictions require this training program prior to establishing eligibility to sit for the registration examination.[28]

Licensing examinations are high-stakes tests and carry with them the requirement of being "professionally sound and legally defensible." They must be very secure, reliable, and valid in distinguishing those equipped to practice from those who are not. The advances in technology and in psychometrics made it possible to create problems and exercises that could be administered on a large scale in repeatable fashion. These complex problem cases can be scored by the computer using mathematical models and algorithms developed by psychologists and programmers. These algorithms mimic the professional judgment of expert architects. Tests like this are more varied, more powerful, and shorter than paper-and-pencil case studies and can be scored and delivered much faster. Simulations have been used extensively in the military and in medicine for training purposes, but not in high-stakes testing because of the difficulty in developing reliable scoring methods.

As in teaching assessment, development for NCARB's examination took several years—five to complete the scoring methodology, programming, and authoring/production. As the body of psychometric research grows and as companies gain experience with the development of such examinations, the lead time should decrease to between one and two years. Even so, the lead time from drawing board to making an examination operational is long, and the cost is high.

Although the capability now exists to develop much richer assessments and measures of know-how and functioning in the workplace, the deterrents of lead time, cost, and an insufficient cadre of developers remain. Contrast this to the ease and rapidity with which multiple-choice questions can be put on computer and administered. Which is likely to win in the marketplace? The simple, inexpensive, and limited approach, or the more elaborate, complicated, performance-based measurement? The value-added benefits to the certifying body and consumer must be sufficient to support the more authentic performance measures.

Examples from Three Universities

These same issues face the academic community when it participates in the certification market: definitions of job-related competencies, selection of educational and training curricula, outcome criteria, and quality assurance. Both the market and technological options bring to the fore issues of faculty time to convert knowledge to software and lectures into computer scripts, and to support high-quality productions and provide means for student dialogue. It is time consuming and costly.[29] Will faculties take the easy route of replicating what is already in existence? What learning models will dominate university certificate programs?

Approaches strikingly different from those above are found at established universities, where most graduate certificate programs are structured in familiar ways: on site, face-to-face lectures, students enrolled for degrees. They augment master's or doctoral programs, sometimes growing out of research in new areas. Certificate programs provide the administrative means (at some institutions) to offer interdisciplinary programs and to limit program approval to bodies within the university. For the most part, the usual rules and regulations apply, though often there are policy issues of credit toward the degree, credit toward more than one credential, locus of program responsibility, and faculty compensation and reward. But issues of quality assurance do not arise because neither the faculty, the accrediting agencies, the regulatory agencies, nor the consumer questions the educational model.

Thus far, graduate school certificate programs for non-degree students and for adults in the workplace are in a minority. Programs for these adults, either credit or non-credit, are offered usually in the professional schools and continuing education divisions. Many are in the fields of business and health sciences. Universities without walls, such as Walden, Graduate School of America, Apollo's Phoenix, and International University, seem to be moving rapidly into this arena, using their technology bases and distance-learning capability as the platform. Here, too, issues of the validity, authority, and authenticity of the credential arise when the focus is on employment and the educational models involve technology-based distance learning.

How are universities responding to quality assurance and the changing modalities? Among established universities, those with strong central coordination are likely to have the most finely tuned certificate programs, whether traditional or distance-based. Administrative support, funding, and appropriate procedures are critical to success. Those with well-developed technology infrastructures are likely to push the frontier of distance learning in both certificate and degree programs.

The University of Washington (UW) is one such university. UW offers 65 certificate programs (not including a similar number of CPE programs in professional schools), both for credit toward a degree and not for credit. Typically, they are an academic year in length (nine months). Those for credit award between nine and fifteen credits. Some are interdisciplinary. Twelve are distance programs. Many more make use of technology though the primary modality is face to face. Programs are offered through individual colleges and UW Extension. An evening degree program, fully state supported, offers both bachelor's and graduate degrees. Many of the courses involve distance learning.

UW uses several techniques to ensure quality: faculty support in using new media, technology support in delivery, central coordination of the process and student assignments, and a network of specified testing centers.

Faculty with the strongest interest in creating distance-learning certificate programs are in the professional schools and the health science fields.[30] Faculty are provided extra compensation, technical support, and workshops in producing Internet and video materials. The expectation is that instructional materials will be appropriate for the new media and that efforts will be made to ensure good quality and proper adaptation or development.

Technologies employed include e-mail, Web sites, online computers, TV/videotape and audiotape, teleconferencing, and streamed video over the Internet. UW has its own proprietary TV network, is the primary anchor in a statewide electronic network including schools and colleges, and, through its Northwest Net, provides Internet services to six states. Thus, the technical expertise to deliver the courses equals the richness of the academic programs that can be adapted to new educational/business models.

The UW Educational Outreach Division coordinates the registrations and assignments of distance-learning students in most certificate programs. The registrations come into the central office and are routed to the instructors, and the responses flow through the central office via mail, fax, and e-mail. Final examinations are required and are offered at testing sites around the state. UW reviews proctors' credentials. The university does not permit exams via the Internet or in venues outside the designated centers because it cannot ensure the security of the examination or the identity of the student.

Vice Provost Louis Fox points to the same academic policy issues others have faced: residency requirements, transcript designations, credits for matriculation across institutions, financial aid, and ownership of course content and software. But two sizable barriers must be overcome in expanding technology-based distance learning so it becomes a significant and integral part of higher education—*economics:* achieving volumes of students and fees to offset development and operating costs; and *branding:* the validity of the certificate and quality assurance of the programs. Few universities have the student volumes, the developmental funds, or the quality assurance procedures of an Open University. To be successful, Dr. Fox believes that universities must partner with other universities.

North Carolina State University (NC State) is also increasing its offerings at the postbaccalaureate level. Its certificate programs usually are initiated at the college or departmental level; 25 programs are currently offered in the fields of computer science, English, psychology, public administration, textiles, and education. Most require three to five courses worth nine to twelve credits, though the computer science program requires seven courses worth 22 credits. Serving students at a distance through extension and continuing education is part of the mission of the land-grant institution, and for some years, NC State has offered graduate-level certificates in textile manufacturing and in training and development and master's degrees in textiles and engineering through distance education.[31]

The North Carolina legislature is pushing the expanded use of electronic means to offer education off campus to meet needs throughout the state; using technology for educational delivery will also limit the number of new facilities needing to be built and reduce operating costs. NC State has been named as one of the lead institutions in doing so, in part because it has the technology infrastructure and talent to support it. To more fully understand the issues of organizational approach and standards, the provost's office implemented Project 25, in which 25 courses were offered simultaneously to on- and off-campus students. The provost was concerned about faculty participation, involvement with students, adaptation of existing course materials, quality of student participation, student performance, and several other variables. The project included an evaluation design to measure outcomes among faculty and students. The results were positive: student performance was similar in both groups, faculty were generally enthusiastic, flexibility was valued, faculty were responsive to students at a distance, and there was evidence of market demand.

Two of the courses were in the College of Management. Two professors, Dr. Cecil Bozarth and Ms. Claudia Kimbrough,[32] reformatted their courses in Operations Management and Marketing Methods, respectively, and adapted them to a new online format using Office 95, Excel, Web sites, a class home page, Net Forum, and audio. Students could open spreadsheets and follow a voice lecture. Communication was by phone and e-mail. Dr. Bozarth developed techniques to ensure the validity of student work by encoding information on spreadsheet problems to monitor and identify the student doing the work. He also required three on-campus proctored examinations. Dr. Kimbrough used essays via e-mail, chat groups, and proctored examinations. Both reported positive experiences with the distance learners. The individual faculty-student interaction was actually greater than with on-campus students. Dr. Bozarth reported a bimodal performance distribution for distance learners compared with a more normal curve distribution for on-campus students. He believes that didactic courses are well-suited for an online medium but wonders how effective the model would be with high-level technical courses.

The same issues mentioned above were identified in NC State's initial efforts: the large amount of faculty time and effort required to design and produce a course suitable for the Internet; the need for faculty support in instructional design and courseware production, both through workshops and troubleshooting; compensation or release time for faculty; incentives for faculty participation in these new courses and the relationship to tenure decisions; academic and personal advising for students; accommodating large numbers of students requiring considerable one-to-one communication and, at the same time, obtaining the critical mass necessary to make such courses cost effective.

To begin to overcome these barriers, Senior Associate Provost Frank Abrams, Jr., and Vice Provost and Dean James Anderson are administering funds set aside for faculty development, reduced faculty load, and technology workshops for faculty. The dean is leading efforts to design a Virtual Advising and Success Center. Both individuals believe it is important to provide support in *all* areas and to develop learning models with high standards.

Increasingly, universities are offering certificate and degree programs online,[33] and, in some cases, in cooperation with businesses. One such program is that produced by PBS The Business Channel in conjunction with the MIT Center for Advanced Educational Services. Students are high-level corporate executives. Professor Shlomo Maital[34] offers an eight-week course, "Economic Concepts for the Sales Force: Eight Essential Tools." The course involves live videoconferencing sessions that are distributed via satellite to corporations. Chat groups, access to the Web, e-mail, and a bulletin board are used. Although the broadcast is one way, there is fax/phone capability during broadcast for questions. Teaching assistants work individually with the students to complete their assignments.

PBS The Business Channel identifies the program need and finances and produces the program; it is the link with the corporate customer. The university is responsible for content. PBS The Business Channel reviews the curriculum to ensure that it meets market need. A production team at MIT is led by a coordinator who works with five to seven people at PBS The Business Channel to mount the program. Lead time is months, not years. The economic concepts course is the first for PBS The Business Channel and MIT; seven are scheduled. The cost is $2,000 per student.

What does Professor Maital conclude is important to ensure and maintain standards? Begin with the understanding that virtual classes are productions; they must be visually engaging, and the professor must be a performer if TV or videoconferencing is employed. Central to the endeavor is designing educational experiences that best suit the learner, keeping in mind that the learning is *not* in a classroom with an instructor. Two-way communication is a must; without it, the course reverts to the correspondence course model. When asked whether distance students require more faculty time than on-campus students, Professor Maital answered "yes," but he sees that as a "huge advantage because interaction with students is what education is all about." Full utilization of the multiple communications channels created a strong sense of community among the students and professor—a "remarkable degree of intimacy" as he said. Students often like it better than the typical classroom. Professor Maital attributes this to two factors: the visual materials are superior to classroom chalk and blackboard, and the student controls his or her learning environment and can pace activities. The nature of the course assignments, i.e., cases based on the student's company and job, coupled with the frequent and multiple means of communication among the senior corporate managers, ensures the validity of the student's work and identity.

GOING GLOBAL

Determining and recognizing competence in the workplace and professions is not limited to markets in the United States. Well-trained and highly skilled workers contribute significantly to global competitiveness. Underdeveloped countries emphasize education and training, including distance learning.[35] U.S. testing and certification enterprises—both university and non-university—are going global. Similarly, institutions, associations, and government agencies in other countries are offering credentials in job-related fields, some of them international in scope.

From Germany, with its government/industry-sponsored postsecondary apprentice programs, to Japan, with its leadership in the development and certification of English-language skills among corporate managers and executives, governments and their private sector companies recognize that the traditional academic track is not sufficient to ensure the requisite talent base.

The globalization of commerce has placed a premium on English-language skills at the executive level. Two international testing programs dominate the certification market: The Test of English in International Communication (TOEIC), offered by The Chauncey Group International (co-developed with Japan), in 25 countries, and the Cambridge (UK) battery of exams and training materials which is heavily represented in Europe and somewhat in Asia. The Chauncey Group has recently established a Paris office to service its corporate TOEIC clients and to represent other of its programs.

For some years, the Educational Society for Resource Management (APICS) has conducted training programs and certification testing through chapters located in 10 countries outside the United States. These courses focus on most aspects of the manufacturing process and major functions within manufacturing companies. They enable an executive in manufacturing to demonstrate current knowledge of managing a manufacturing enterprise through a series of 11 examinations leading to two certificates.

Increasingly, professional associations' licensing examinations are becoming models for exam development in other countries, or U.S. associations are moving beyond domestic borders to offer translated versions. Consider, for example, the National Administration Board of Architectural Registration of the Peoples Republic of China, which modeled its exam on the NCARB registration exam and is designing a computer-delivered test. With the assistance of Mr. Balen, executive director emeritus of NCARB, Japan is now examining the comparability of its architectural exam with that of NCARB. The National Association of Boards of Pharmacy is moving in several directions, including developing examinations in disease management, e.g., HIV and diabetes, to be delivered via the Internet to practicing pharmacists around the world.

Under the auspices of the National Education Examination Authority (NEEA), a division of the State Education Commission in the Peoples Republic of China, The Chauncey Group created an advanced-level computer science examination for technical specialists already in the workforce in China. The NEEA provides many certification examinations for workers who are studying and learning on their own ("self-taught learners"). The Ministry of Personnel administers certification exams to large numbers of individuals in the workforce. These examinations are an important way to upgrade skills and to demonstrate the talent base in the workforce.

Perhaps the most extensive, structured, and systematic developmental efforts have been undertaken by the National Council for Vocational Qualifications (NCVQ),[36] now merged with the Qualification and Curriculum Authority, in the United Kingdom. The NCVQ was formed in 1986 to develop competence-based qualifications in accordance with employment standards in various occupations and professions. The goal was a comprehensive array of performance-based assessments covering most jobs and professions in the country. Unlike many examinations in the United States which target the minimum skills and knowledge necessary to enter a profession, the national vocational qualifications (NVQs) confirm full occupational competence. The assessments provide direct evidence of ability to perform in the workplace. NVQs are awarded at five levels.[37]

1. Range of work routine.

2. Significant range of work, some of which is not predictable; a degree of autonomy; no supervision required.

3. Broad range of activities in a variety of contexts; complex work; supervision of others.

4. Broad range of activities that are technical and that require significant responsibility; managing and directing other staff, e.g., technical occupations and lower-level management.

5. Significant range of complex techniques across a wide range of unanticipated contexts; managing or co-managing an entire organization, e.g. middle

and senior management and professionals such as engineers, doctors, and lawyers.

The structure for developing NVQs and the assessment of competencies is established at the national level. While the framework and processes are established nationally, many parties are involved. "Lead bodies" set the standards and requirements within an industry or profession and comprise members from commerce, industry, trade unions, professions, training, education, and the awarding bodies. Some awarding bodies are industry or profession specific, and others are recognized organizations, such as City and Guilds, the Business and Technical Education Council (BTEC), and the Royal Society of Arts (RSA). Awarding bodies must be accredited by the Qualification and Curriculum Authority.

Many kinds of organizations design and deliver learning opportunities and serve as "assessors" in the process. These include private training providers, consultants, individual employers or consortia of employers, and education providers. To provide these services, an organization must be recognized by an awarding body by demonstrating that they have trained assessors and an established quality assurance program; they also must submit to an external audit. There are standards and qualifications for assessors, and awarding bodies require their assessors and verifiers to demonstrate competence in this role.

For example, the LCCI Examination Board is an awarding body that provides guides for trainers and assessors as well as materials and guides for candidates. It operates 8,000 centers in 24 countries and offers qualifications in 15 areas (some available at level 4), including an Executive Diploma in Business Accounting. NVQs are also offered in jobs ranging from distribution and warehouse operator, to information technology specialist, to school administrator, to sales and sales management.[38]

A few universities have begun to offer NVQs, mainly through their business schools. Some professional bodies have converted their own credentials to a competency-based model but have not sought accreditation by the Qualification and Curriculum Authority.

The process is as follows: A candidate supplies evidence of performance, usually a portfolio of work, letters from his or her employer, and a summary of units completed (each NVQ has a number of units) to the assessor. Alternatively, a candidate may participate in a training program under the supervision of a recognized assessor. An internal verifier ensures the quality and completeness of the portfolio. An external verifier from the awarding body must approve the work of the internal verifier. Finally, the awarding body grants the certificate.

To date, approximately 10 percent of the workforce has obtained NVQs. A press release from the Qualification and Curriculum Authority indicated that

41 percent of the vocational certificates are NVQs; 97 percent of those who have them recommend them, and 96 percent of employers are aware of them.[39] Most NVQs are at the lower three levels.

A number of reports have been commissioned, articles written, and recommendations made about the system of NVQs, higher education, and lifelong learning.[40] All attempt to rationalize the links among formal education, prior learning, and the workplace. Three themes are relevant.

- The recommendations to create a national transcript system for accumulating credits from various sources, whether institutions, prior learning, or workplace or NVQ units.
- Attempts to structure and order hierarchically the credits and achievements attained through formal education, NVQs, and Accreditation of Prior Learning.
- External quality assurance programs as they pertain to educational programs.

The Dearing Report addresses all three. It recommends a national registry for the accumulation of all credits. There is also a move to convert whole courses to a modular structure. Individuals will be able to acquire course credits from different institutions. Pressure to develop a central repository will increase.

The Dearing Report also suggests a qualifications framework that aligns types of programs, accumulated credits, and educational levels up to the doctorate and Level 5 NVQs.

According to the report, the framework should be broad enough "to cover the whole range of achievement . . . , well understood within higher education and outside it, and incorporate provision for credit accumulation and, increasingly, scope for the transfer of credits earned in one institution to another."[41] It should be based on achievement, not time in class; encompass vocational as well as academic qualifications; and enable a person to build up a portfolio of accomplishments over a working lifetime.

A national transfer system for academic credits, the Credit Accumulation and Transfer Schemes (CATS for England, Wales, and Northern Ireland, SCOTCATS for Scotland) is in operation. Points are assigned to units and courses, and these general credit ratings are accepted widely by a number of universities, thus facilitating the transfer of credits from one institution to another. The Open University operates a small registry primarily for credits awarded for learning outside higher education.

The Dearing Report also recommends establishing a Quality Assurance Agency to deal specifically with "franchising" programs from a parent institution to others elsewhere in the country and the world. Rather than establish a separate authority, higher education is seeking to accommodate this recommendation within initiatives already under way.

These reports are notable for their attempts to develop an orderly educational and training framework. The government has accepted recommendations emphasizing criterion-referenced learning outcomes, national standards, and more effective external quality assurance. The means for achieving all of these goals is not yet fully established. The higher education marketplace, like other labor markets, is fragmented and imperfect. However, the tradition of examinations, assessments, and focus on outcomes that has anchored the U.K. academic and vocational systems would lead naturally in these directions. No formal structures currently link the awarding of higher education credentials with workplace assessments, but ferment in the market created by distance learning universities, NVQs, lifelong portfolios, and the overlap with university credentials will lead the British to continue to try to rationalize their systems of education and work.

The UK model of NVQs has moved beyond its borders. Similar initiatives are in place in Australia, Mexico, and Singapore; they are under way in Canada and New Zealand. In Canada, the Association of Physical Therapists has established standards based on the U.K. model.

THE LEARNER, JOB RELATEDNESS, AND EMPLOYABILITY

Issues of quality, standards, and learner outcomes pervade educational circles. The learning and assessment models and the structures within which they function are very different in the university and the non-university sectors. Among the professions, licensing bodies, and national boards, the focus—indeed the requirement—is *job relatedness*. Standards of professional practice or workplace performance set the criteria of successful certificate programs. Certifying examinations and assessments measure *competence to perform*, and the curriculum (if any) is linked to job requirements, sometimes generic across multiple functions, other times narrow and specific. Outcomes are all that matter. The certificate results from a yes/no decision: the candidate does or does not meet the minimum standards for entry into a job or profession or for full occupational performance.

Validity is in the credentialing instrument or assessment process (such as the NVQs). Examinations and assessments are based on the expert judgment of practitioners who define the discipline, specify the assessment, and develop the exercises, problems, and test questions. Seat time, class attendance, homework, and grades don't count, except to establish eligibility to sit for the exam. Only demonstrated performance counts. Thus, the quality of the assessment, the security of the content, and protection against impersonation are vital.

In the academy, the focus is most often on the body of knowledge defined by faculty and the process by which that knowledge is imparted and absorbed. The process itself is a key component of the educational program. The faculty member is at the center, determining the subject matter and evaluating student outcomes through discussion, homework, and class examinations. There is no attempt to answer the yes/no question related to employment competency.

In this model, validity is in faculty judgment, and indirectly, in the academic standing of the faculty member and institution. Student performance is not measured according to an external criterion; rather, it is judged relative to that of other students. Evaluations are local, based on face-to-face dialogue, papers, and class exams. However, when a postbaccalaureate certificate purports to represent readiness for employability, the certifying agent cannot escape the external criterion of job relatedness. Thus, these questions arise: What assures the link between course content and job? What is the relationship of grades to job performance? And how is this link made when credits are earned from many sources/several institutions or when they are compiled in different ways via self-study, online classes?

Just as the validity models of university and non-university providers differ, so the ways in which the two sectors address *standards and quality assurance* differ. In the non-academic sector, competence and criteria are determined by professional associations, expert practitioners in the field or industry, and lead bodies designated or accepted by government agencies. Some of these organizations come together in the Council on Licensure and Enforcement Regulation (CLEAR) to discuss and develop standards. Or, these organizations themselves may have their programs accredited by organizations such as the National Organization for Competency Assurance (NOCA), established in 1977, which conducts a thorough review of both the organization and the psychometric aspects of the assessment.[42] The examinations are reviewed with reference to both the Uniform EEOC Guidelines and the Joint Technical Standards of the psychological and measurement organizations.[43] The Joint Technical Standards constitute the "gold standard" for measurement and assessment in the United States. In addition, the Association of Test Publishers is undertaking a standard-setting exercise for computer-based tests. Ever mindful of the legal ramifications of assessment as it relates to employment and strongly committed to high professional standards, some testing companies (such as Educational Testing Service and The Chauncey Group) have their own standards of quality and fairness, which go beyond the Joint Technical Standards. ETS and The Chauncey Group voluntarily established a program of outside audits.

In higher education, regional accrediting bodies and some professional associations determine the criteria by which universities and their schools and colleges— e.g., faculties, degree offerings, and programs—are evaluated. The Distance Education and Training Council (DETC) and the Global Alliance for Transnational Education (GATE) focus on distance learning and international programs. Most often, regional accrediting criteria pertain to inputs, e.g., resources, faculty-student ratios, faculty credentials, and proportion of full-time faculty. For years, there has been a call for student outcomes criteria and assessment in the academy. Though a few institutions focus on outcomes, (e.g., Alverno, Phoenix, Open University), the practice is far from the norm.

In the case of postbaccalaureate certificates, the locus of regulatory or quality control authority is the department, the school, the university, or a coordinating board (or all of the above). In professional disciplines served by universities, such as nurse practitioners, medical specialties, or substance-abuse counselors, the university prepares practicing adults for external examinations specified by regulatory boards or professional societies. For those programs without external examination requirements, establishing an institutional audit function using external expert practitioners may be a reasonable course of action. The future postbaccalaureate landscape poses real challenges for accrediting bodies and universities in terms of criteria for educational outcomes—particularly as they pertain to employability.

The stakes for the student consumer and employee are high. For the certificate to have currency, learning must lead to the acquisition of job-related knowledge and the ability to perform. The demand for evidence of current skills in the workforce is growing. The tide of the adult education market cannot be turned back. People want more education, and more people want education. Technological delivery will begin to displace or make obsolete existing learning/business models. Advances in psychometrics and educational programming and production are sufficient to facilitate the creation of new, valuable educational forms.

What is not yet clear is how committed universities are to drive and shape market forces. All the players—universities and others—face the same obstacles:

- lead time to develop new courseware or productions;
- production and development costs;
- clearly delineated and well-publicized standards for educational components;
- competency and assessment models that are authentic and attest to the validity and usefulness of the certificate; and
- economies of scale to recover costs of development and delivery.

Perhaps the question is not *whether* colleges and universities will adapt to these expanding markets (higher education has been ever adaptable throughout this century), but, rather, *how*.

- Will university programs get the attention they need to be successful?
- Will faculty receive incentives, e.g., financial rewards, release time, modified criteria for promotion and tenure or for developing technology-based courses, or will universities take the easy way out and simply replicate what already exists?
- Will learning models that take into account job relatedness and employability be devised and used?
- Where in the institution is the catalytic agent that will make things happen?
- Where is the leverage for a new kind of quality assurance? Does it lie with accrediting bodies, federal or state agencies, or voluntary, institutionally established external audit programs?

Now that the state, university, and corporate networks are sufficiently widespread to democratize access without regard to geography, the challenge for those whose mission is education and human development is to ensure the authenticity of educational content, the robustness of assessment processes, and the authority of certifying bodies.

Caveat emptor for the student consumer is not good enough if colleges and universities, professions, accrediting bodies, and testing companies are fully committed to serving the public interest. Success for these organizations must be viewed not just in market terms, but in the context of whether learning translates into excellent performance in the workplace.

In his account of his 10-year tenure as director of the Metropolitan Museum of Art, Thomas Hoving reported that his single-minded passion was to transform what had become a comfortably stodgy, increasingly remote, and elitist institution into something splendid, glorious, and elegant; to make it come alive, and to help it regain its leadership position. He "made the mummies dance."[44] Creative leaders and imaginative faculties can do the same for universities and the adult markets they serve.

NOTES

1. Referenced in Michelle Neely Martinez, "The Collective Power of Employee Knowledge," *HR Magazine*, February 1998, pp. 88-89.
2. Hal Lancaster, "Managing Your Career," *Wall Street Journal*, 18 August 1998, Dow Jones & Co., Inc.
3. Anthony P. Carnevale and Stephen J. Rose, *Education for What? The New Office Economy*, Executive Summary. Princeton, N J: Educational Testing Service, 1998.
4. The Institute for International Business Communication in Japan is working with Japanese companies to fashion a Global Awareness Assessment Program. The Global Executive MBA program at Duke is another example.
5. Carnevale and Rose, *Education for What?*, p. 2.

6. *Real Hourly Wages by Education, Using CPS Education Definitions Beginning 1992* (1996 Dollars), Economic Policy Institute, Datazone. Undated. <http://epinet.org/datazone>.

7. L. J. Finocchio, C. N. Dower, T. McMahon, C. M. Gragnola, and the Taskforce on Health Care Workforce Regulation, *Reforming Health Care Workforce Regulation: Policy Considerations for the 21st Century*. San Francisco: Pew Health Professions Commission, December 1995, pp. 27-28. (Hereafter cited as Pew Commission report.)

8. "Brushing Up," *Time* Select Business Report, *Time*, 20 July 1998.

9. Theodore J. Marchese, "Not-So-Distant Competitors," *AAHE Bulletin*, May 1998, p. 5.

10. Wayne Patterson, *A Survey of Graduate Certificate Policies, Procedures, and Programs*, Council of Graduate Schools, 37th Annual Meeting, November 1997.

11. Marchese, "Not-So-Distant Competitors," p. 5.

12. Interview with Lauren Hebert, Director of Strategic Services, Integrated Computer Management (ICM), September 1998.

13. Jill M. Galusha, "Barriers to Learning in Distance Education," University of Southern Mississippi, Undated. <www.infrastruction.com> - Microsoft Explorer; "Certificates: A Study of Our Status and Review of Successful Programs in the U.S. and Canada," *Background Readings, Part 1, Postbaccalaureate Futures*, Joint Project of the University Continuing Education Association, Council of Graduate Schools, and Johns Hopkins School of Continuing Studies. Washington, DC: September 1998. (Hereafter cited as *Background Readings*, Part 1.) *Note:* Numerous issues, from the approval process to program structure, administrative oversight, student record systems and academic support, and target audiences are discussed in these and other papers. What is missing in much of the descriptive literature is discussion of how technology will change the programs, and of what assures quality of the enterprise in the new modes. What about differences in course/content production necessary in new media and in methods and validity of student evaluation and performance in a distance-learning environment?

14. David F. Noble, "Digital Diploma Mills: The Automation of Higher Education," *Background Readings. Part 1*; Lisa Guernsey, "Is the Internet Becoming a Bonanza for Diploma Mills?" *The Chronicle of Higher Education: Articles*, 19 December 1997.

15. Western Governors' University Web site, <www.wgu.edu>.

16. Telephone interview with Louis Fox, Vice Provost, University of Washington, July 1998.

17. Goldie Blumenstyk, "Elite Private Universities Get Serious about Distance Learning," *The Chronicle of Higher Education*, 20 July 1997.

18. Pew Commission report, p. ix.

19. "News Release," Joint Commission on Accreditation of Healthcare Organizations, Oakbrook Terrace, IL, 23 January 1998. (Hereafter cited as Joint Commission.)

20. Interview with Nancy Deal Chandler, vice president for education, Joint Commission, September 1998. *Note:* The descriptive information in this section is based on the interview with Ms. Chandler; opinions expressed are those of the author.

21. Interview with David Foster, president, Galton Technologies, Inc. Mr. Foster was instrumental in the development of the Novell program and now heads his own consulting and test development firm.

22. Information in this section is based on interviews with David Foster, Galton Technologies, Inc.; Lauren Hebert, ICM; and on personal experience of the author.

23. Interview with Tony Abena, president & CEO, The Gartner Institute, subsidiary of The Gartner Group, Eden Prairie, MN. <www.gartner.com>.

24. The National Board was organized in 1987, based on the Carnegie Task Force on Teaching as a Profession report, "A Nation Prepared." It was to reconceptualize the profession of teaching and to establish high standards for excellence <www.nbpts.org>.

25. *Guide to National Board Certification, 1998-1999*, National Board for Professional Teaching Standards.

26. Mari A. Pearlman, "Designing in Validity: The National Board for Professional Teaching Standards Certification Assessments." Paper presented at the annual meeting of the American Educational Research Association, March 1997.

27. Drew H. Gitomer, "Challenges for Scoring Performance Assessments in the NBPTS System." Paper presented at annual meeting of the American Educational Research Association, March 1997.

28. Many of the NCARB programs were developed under the leadership of Mr. Sam Balen, who for years was executive director of NCARB and who now, as executive director emeritus, continues to work with the Chinese and Japanese authorities to develop examinations linked to the NCARB registration examination.

29. Developing a course in the Open University can cost between $2.5 and $3.5 million. Reported by John Palatella, "The British Are Coming, The British Are Coming (A Lesson for American Educators)," *University Business,* July/August 1998.

30. Information in this section is based on an interview with Vice Provost Louis Fox of the University of Washington and on UW's Web page <www.u.washington.edu>. Any factual errors are those of the author.

31. Information in this section is based on interviews with Senior Associate Provost Frank Abrams, Jr., and Vice Provost and Dean James Anderson. Any factual errors are those of the author.

32. Both professors participated in Project 25, and Dr. Bozarth was on the planning and coordinating committee.

33. The MBA programs are those of Duke University, Florida State University, Phoenix University, Stanford University, and the University of Missouri. MIT's program in System Design and Management offers a 13-month degree program or a 10-course distance learning certificate.

34. Professor Shlomo Maital is visiting professor at the MIT Sloan School of Management and a member of the faculty of the School of Industrial Engineering and Management at the Technion Israel Institute of Technology. Information based on correspondence with Professor Maital, <smaital@MIT.edu>, and an article by him entitled "Alternative Teaching Methods: Virtual Classes" in the *Handbook for the Teaching of Economic and Consumer Psychology,* edited by Paul Webley and Christine Walker. Information about PBS The Business Channel was provided by Ms. Marty Feinberg, director of program development and Mr. Frederick Ricci, director of executive education.

35. Michael Potashnik and Joanne Capper, "Distance Education: Growth and Diversity," *Scoop! Direct,* 1 March 1998 <http://www.scoopdirect.com>.

36. Background information for this section was provided by Mr. Graham Debling, president of Graham Debling Associates, Ltd., who previously was director of the Learning Methods Branch, Department for Education and Employment in the United Kingdom, and by Ms. Susan Simosko, president of Susan Simosko Associates, Inc. The author is indebted to Mr. Debling and Ms. Simosko for their assistance in explaining the complex system of NVQs and GNVQS and their contexts. Any errors are the responsibility of the author.

37. Lynn Chadwick, "Introduction to National Vocational Qualifications," UK TeleCottage Association Training. Undated. <http://www.icbl.hw.ac.uk/telep/telework/ttrfolder/twvqfolder/nvqlfolder/nvql.html>.

38. National Vocation Qualification, LCCI Examination Board <http://www. lccieb.org.uk/nat-voc-qual.htm>.

39. Qualifications and Curriculum Authority Home Page, <www.crownbc.com/qca/>.

40. R. H. Fryer, *Learning for the 21st Century, First Report of the National Advisory Group for Continuing Education and Lifelong Learning,* November 1997. <www.lifelonglearning.co.uk/index.htm>. Sir Ron Dearing, *Higher Education in the Learning Society,* The National Committee of Inquiry into Higher Education, 1997 <www.leeds.ac.uk/educol/ncihe>. *National Report—Qualification and Standards—Part 2,* National Council for Vocational Qualifications <http://www.leeds.ac.uk. educol.ncihe/nr-146.htm>.

41. Fryer, *Learning for the 21st Century,* Part One, Agenda Point 5, Part 4, Section 4, Points 3 and 4; Dearing, *Higher Education,* p. 9; *National Report,* point 10.23.

42. The National Commission for Certifying Agencies (NCCA) is the accrediting arm of NOCA. It accredits organizations with certification programs. The review includes evaluations in terms of nine criteria, among them: organizational structure, resources, public information, governance, board membership, responsibilities to applicants, candidate testing, and independence of testing program. It reviews testing programs with reference to EEOC guidelines or APA/AERA/NCME standards as appropriate. There are 215 members (members do not have to have certification programs) and 40 accredited organizations. *Source:* Ms. Bonnie Aubin, executive director.

43. Developed and published by The American Psychological Association, The American Educational Research Association, and the National Council on Measurement in Education.

44. Thomas Hoving, *Making the Mummies Dance.* New York: Simon and Schuster, 1993. When Mr. Hoving told his boss, Mayor John Lindsey, that he was going to the museum, the mayor said, "Seems to me the place is dead. But, Hoving, you'll make the mummies dance."

CHAPTER 11

Intravenous Learning

Donald N. Langenberg

The explosive evolution of information technology is changing our world profoundly, and at a breathtaking pace. This has become apparent—sometimes painfully so—to almost everyone, including educators. We all are scrambling to incorporate technology into our academic programs and institutional operations. We are inventing new kinds of education institutions. As we do these things, we are struggling to understand the implications of what we are doing and to divine what the future may hold for us and our institutions. We talk about technology-enhanced learning, Web-based courses and programs, distance learning, and virtual universities. We debate whether technology will affect the quality and character of our education enterprise positively or negatively. Some are pursuing the indefinite future enthusiastically, pell-mell. Others are asking that the world be stopped so they can get off. But like it or not, all of us are in a situation that resembles a fast-paced Darwinian evolution, one in which "survival of the fittest" has assumed a more immediate and pressing meaning than most scientific concepts.

Donald N. Langenberg is the chancellor of the University of Maryland System and professor of physics and electrical engineering.
Note: This chapter is adapted from and based on the author's opinion piece, "Diplomas and Degrees Are Obsolescent," published in the *Chronicle of Higher Education*, 12 September 1997.

Another less commonly recognized facet of this evolution has profound implications for education. Throughout most of the twentieth century, the economies of the "developed" nations have been dominated by industries whose success depended on such factors as massive capital investment, availability of (largely unskilled) labor, and ready access to natural resources and other physical assets, e.g., transportation systems capable of handling large masses of material objects. These industries have tended to be relatively stable over time. Prominent in most were large, hierarchically organized corporations. (Agriculture is somewhat of an exception, but the food industry is not.)

This is the economy for which most American universities were designed, beginning in the nineteenth century with the great public land-grant universities. These were chartered explicitly to educate "the children of the industrial class" in economically important fields like "agriculture and the mechanic arts." The Industrial Age required educated and professionally trained workers like engineers and managers—but only to the extent of 10 or 20 percent of the workforce. The rest of the workforce—80 to 90 percent—continued to be composed of unskilled laborers and skilled trade workers for whom postsecondary education was unnecessary. The idea was to educate and train a small fraction of the nation's high school graduates (only to the baccalaureate level in most cases) and to send them out on relatively predictable career paths that were expected to look much the same when they retired as when they started.

All that has changed quickly, even suddenly. Over the past half century, the ratio of jobs requiring postsecondary education to those that do not has inverted. Today, only 10 or 20 percent of jobs can be described as "unskilled." All the rest require some degree of college- or university-level education. And many of the latter are in businesses utterly unlike those of the Industrial Age. The businesses of the Internet Age rely on a transportation system that moves bits, not bodies or boxes. They require little in the way of physical assets. Adventuresome entrepreneurs with a good idea can launch a business with a few computers in a basement, take it public in months, and attract tens of millions of dollars in capital; it can hit the billion dollar revenue mark within a few years. (And, evidently, it need not turn a penny of profit along the way.) Some "e-businesses" have within a very few years become larger (in terms of market capitalization) than traditional corporate behemoths that have existed for a century or more. All this is happening at a frenetic pace. Frequent references are made to "Internet time." This is usually left undefined, but it appears roughly equivalent to "pretty damn quick" (PDQ). It also may be related to the 18-month doubling time for computer capacity embodied in Moore's Law.

It is rapidly becoming clear that *the* key asset for any business or other organization in the Internet Age is not financial capital, physical facilities, or cheap labor; it is creative, knowledgeable, adaptable, professional people! The twenty-first century will require exactly the kind of people our colleges and universities purport to produce. I say "purport" because it also is becoming increasingly clear that institutions designed to meet the needs of the Industrial Age are in many ways ill suited to the Internet Age.

It is not that our colleges and universities are generally failing to give their graduates broad education in the liberal arts and sciences or to equip many with immediately marketable job skills. They have their deficiencies, to be sure, much discussed and all-too-well advertised. They could do better, but they are doing a pretty good job by any reasonable comparative standard. The problem is the growing volatility of much of what their graduates know and can do on commencement day.

In some disciplines, this is not new. There is a story about the medical school dean who told his graduates at a commencement at the beginning of the twentieth century, "Gentlemen, I must inform you that half of what we have taught you is wrong—and we don't know which half!" Coming, as it did, at the dawn of medicine's transformation from mysterious art to science-based profession, that certainly was true. Nevertheless, the rate of transformation was then sufficiently leisurely that most of the physicians listening to the dean could expect to reach retirement practicing medicine pretty much as they had at the beginning of their professional careers. In short, an M.D. from a good medical school was both a necessary and a sufficient entrance ticket to a stable lifelong career.

The present is very different, and not just in medicine. Bill Wulf, president of the National Academy of Engineering, is reported to have asserted that the half life of a good engineering education is now 5 ± 2.5 years. Software engineers expert only in Cobol programming of mainframes have long since gone into retirement. Farmers who have not yet adopted Global Positioning Satellite technology in distributing fertilizer on their fields have slid another rung down the competitive ladder toward bankruptcy. So has the manufacturer who is not conducting e-commerce with his suppliers. Teachers who are not infusing their classes with Web-based technology are short-changing their students.

The time scale of the evolution of much career-related knowledge from novelty to obsolescence has decreased by an order of magnitude, from something like a human generation to a computer generation, i.e., from thirty years to three years. While a college degree has become a necessary step in the majority of people's career courses, it also has ceased to be a sufficient step for most. Moreover, the career is increasingly unlikely to be either stable or lifelong.

The essence of the challenge for our colleges and universities is that the current situation invalidates the traditional notion that the best way to educate a person is to administer one huge intensive dose of learning early in life, to declare the person "educated for life" in elegant language on a diploma, and to bid him or her farewell. Our education institutions—elementary, secondary, and postsecondary—are all designed to educate children, not adults. That must change! We must accommodate the structures and cultures of our education institutions to the modern reality that most people will need to engage in formal learning for most of their lives, consistently if not continuously. Our institutions must adapt themselves to deliver learning to their students not in one massive dose, but in a manner more like a lifelong intravenous drip.

As we contemplate the thoroughgoing reform of our education system, it quickly becomes obvious that this must be accomplished at all levels. We cannot succeed if we focus on just one segment of the system, e.g., higher education.

One of the most exciting recent developments in education reform has been the emergence of statewide partnerships among businesses and institutions of elementary, secondary, and higher education. Often labeled "K-16 partnerships," these initiatives can be powerful ways to reform our elementary and secondary schools—for example, by creating mechanisms for direct participation by higher education and business in the planning, design, and implementation of reform initiatives and by publicly demonstrating higher education and business support for and commitment to the success of those initiatives.

Many reformers believe that establishing rigorous standards for all students and assessing student performance in terms of those standards will help restore the quality of our high school graduates to levels more acceptable to parents, employers, and educators. In Maryland, our K-16 partnership is developing a comprehensive assessment program in which successful completion of elementary and secondary education will depend more on what the student knows and can do rather than on how long the student has been in school. Maryland high school graduates will be required to demonstrate through a battery of tests that they can comprehend, analyze, synthesize, and integrate information in broad subject areas; that they can reason, calculate, and solve problems; and that they can communicate through a variety of media.

If such reforms succeed, they will require substantial changes in the ways colleges and universities judge high school graduates' ability to succeed in higher education. At the very least, college and university admission standards must be aligned with high school graduation standards.

But the changes in higher education that secondary school reform will demand are much more far-reaching and profound than merely tinkering with admissions processes. For example, we must acknowledge that any substantial reform of elementary and secondary education inevitably will require comparably substantial reform of the education and training of those who teach in and manage our schools—thus, reform of schools of education. Moreover, the reform movement probably will contribute to the mounting pressure on higher education to address such issues as escalating tuition, decreasing retention and graduation rates, the need for improved coordination of requirements and curricula among high schools and two- and four-year colleges, and the inexorable aging of our student populations as people return to school to upgrade their skills or to prepare for different jobs throughout their working lives.

The most provocative and powerful impact of K-16 partnerships on higher education is to be found in the implications of two principles underlying most reforms. The first principle is that our education system ought to have no boundaries or barriers between its segments, combining education from cradle to grave into one seamless whole. The second principle is that what counts in the real world is what one knows and can do. Therefore, that is precisely what should determine a student's progress through the education system—including college. Both academics and employers complain frequently that college graduation requirements based primarily on passing variously defined sets of courses manifestly fail to ensure that graduates have the skills and essential personal qualities to succeed in postbaccalaureate and professional training and in the workplace. What are these skills and qualities? They include initiative, persistence, diligence, vision, perspective, personal integrity, and the ability to communicate effectively, to think creatively as well as critically, and to work with others in addressing novel problems. If such traits and abilities are essential to the success of our graduates, shouldn't graduation depend substantially on a student's ability to demonstrate them? And, if we insist on such a demonstration, shouldn't we also insist that our faculties, programs, and curricula prepare our students toward that end?

Many will claim that our colleges already provide just such preparation. But if we listen to those who employ our graduates or to those who provide the next level of education, we hear that there is an enormous chasm between what we claim we're doing and what they find we actually achieve.

Over the past few decades, colleges and universities have adopted some practices intended to rationalize the transition from high school to college (Principle 1) and to assess (albeit indirectly) certain desired personal qualities (Principle 2). For example, we offer some remedial courses. (But why are students who are not fully prepared for college work admitted to college in the first place?) We certify "advanced placement" courses in some high schools as providing the equivalent of college work. (But why are "AP" students still in high school?) We weight high school students' grade point averages more heavily than SAT or ACT scores in admissions because those grades reflect personal characteristics (e.g., persistence and diligence) that are important to success in college.

But such adaptations remain the exception rather than the rule in our current education system. That must change. We must move much more rapidly and aggressively toward an education system worthy of being called a system—one in which students' passage from one phase of learning to the next is based on their readiness rather than their age; one in which students are evaluated on their mastery of knowledge and skills rather than their completion of course units; one in which students gain certification to do things rather than do things to gain certification.

For anyone who has spent a lifetime in American schools and universities, it is hard even to think about such drastic change. In their 1958 book, *Higher Education in Transition: An American History, 1636-1956*, John Brubacher and Willis Rudy recounted the fascinating evolution of the present layered structure of the American education system. Beginning with village schools and academies, we added colleges patterned after English four-year colleges, upward extensions of elementary schools originally intended to prepare a few students for college (termed preparatory schools, then high schools), and post-college graduate and professional schools based on the German model. Then we inserted transitional institutions—the junior high school or middle school, and the junior college, now commonly called the community college.

At every stage of this accretive process—particularly during the late nineteenth and early twentieth centuries—educators vigorously debated the purposes of each layer of the system, as well as the circumstances and conditions that should attend a student's transition from one layer to the next. Traces of these debates persist today, but the sedimentary layers of the American education system have hardened into something with the apparent permanence and inevitability of stone.

It is time to revive the vigorous debates of a century ago and to reconsider the whole structure of the system from bottom to top. The changes that I envision are analogous to what is happening in the world of computers as we move from the era of independent mainframes to that of interconnected desktop machines. If we succeed in making the right changes, our education institutions will function as a seamlessly integrated and fully interoperable system and will be truly accessible to any appropriately prepared student at any age. True accessibility means minimizing the constraints of time and location by adjusting educational delivery to the student's circumstances rather than forcing the student to accommodate to the education institution's convenience. Requiring a student to be in a room with a professor on a campus precisely 45 times will become abnormal. Learning will occur wherever there's a Web connection. "Courses" will cease to be delivered in one-size-fits-all packages. Movement among institutions will be free of the impediments that now often accompany the transfer of credits. Students may simultaneously enroll in high school for some subjects and in college for others, or they may study at several real or virtual universities at once. A universal "college credit banking system" will evolve from the rudimentary examples now in existence. A student's academic progress throughout his or her lifetime will be marked by frequent certifications based on demonstrated performance. The record of these certifications—called a "performance profile," perhaps—will resemble a traditional academic curriculum vitae (CV) but in practice might well take the form of a personal multimedia Web site.

Such an education system would make sense in terms of how humans learn. Cognitive scientists tell us what we teachers have long suspected—and long ignored: Different people learn different things in very different ways and at very different rates. Fortunately, emerging technology promises to help provide just the customization and connectivity that a new education system would require. We soon will have the opportunity—and the obligation—to adapt our educational products (e.g., courses) to the specific cognitive profile of each student, with lectures for those who learn best by listening, sophisticated visual images for those who do better with pictures, and interactive hands-on virtual reality for the plurality who learn best by doing. If Levi Strauss can custom manufacture blue jeans to the specific personal dimensions of millions of individual customers, then eventually we ought to be able to similarly mass customize our products. We also have the opportunity and the obligation to complement our growing electronic connectivity with increased inter- and intra-institutional connectivity. We can eliminate artificial distinctions between on-campus and distance education students, between "traditional" and adult students. And we can reduce the compartmentalization and departmentalization of knowledge.

A seamlessly integrated, cradle-to-grave education system is within our reach, if only we can muster the courage and the will to create it. That won't be easy, for we have come to believe that our present fossilized education layer cake and all its features are somehow eternal and inevitable.

Standards-based reform of elementary and secondary education cannot succeed without substantial participation by colleges and universities. If reform does succeed, its underlying principles must inevitably change the practices of those same colleges and universities, and of the workplace as well. The integration of the workplace with higher education under rubrics like "cooperative education," "continuing education," and "professional development" is already farther advanced than we in higher education commonly acknowledge. That integration needs to broaden and intensify and to extend into the high school regime. (IBM recently took a step in the right direction when it announced that henceforth it will require job applicants to provide high school transcripts instead of diplomas.)

If we believe that 18-year-olds can and must demonstrate through performance measures that they meet high education standards, then we should embrace the same idea for all students of whatever age. If we can do that, we stand a fighting chance of creating an education system through which all our citizens move smoothly and efficiently, at rates limited only by their intrinsic abilities, building as they go richly detailed performance profiles that will serve as far more informative indicators of their capabilities than mere diplomas and degrees. Isn't that what we really need?

The tradition of awarding diplomas doubtless will remain important. We will continue to desire ceremonies of completion and commencement at certain milestones in our lives. Like many academics, I enjoy donning my medieval costume and intoning Latin phrases such as *summa cum laude*. But perhaps we can preserve such customs for their emotional and sentimental value while downplaying the counterproductive discontinuities between stages in a student's education that they now represent.

We musn't allow milestones to become millstones. We musn't continue to see diplomas as emblems of the end of an education, or degrees as either necessary or sufficient keys to continued learning. We must rethink the methods by which we encourage, evaluate, and mark the progress of learners of any age. One indication of our success may well be the displacement of degrees and diplomas by more informative—if less hallowed—means of certifying learning. Whatever form a student's performance profile may take—Web page, smart card, electronic merit badges, or multimedia portfolio—it must convey more useful information and have greater predictive value than the pieces of paper we now bestow at graduation ceremonies.

The changes and conceptual shifts I have described here pose enormous challenges for all educators. Among those challenges is the acknowledgment that degrees and diplomas are obsolescent—or at least should be.

PART 4

• • • • • • • • • •

Balancing the Private
and Public Good

CHAPTER 12

Research Universities in Transition

Myles Brand

A merican higher education has emerged as the best in the world. Led by its public and private research universities, American higher education has surpassed the great systems in England, on the Continent, and in Asia. This ascendency has occurred since World War II, and it has been driven by enormous investment from the federal and state governments.

Federal government research support has increased from $22 million in 1930, to $405 million in 1960, to $15 billion today. State funding for public higher education also has increased to meet growing demand from middle- and lower-income students and their families. While it is true that loan programs now dominate financial aid, funds from federal sources have increased from $2 billion for the 1950-51 academic year to $12.5 billion. Currently, nearly two-thirds of high school graduates pursue some postsecondary education, with almost 15 million students enrolled (compared with one million in 1930 and 3.5 million in 1960). Approximately 80 percent of these students attend public universities, compared with 50 percent prior to World War II.

But in some ways, American higher education is becoming a victim of its own success. Growing awareness of the advantages of postsecondary education will lead to the enrollment of an additional five to ten million students annually in the early decades of the new millennium; for the most part, these new students will be returning adults seeking skill enhancement and certifica-

---

Myles Brand is the president of Indiana University.

tion for workplace advancement. Their tuition dollars will attract new providers into higher education that differ markedly from the traditional ones, such as small New England colleges and major research universities. These new providers will include for-profit corporations, both those whose core business is educational services (such as the University of Phoenix and Walden University) and those who augment their activities to include educational services (such as publishing houses and entertainment conglomerates), as well as not-for-profit consortia (such as Western Governors University). Many of these will use newly developed information technology as the primary mode of delivery.

In addition to emerging competitors, higher education—particularly the lead research universities—has come under increasing public scrutiny. Since winning the Cold War, we have been without a common enemy, so we have directed our aggressive tendencies toward ourselves. Public criticism of higher education is further compounded by the recent conservative turn in American politics. Those who have not forgiven universities for the upheavals during the Vietnam War believe that campuses continue to promote a left-of-center agenda (consider the attacks on "political correctness" of several years ago).

Finally, but not least importantly, higher education has experienced increased fiscal constraints. Except in bio-medicine, research funding continues to be under pressure. For most public universities, incremental state funding will be at best modest because of the high priority placed on other needs, such as K-12 schools, the criminal justice system (including prison build-out), and entitlement programs—especially health care. Moreover, tax reduction often has taken precedence over investment in higher education. The only area in which funding is presently increasing is financial aid, and that mostly through tax rebates and loan programs. While these increases are welcome because they provide direct student support, they do not reduce the pressure on universities' operating budgets. Indeed, they act as incentives for nontraditional competitors. Tuition increases cannot be expected to continue to make up for constrained state and federal support.

Growth, competition, changing public perceptions, fiscal constraints, and new technology are all contributing to an environment of change. As a result, higher education is entering a singularly important period. Change, no doubt, will be a constant in higher education's future; but the scale and rate of change are especially acute during this current transitional period.

Here I will focus on the transition underway in research universities, with an emphasis on *public* research universities. While much of serious interest is occurring in other sectors of higher education, notably community colleges and nontraditional providers, my attention is on that group of institutions most responsible for providing the basic and applied research, scholarship, and creative activity that drive global competitiveness and improved quality of life, while simultaneously educating most of tomorrow's leaders and professionals. In particular, I focus on teaching and learning—especially as they relate to faculty responsibilities and obligations, the role of new information technologies, and the relationship between universities and their external partners. While these topics do not exhaust the challenges facing public research universities, they do represent the key factors in this transitional period.

TEACHING, LEARNING, AND DISTRIBUTED EDUCATION

I am reminded of the time I met a senior faculty member at term's end. He said that his teaching excelled that semester; his lectures were well planned, the course readings relevant, the jokes well delivered. But then, he lamented, "They didn't get it." The final exams made it clear that the students had not mastered the material.

The fact of the matter is that the faculty member did not get it. If learning did not occur, then his teaching could not have excelled. Learning—not teaching—is the goal; teaching is instrumental to learning.

As we have become aware, this is a crucial shift in perspective. Successful instruction occurs when learning takes place. Learning may consist of information transfer; as such, the lecture format—"the sage on the stage"—is reasonably useful. But learning also involves self-discovery catalyzed by the teacher. Learning also can occur in the absence of a teacher, as when a piece of software—or even a book—is the catalyst.

It is clear that continuous learning will be required for workplace success in the future. Shifting the focus from teaching to learning naturally shifts attention to the student. How can we optimize the conditions under which a student learns? How can faculty members both enhance their abilities to transfer information and also provide ample opportunity for students themselves to make discoveries? How can research universities best organize themselves to be responsive to the new, emerging population of adult students? How can professors best teach students how to learn by themselves?

Some answers to these questions can be found in the use of the new information technologies—in particular, application to the campus experience of the techniques used in distance education. New and emerging information technologies offer prospects of providing students anytime, anywhere, with seamless virtual learning environments and a wide range of distributed learning opportunities, ranging from the full array of library resources to convenient student services.

But there is much to be accomplished before virtual learning environments of this type can be realized. Despite the bravado of the vendors and the exaggerated claims of nontraditional providers, technology has not yet evolved to the requisite levels. Moreover, these potential levels of technological advancement require that universities make substantial developmental investments and undergo concomitant cultural change.

The completion of high-speed, broad band-width networks, such as Internet2, will require connectivity among university campuses and the private sector. And the development of nationally distributed digital libraries promises to moderate through common usage the growing costs of library materials, especially journals and foreign acquisitions. Although the technology for digital libraries is not yet wholly serviceable, the major impediment may prove legal rather than technical. Evolving trends in intellectual property law may inhibit digital library access. (See Chapter 7, "Risk, Tribe, and Lore: Envisioning Digital Libraries for Postbaccalaureate Learning.")

Research universities that wish to avail themselves fully of these emerging technologies must equip and refurbish classrooms; lay fiber throughout the campus, including dormitories and off-site residences; and provide training for students and faculty. Students tend now to have the background and desire necessary to use these technologies; even for those lacking skills, the learning curve is rapid. The same is true for many (though not all) faculty members. Professional development for faculty, an area too often underfunded, or even overlooked, must be a major emphasis. While some few faculty members may continue to use desktop computers as large paperweights, the issue is mostly generational; incoming faculty tend to be more aware of the benefits of the new information technologies and more committed to developing the skills they require.

The ability to complement successful classroom instruction with the new information technologies will require initial investments and funding for continuing operations. I estimate that research universities need to devote between 7 and 10 percent of their operating budgets to information technology, up from a current average commitment of less than 5 percent. For public universities, this is significant. Because states are slow to provide incremental support for information technology, and because additional student fees can offset the costs only partially, significant resource reallocation is required.

Although I am arguing that virtual learning environments will enhance pedagogical success, I am *not* suggesting that technology-driven instruction should replace direct faculty interaction. Rather, I advocate thoughtfully supplementing and enhancing classroom activity with the new information technologies. In fact, I believe it is misleading to distinguish between campus-based and distance education. It is better to conceive of the entire process as *distributed learning*, where the defining variable is not geography, but rather the extent and manner in which instruction is mediated.

Peter Drucker, the renowned business futurist, claims that traditional campuses will disappear in favor of wholly technologically delivered higher education. (See Robert Lenzner and Stephen S. Johnson's interview with

Peter Drucker in *Forbes Magazine*, 10 March 1997.) In fact, the campus-based research university will continue to be focally important. Recent high school graduates will continue to desire and require campus environments. While information technologies are likely to play increasingly important roles in the learning process, they will not substitute for, among other things, the intellectual and social developmental aspect of a college education.

Distributed learning spans the boundary between campus-based and noncampus-based instruction. In developing the capacity for supplementing traditional campus-based instruction, universities are *ipso facto* developing the capacity for off-site, asynchronous delivery of instruction. The infrastructure required for a technologically sophisticated, campus-based learning environment naturally lends itself to expansion for off-site delivery. Similarly, course materials—especially Web-based ones—developed for campus use are expandable to courseware for students not geographically proximate.

As I noted earlier, the growth sector in higher education is among non-traditional students, most of whom are seeking to enhance career-oriented skills; they are not necessarily interested in standard degree programs. These new students will be more accepting than traditional-aged students of educational services delivered mostly or wholly by information technology, and thus may be less likely to want a campus experience. As adults with careers and families, they seek convenience more than social development and broadening experiences. They likely will pay a premium for this convenience, especially for a proven product. For-profit providers are currently targeting this segment of the student population, but they do not have a corner on the market. Indeed, name brand recognition should give research universities a market advantage. Undertaken as an auxiliary operation, and built through the expansion of campus-based distributed education infrastructure and course materials, this distance education seems to promise a revenue stream that itself can support the increased cost of technology and, potentially, can provide funding for the institution's other missions, including research and scholarship.

Research universities have long been engaged in educating nontraditional students. Continuing studies and outreach activities, though not highly visible at these universities, are nonetheless integral to their mission. For example, since the 1930s, Indiana University has been engaged in correspondence education. Today, IU's Division of Extended Education, which serves more than 25,000 students annually, is second in size only to the correspondence school of the University of Maryland, which serves the armed forces. (Interestingly, IU's enrollment has not declined in recent years, despite the growing availability of electronically delivered education. It will be some time—longer than enthusiasts project—before the general population is fully wired and feels comfortable relying on this mode of communication.) Research universities in fact will seek to expand their efforts in this arena; indeed, that already is occurring.

However, before research universities begin to spend the revenue from burgeoning continuing studies programs, they must clear several hurdles. Universities typically have little expertise in conducting these activities to generate "profits." Research universities simply are not experienced in competing directly with the for-profit sector. Over time, they can learn to be successful—more likely than not by hiring specialized talent. But few, if any, major universities have done so. In fact, in the vast majority of cases, off-site distributed education requires continuing subsidies. With some selected programs as exceptions, revenues are not outpacing costs.

Moreover, unless these universities are to undertake off-site distributed distance education in a way wholly divorced from their normal activities (an approach that has little to recommend it), substantial cultural change is in order. This will be difficult to accomplish. While only a minority of faculty need be directly engaged in off-site, distributed education, the standards of quality and the commitment to a shared, collegial environment dictate faculty involvement in the oversight and governance of any expanded effort. Many faculty members, however, are uncomfortable with this approach and prefer instead to restrict the institution's focus to its traditional, campus-based instructional mission. They are skeptical about the financial benefits and conservative about trying to serve new student populations. This skepticism, profound in some cases (particularly among liberal arts faculty), results in part from the concern that developing off-site, distributed education will contribute to the degradation of academic life and a reallocation of work time away from those areas which many faculty value most: research and contemplation. In the end, the most forceful response to these concerns is that research universities—especially the public ones—have an obligation to provide high-quality instruction to a broad spectrum of students. This obligation has existed since our institutions were founded. Leaving the field to for-profit corporations and nontraditional providers abridges this obligation and deprives a large population of students of access to the higher quality instruction research universities can provide.

While these challenges to engagement in off-site, distributed education are serious, they are not defeating in the long run. The successful research university will negotiate these issues and will find ways to meet the cultural challenges. One of these challenges—faculty roles and responsibilities—stretches beyond the incipient changes prompted by the expansion of information technology and, in fact, is at the heart of the issues facing research universities as they navigate this transitional period.

FACULTY ROLES AND RESPONSIBILITIES

It is commonplace to say that faculty members have a tripartite mission of teaching, research, and professional service. However, this generalization masks a great deal. At the research universities that are our focus, and increasingly at all universities and colleges, a value hierarchy exists in which research and scholarship are at the top of the pyramid, followed by teaching and then professional service. But this hierarchy becomes dysfunctional when it fails to reflect the goals and needs of the students and public which support these institutions.

Research, scholarship, and creative activity receive notice beyond the confines of the campus. Publication (public performance and exhibitions in the case of the arts) enables individual faculty members to gain recognition and standing among their peers, both nationally and internationally. This recognition becomes a source of professional and personal self-esteem. Interestingly, information technology magnifies this situation; with the growing ease of communication, one's colleagues become those who share disciplinary interests rather than geographic proximity.

In contrast, success in teaching and professional service receives mostly local campus recognition (at best), though likely on an even smaller scale than that—often among only a few colleagues and students. With recognition—especially when it exceeds the confines of the campus—comes rewards, such as salary increases and promotions. Thus, from an individual faculty member's perspective, it is rational to value research and scholarship most highly and to organize one's time to focus most on that area.

But again, universities do not exist in isolation; they belong to an integrated educational system that has integral social responsibilities. The issue then becomes structuring academic work and rewards so that the value of research remains high even as the obligations of enhancing learning and providing expert professional service are met.

In recent years, one good approach to this issue has emerged in which the unit of analysis is shifted from the individual faculty member to the academic department or school. Departments—not individual faculty members—are responsible for a certain level of teaching and service productivity. This approach recognizes that faculty members change their emphasis on research over their careers; rather than punishing them for this shift, it permits the group to take advantage of it to meet the unit's teaching obligations. Individual faculty members gain in prestige by being associated with highly ranked departments; thus, there is internal peer pressure to work toward the good of the department, which translates into meeting the unit's obligations—including its teaching obligations.

This approach is reinforced by attaching financial incentives to teaching productivity. Several years ago, Indiana University decentralized its budgetary systems under the rubric Responsibility Centered Management (RCM); academic units retain tuition and state funds for the students they serve. In turn, academic units reimburse the university's support areas, such as the library and student affairs. This enrollment-driven model provides direct incentives for good teaching and conscientious attention to student needs. For example, despite strong student demand and the dean's urgings, one department had resisted opening new introductory sections because the faculty preferred to teach upper-division and graduate courses in their areas of specialty. With the advent of decentralized budgeting, this department not only opened new introductory sections to meet student demand but now seeks additional introductory students because it has a direct financial incentive to do so. With the additional resources, the department has enhanced its programs, even by hiring additional faculty members. Providing incentives for departmental responsibility through decentralized budgeting is becoming widespread, and many major public research universities are adapting it to their own contexts.

Although this approach has brought about improvements, it has not been entirely successful. Peer pressure at the unit level for faculty members to focus their attention on service or teaching is countermanded by continued reliance on the underlying hierarchical value system, which depicts faculty who emphasize teaching—even temporarily—as "less valuable."

Increased demands on academic units also have been met unfavorably. To meet teaching obligations, adjunct, temporary instructors are hired—especially to staff introductory courses. Employing part-time faculty is not inherently bad, but generally speaking, these instructors lack the qualifications and standing of regular faculty. Some must piece together several part-time positions, creating a travel burden and decreasing their capacity to work with students outside the classroom in other than the most perfunctory manner. When part-time faculty provide special expertise or serve to meet unexpected enrollment demand, their employment is sound; but when they are used to relieve the regular faculty's teaching obligations, the practice benefits neither the students nor the university.

A second unfortunate response is the enlargement of graduate programs so that teaching assistants oversee the majority of introductory courses. This practice is not universal, but it is widespread among disciplines that have significant service obligations in general education, such as English, mathematics, and foreign languages. Like part-time instructors, teaching assistants typically are enthusiastic, conscientious teachers. But they tend to lack experience in the classroom, and because they themselves are students, they can be distracted from their teaching assignments. This is further complicated by the reality that in almost all fields, the majority of graduate students will not find tenure-track academic positions. Increasing numbers of teaching assistants are beginning to understand that their primary role is to substitute for regular faculty; that, in turn, has led increasingly to unionization. There needs to be better alignment between training the next generation of faculty members and opportunities in the academic marketplace. Under the guise of permitting free choice to incoming students, some departments have grown their graduate programs simply to meet their teaching needs. That is not acceptable. Instead, regular faculty must take primary responsibility for the department's teaching obligations—especially at those public universities that tend to have high student/faculty ratios.

Attempts to change the value hierarchy of research, teaching, and professional service have been modestly effective, but these attempts by themselves will not overcome peer pressure. Peer pressure can be ameliorated only by changing the unit of analysis from the individual faculty member to the academic unit (such as the department) and developing a decentralized budgetary system that rewards each unit for teaching productivity. Even so, teaching is devalued—even more so when there is too great a reliance on teaching by nontenure-track faculty and teaching assistants. One consequence is that faculty have little energy or inclination to provide the human resources necessary to enhance off-site distributed education—and thus, little ability to accommodate the new population of postbaccalaureate learners.

ADDITIONAL STRUCTURAL CHANGES IN THE ROLE OF FACULTY

The successful university of the future will balance its research activity with the ability to meet fully its instructional obligations—including those that are off site. Further development of the differential model is one possibility to explore. Caution should be exercised because the stakes are high. But careful thought combined with a timetable that is steady but not precipitous may well lead to a rational restructuring of faculty work.

The leading idea is to institutionalize faculty roles that involve differentiation of teaching, research, and professional service. "Pathways" in each area would be distinct. Faculty members would choose areas of emphasis for specific durations—perhaps three to five years—and would retain the option to continue on that pathway or to pursue a different one. Reward structures and departmental budgeting would each be aligned with this approach.

For example, one area of focus would be research. Faculty within this area might undertake some teaching, especially at the graduate level, but their primary assignment would be research. They would be expected to achieve genuine excellence in this area, and their performance would be evaluated explicitly on the basis of the quality and quantity of their research results. For faculty in the sciences, success in the grant process would be one major factor in evaluation, as articles and books would be for faculty in the humanities. Those who focus on research would enhance the prestige of their academic department and university, but they would not assist a great deal in generating student revenues. Given this fact, departments—the primary budget units—could afford only a limited number of faculty whose focal area was research.

Other faculty might choose or be assigned a teaching pathway. A good teacher must be knowledgeable; the half-life of scientific knowledge is currently estimated to be five years. The best way to remain knowledgeable and to continue to be intellectually excited about one's field is to engage in research and creative activity. So, even with an emphasis on teaching, engagement in research is appropriate; indeed, it is required. But the *dominant* activity would be teaching. Expectations for the quantity of research (though not its quality) would be adjusted. Teaching obligations would include not only classroom instruction, but also advising, curricular development, honors and dissertation supervision, and so on. In addition, some faculty with this focus might take primary responsibility for the delivery of off-site distributed education. Given the incentives of an enrollment-driven budget, the majority of faculty in an academic unit are likely to focus on teaching.

The third area of emphasis is outreach and service. In some disciplines, such as education and business, the need for such contributions is clear. Indeed, many professional schools already have faculty members who have chosen outreach and service as their primary pathway.

Within the differential model, faculty would have the ability to change pathways. One way to proceed might be to develop formal agreements between faculty members and department chairs or deans. For example, a faculty member could be assigned to the research pathway under an agreement to reach a predetermined level of productivity; he or she would be reassigned if the specified level of productivity were not attained.

This division of labor already exists in many academic areas. But this extended differential model includes an explicit recognition of alternative roles for regular faculty and sharper divisions between pathways. Some faculty members already devote the vast majority of their time to research (for example, those in the sciences who buy down their teaching commitments with federal grants). This model recognizes this use of faculty time as primary, and it sets appropriate standards and review procedures.

The differential model continues to place high value on research, but it also reinforces the economics of a decentralized budget. In so doing, it creates peer pressure that permits only a limited proportion of the faculty to pursue the research pathway.

Administration must reinforce this model by ensuring that the reward system recognizes excellence for all three pathways. Assignments are differentiated in terms of focus, but salaries and promotion and tenure requirements should not differ. Equity in rewards among all pathways must be enforced. Similarly, administration—both at the local and university levels—must set and maintain guidelines for the number of part-time and teaching assistants. This expanded differential model of faculty work cannot be imposed; rather, it must be coupled with a pattern of reinforcing incentives, and it must be accepted on the basis of reasoned consideration of the obligations of individual academic units and the university as a whole.

When we consider reinforcing incentives, the issue of tenure becomes crucial. The differential faculty workload model will be viable only if tenured appointments are available on all pathways. After all, faculty members will be expected to change pathways during their careers—perhaps several times— and their tenure status should not be placed at risk because of a shift in focus. We not only must permit, but also must encourage and respect, faculty choices. By trying to force all faculty members into the same mode by requiring the traditional tripartite division of teaching, research, and service at all times, we fail to be realistic about faculty members' changing interests and abilities, and we fail to utilize their talents to the fullest extent. In essence, the differential model of faculty work will become institutionalized through its incorporation of the tenure system.

I personally suggest that pathways be specified only for tenured faculty members. Except in certain professional areas, junior faculty members would be placed too much at risk in selecting non-research pathways, given the extant value hierarchy. More important, an institution would be justified in making a long-term commitment to a faculty member—often as long as 30 to 40 years—only if that faculty member had the ability to succeed on more than one pathway.

However, there is one critical qualification. Expectations for tenure sometimes rise to almost unrealistic levels. Current practices have led to cynicism and disillusionment among many who have undergone the probationary period and review process. Judgments for tenure should consider demonstrated ability and commitment to high-quality teaching and the ability to establish and maintain a research program. For the most part, good teaching is a learnable skill, and no one should be tenured without having acquired it. In terms of research, the institution should be convinced that the individual has an excellent quality of mind and demonstrates knowledge of what is involved in conducting a sustained research program on a deep problem or vital issue. The current expectation of quantity for research productivity often goes beyond what is necessary to obtain the required accuracy in judgments.

Adoption of the differential model of faculty work, in sum, would better position universities to respond to the needs and demands of students and the general public. These institutions would continue to be the nation's research and creative engines; indeed, specific and determined development of a cadre of those engaged in research will provide opportunities to enhance the role of universities in research. At the same time, the differential model encourages a focus on teaching for the majority of faculty and, to a greater extent than presently, provides them with equitable rewards and respect.

Some who are focusing on serving primarily the new class of students—including those who approach the matter from the perspective of an information technology-rich environment or from that of the for-profit nontraditional provider—would find this suggestion too tempered and conservative, indeed, insufficiently innovative to be successful. Given the demands of the burgeoning nontraditional student population, especially at the postbaccalaureate level, and given the opportunity to "reinvent" higher education, this proposal is basically reactive, not forward looking. From this perspective, radical change is the order of the day.

But faculty members at research universities are likely to react to this proposal quite differently. From their viewpoint, the proposal verges on the radical. In institutionalizing differential faculty roles, one of the longstanding basic assumptions of the academy is relinquished—namely, that all faculty members at all times have the same responsibilities. Never mind that this equalitarian assumption is rarely upheld in practice! The point is that an explicit retreat from it is threatening to the culture. This cultural mismatch will make acceptance of the formally differential model difficult; indeed, it will make *exploration* of the model difficult.

Neither party is correct; rather, the truth lies somewhere in the middle. The success of American higher education has been driven to a great extent by research universities. Though they number only 100 out of approximately 3,500 public and private nonprofit universities and colleges in the country, they have set the agenda for others, provided the research and development that is the economic engine of the country, and educated a majority of professional and political leaders. While there is room for the development of nontraditional providers to service the new class of students, research universities should not redefine themselves in the image of such providers.

However, it does not follow that research universities should not change at all. These institutions must be responsive to the new class of students. The research university of today, and faculty members' roles therein, are not the same as 100, or 50, or even 25 years ago. External pressures and internal maturation have affected research universities in myriad ways. That process will continue. The goal is to reform and restructure these institutions so they can responsibly accommodate the new demands placed on them, without losing those elements that have made them strong. The challenge is to balance change with the retention of fundamental strengths. An expanded and institutionalized differential model of faculty work could achieve this balance.

PARTNERSHIPS

Another key transitional factor related to both the shift to learning from teaching and the changing responsibilities of faculty members is the relationships between universities and their external constituents. Most traditional universities have long favored the idea that they are separate from the forces and institutions that surround them. This splendid isolation was interrupted first after World War II, when the federal government adopted policies and provided funding to make universities the major centers of basic research and technological innovation. It was interrupted again in the late 1960s and early 1970s when students demanded engagement in the social and political issues of the day. Both events changed universities, but faculty retained an interest in being separate from the world—especially when it came to forming close alliances with the corporate sector.

Not all universities follow this pattern. For example, urban campuses tend to develop strong working relationships with their surrounding communities. Indeed, the distinguishing characteristic of a successful urban campus is its ability to be involved directly in the business and life of its host city. But for the major public and private research campuses, such as those that belong to the Big Ten, the Pac 10, and the Ivy League athletic conferences, direct involvement with external constituents remains elusive.

However, the environment has changed, and successful institutions in the future will need to exhibit a high level of integration across a wide range of sectors. The best approach to integration is partnerships. Friendly relations with proximate communities or industries are important, but they are only a partial answer. Working partnerships which integrate the goals of both organizations are more productive over the long term. Partnerships, which can involve binding contractual relationships, press each party to be flexible, especially with regard to their cultures. Campus cultures are notoriously slow to respond to business-university partnerships, in part because they are protective of their commitment to full disclosure of research results. Corporate culture, on the other hand, values the ability to act quickly and to take proprietary positions with regard to information and research findings and is loathe to turn almost every activity into a teaching and learning experience. Nevertheless, universities cannot remain entirely outside the fray. Public research universities, in particular, must contribute to the economic development of those states which support them.

The value of partnerships is evident in the relationship developing between Indiana University, a traditional public research university, and Walden University, a for-profit provider focused on postbaccalaureate, nontraditional students. The collaboration, which began in 1991, includes imaginative programming that benefits both institutions.

Walden offers its postbaccalaureate degree programs primarily through various modes of distance education; a brief residency requirement can be satisfied during a three-week summer session that convenes annually on the IU Bloomington campus. During that time, students have full access to IU's library, information technology, and other resources. This past summer, approximately 500 Walden students enrolled in the Walden summer session, and a graduation ceremony for those completing their programs was held on campus.

Through contractual arrangements, Walden students live in the residence halls and attend classes with IU faculty, who are paid on a compensation basis. Campus services—including library access—are purchased or otherwise compensated. Walden enjoys an especially robust relationship with the IU Schools of Education and Continuing Studies. For example, the development, delivery, and marketing of IU's Continuing Studies M.S. in Adult Education are coordinated with Walden's Ph.D. in Education, with specialization in adult education leadership. While this is an example of program articulation rather than a joint degree program, discussions are underway for joint degree programs in other areas.

Some Indiana University faculty have expressed concern about the collaboration with Walden University. Apart from expressions of elitism, some query the benefits to IU. Indiana University is able to take advantage of Walden's business experience in developing and administering programs tailored to nontraditional students. Also, because it is public, IU must gain approval for new degree programs—a time-consuming and sometimes troublesome process. Walden, in contrast, is able to institute new degree programs rapidly in response to market opportunities. As long as IU can assure quality control, there is the potential for joint programming for off-site distributed education. There are also advantages for Walden University, including use of library and technology resources, residence opportunities for students, and the marketing gains achieved through association with a highly regarded university. The partnership benefits both parties.

Research universities must be prepared to partner not only with public agencies and businesses, but also with other education institutions, including nontraditional higher education providers. Public research universities, in particular, have an obligation to collaborate with external groups, since doing so widens access for students and enhances economic development for their states. Successful working partnerships achieve a degree of integration such that it becomes impossible to tell where the university ends and the rest of the world begins. Nevertheless, it would be a mistake to conclude that research universities should rush headlong into such partnerships. Care must be taken in initiating these partnerships, and they must be assessed diligently. Not every opportunity is meritorious.

Western Governors University (WGU) appeared (at least at first) to be an example of exaggerated expectations. The western states are facing significant growth in the population of traditional college-aged students, with as much as a 10 to 20 percent increase forecast for the next several years. Add the increasing educational needs of the new class of nontraditional students, and states face a serious problem. During the mid 1990s, under the leadership of Governor Roy Roemer of Colorado, a group of governors determined that rather than spending hundreds of millions of dollars on new construction, their states could best serve the increasing numbers of students through electronic educational delivery systems.

Last fall, WGU opened its virtual doors. But the expectations of high enrollments were unfulfilled. Initially, 10 students enrolled. WGU officials say that hundreds of students in 26 states have now signed up for classes, and they expect those numbers to continue to increase.

The state of Indiana joined WGU this past year. Although serious doubts remain that WGU or similar enterprises will be able to meet the demands of the new class of nontraditional students, the consortium sets a precedent because it seeks accreditation on the basis of proficiency. If WGU succeeds in this attempt, it will break new and useful ground. For nontraditional students, proficiency and other outcome measures of knowledge and skill should be a significant factor in certification. Accreditation measures such as "seat time" are not entirely appropriate for this group of students.

This fall, Great Britain's Open University began enrolling students in its American sister institution, United States Open University. The Open University reports enrollment of 164,000 students in 41 countries, and the university was ranked eleventh of 98 U.K. universities for the quality of its teaching. Open University officials believe the school's reputation for high-quality course offerings will earn it steadily growing enrollments in the United States. Competitors, of course, are skeptical, saying that with so many U.S. public universities and private companies expanding their online curricula, there is little room for a foreign alternative. Competition among private companies seeking to reach agreements with traditional colleges and systems to create online courses is also intensifying.

It is impossible to predict how all these contests for market share will sort themselves out. As the marketing and the variety of online courses expand, it is safe to assume that enrollments will, as well. Yet early indicators give little reason to believe that WGU, for example, will significantly relieve the pressure for further investment in higher education in its member states, either for traditional students seeking undergraduate degrees or for nontraditional, postbaccalaureate students seeking career advancement. More marketing of higher education options should increase the number of students overall, but the demand for brand-name higher education will remain.

Caution is compatible with exploration. Research universities should not be risk averse in exploring and entering into partnerships, especially as they enable these institutions to be central participants in the delivery of educational services to the new class of students. But neither should they be overzealous. The development of pilot programs involving multiple approaches is preferable. Universities need to better understand their "best roles" as they meet the challenges of emerging student populations. These roles must be determined with care and caution and with the realization that the institution's reputation and mission should never be compromised.

CONCLUSION

Higher education is in a period of rapid transition. From the eye of the hurricane it is difficult to determine when—or even if—this transitional period will end. But if the past is a guide to the future, the situation eventually will stabilize; some universities will find themselves in an improved competitive position while others will fall back.

The key factors driving this transition are cynicism toward all of America's institutions, including higher education; competition from the private sector, made possible in part by improved information technology; a changing workplace that demands better educated employees; and a re-prioritization of state expenditures for immediate needs (such as the criminal justice system and health care) and away from long-term investment, including that represented by higher education. These factors challenge the underlying principle of incremental growth that has permeated higher education since World War II. Despite these factors, higher education needs to be responsive to a new class of students—namely, nontraditional, postbaccalaureate, non-degree students.

This transition focuses on several key areas: an increased emphasis on learning, the changing structure of faculty work, the movement toward distributed education, and the growing connectivity with external institutions and corporations through partnerships. Each of these areas remains fraught with serious challenges, but research universities ignore these trends at their own risk.

The most successful universities in the future will be those that respond positively to these challenges and do so in ways that preserve the values of high-quality education. As they have done for hundreds of years, universities must be the keepers of our intellectual traditions both by educating the next generation and by pioneering new frontiers in knowledge. But they also must respond to the needs and demands of the public that supports them.

CHAPTER 13

Demand for Postbaccalaureate Education in a Knowledge-Driven Research Environment

David G. Burnett

THE WORK COVENANT IN KNOWLEDGE-INTENSIVE SETTINGS

What is the nature of the future demand for postbaccalaureate education in the private research environment? To respond to this question, some background on the sometimes uneasy relationship of knowledge workers and employers is required. The April 1996 issue of *Fortune* featured a perplexed AT&T manager under the headline "How Safe Is Your Job?" Two years later, *Fast Company* featured Uncle Sam on its cover amid the bold-face text: "Talent Wars: WE WANT YOU!" How quickly things change, it seems, as corporate reengineering and downsizing have given way to growth strategies, and as pink slips have been replaced by signing bonuses for bachelor's degree holders.

Of course, this volatility is hardly new. The employer/employee relationship has always been ambiguous, and employees in all organizations have always been both a cost and an asset. In the private sector, one side of the "equation" is simply managed more aggressively than the other, depending on the business cycle.

Thinkers about our knowledge-driven society teach that a global service economy demands brain power over back power. Most corporate assets at the end of the twentieth century leave the worksite at the end of each day, and

David G. Burnett is head of Pfizer Research University, Central Research Division of Pfizer, Inc.

thus, the stakes in the employer/employee game have been raised. Mismanage these living assets, and chances are that an organization will soon be out of business. The combination of a robust economy, global competition, and the rapid growth of such knowledge industries as finance, entertainment, software, telecommunications, and pharmaceuticals has resulted in enormous leverage for well-educated knowledge workers.

Today, corporate value is defined largely in terms of these intellectual assets, i.e., employee know-how and creativity. David Ulrich defines "intellectual capital" as the product of employee competence and employee commitment. He illustrates the notion by comparing Dell Computer and General Motors: GM has a book value of roughly $65 billion and a similar market capitalization; Dell has a $65 billion market cap, with a book value of some $3 billion.[1]

The example is subject to many caveats, but it makes a point. The market places real dollar value on the intellectual capital that Dell has accumulated and that it believes will successfully generate future products of value.

Under the circumstances, nurturing and managing "intellect" is private sector job number one for the twenty-first century. Future downsizings, such as those of the early 1990s, are unlikely to be rewarded (as they were then) with increases in stock prices. How could a corporation risk alienating its current and future workforce through wholesale firings?

So what effect has the legacy of Chainsaw Al Dunlap had on the work attitudes of well-educated "20 and 30 somethings"? If the benefits of large corporations' past paternalistic practices (we're a family, we are wise about the future, we will take care of you for life if you work hard) cannot be counted on, then what is the employment contract worth? Whom can a well-educated young person trust as he or she contemplates entering the workforce?

Many are skeptical about large organizations. They have preferred to join a consulting firm or to become contract employees, effectively renting their knowledge to the highest bidder, with no strings attached. The most cynical have sought to "job jump" as often as possible, and when they have joined a firm, they have exploited corporate employee development programs to enhance their value to the next bidder for their services.

The rebellious "Generation X" spirit still abounds, but polls show that employees generally are anxious to be part of an enduring, win-win relationship with an employer.[2] Many corporations, in turn, chastened by the mistakes of the 1990s, are striving to rebuild employees' trust through participatory mission and vision creation and the elaboration of shared values. Even as they acknowledge that employment for life is no longer a realistic commitment, employers are committing themselves to the creation of a work environment in which employees' individual interests and talents can flourish. The "talent wars" have brought employees a variety of benefits, many of which are relevant to planners in higher education.

INVESTING IN EMPLOYEE EDUCATION

What impact has this evolution had on corporate investment in the education and training of employees? The traditional educational paradigm of many large organizations was and is training—the up-front investment in teaching employees how work is to be done. Best practices frequently are defined by management and transferred in a structured way to novices, sometimes via mentoring or apprenticeship, but also by professional "trainers," who in fact may not be content experts. This system remains common and critically important. No brain surgeon or brake assembly specialist should lack the training required to do his or her job exactly as it should be done.

In a complex, knowledge-driven environment, however, training is hardly sufficient. Seldom is there time to identify a "best practice," codify it, design instructional materials, train the trainers, and schedule, deliver, test, and certify the outcome. By the time the process is complete, a better practice will have evolved or new knowledge will have come to light. Individuals doing the knowledge-intensive work become the best sources of ideas for how that work could be done better. In such an environment, organizational and individual learning rapidly become interdependent.

THE INTERDEPENDENCE OF PERSONAL
AND ORGANIZATIONAL LEARNING

Recognizing the interdependence of organizational and employee learning, knowledge industries have focused their educational investments on creating conditions for learning in the workplace. A trusting environment, based on the shared values mentioned above, is essential. Learning occurs through trial and error, through experiments and mistakes. Reasonable risk taking in the search for ways to do work better must be recognized and rewarded whether the outcome is successful or not.

So employees are enjoying access to more learning tools and have more incentives to seek new knowledge and apply it. Organizations are devoting more attention to cultural support for information sharing and experimentation. The goal, of course, is to preserve, nurture, and grow the organization's knowledge assets.

It is not a coincidence that "knowledge management" has become the corporate preoccupation of the late 1990s. This term refers to the active development and coordination of tools, technologies, organizational values and habits, incentives, and systems to capture insights deriving from work experience. Step two involves management of the "delivery" of the most valuable of these insights to those who can profitably apply them to their own work efforts. Most serious thinkers about organizations now acknowledge that knowledge management is primarily about people and their behavior rather than systems and their applications.[3]

The critical knowledge that organizations seek to manage and exploit exists in employees. The challenge is to identify and tease out this tacit knowledge, to make it accessible to those who can profit from it, and to ensure that the organizational culture promotes the active sharing of insights by those who know, as well as the active pursuit of those insights by those who need to know. The larger the organization, the greater the challenge to make this happen.

Ideally, knowledge and insights flow throughout a boundaryless organization. Useful knowledge is accessed and applied freely between and among line organizations, teams, divisions, and, on occasion, competitors. Most significantly, the employee is cast in a critical new role: that of teacher, as well as learner. In a successful knowledge-driven organization, each employee must take responsibility for sharing what he or she learns on the job with others.

This vision should please every educator. Employees teach and learn from one another to do their own work better and to help co-workers do the same. Each employee thus realizes his or her own learning and teaching aspirations, and the organization is carried along on a virtuous spiral of ever more efficient and creative work processes.

ORGANIZATIONAL CHALLENGES TO GOOD KNOWLEDGE PRACTICES

Achieving this vision requires surmounting many obstacles. Every organization faces the challenge of integrating diverse organizational learning needs: to sustain best practices, to improve efficiency through continuous improvement efforts, and to challenge existing paradigms for value creation. The tension between the application of new ideas to the existing process and the need to seek actively for a new paradigm is constant.[4]

Other equally vexing organizational learning challenges include thinking globally and acting locally, being innovative but delivering results on time and on budget, promoting teamwork while motivating each individual, honoring specialized knowledge while seeking common understanding; the list goes on and on. Moreover, most business processes can be improved only to certain limits, at which point the incremental gains are not justified by the associated costs, so that continuous cost/benefit judgments are required as well.

The ultimate challenge is to balance organizational needs with employees' needs in a dynamic fashion. Organizational learning must be managed actively in response to environmental conditions, product maturity, market opportunities, regulatory changes, etc. The focus must change as circumstances change. This need for realtime business alignment of teaching/learning activity requires rapid turnaround of ideas with minimal organizational bureaucracy. Successful corporate universities cannot afford to debate curricular refinements for several semesters!

PERSONAL LEARNING AND ACADEMIC CREDENTIALS

At the Research Division of Pfizer, Inc., we are concerned first with the "personal knowledge" of employees we recruit to the division staff. Most are hired directly out of universities, and their academic credentials provide a ready proxy of the specialized scientific or mathematical knowledge they possess. Our scientific and technical knowledge needs align reasonably well with the traditional academic disciplines of chemistry, medicine, statistics, and engineering. We hire "high up on the food chain": M.D.s, Ph.D.s, Pharm.D.s, and B.S. and M.S. scientists. Credentialling—especially at the graduate level—is an important service provided to us by universities. Without this screening mechanism firmly in place, our search for talent would be far more difficult.

We compete with much greater difficulty for information technology talent, much of which is "homegrown" and comes with widely varying academic training. Lacking the well-entrenched vetting system of established academic disciplines, these fields (database development/management, applications, systems engineering, etc.) are driven by experience rather than formal academic credentials. The challenges in this arena only reinforce the importance of continued, highly rigorous, well-funded, scientific and medical training/credentialling at the university level.

Central Research employees benefit from additional investments in their "personal" knowledge, including formal graduate degrees supported by the corporation. We have developed partnerships with Brown University, the University of Connecticut, the University of Rhode Island, and Connecticut College to build the technical and scientific knowledge of our baccalaureate degree holders. We are very pleased with the on-site graduate degree programs (M.A. and M.S.) in biology and chemistry these institutions provide to hundreds of our employees each year. We invest large sums annually in these programs, in addition to the value of employees' time away from labs and offices.

ORGANIZATIONAL KNOWLEDGE AND CONSULTANCIES

Building personal knowledge—in the form of graduate degrees or credits—is not our highest organizational priority. Even though we do benefit from the insights, maturation, and sense of accomplishment achieved by our students/ workers, it is learning applied to work challenges that yields new "value" for the organization as a whole. Awarding credits for personal knowledge is not likely to prove valuable in the collaboration between knowledge industries and postbaccalaureate education institutions.

The primary area of need is the creation and exploitation of organizational knowledge. We wish to expand our understanding of how to apply individuals' specialized knowledge to the general, shared task of making better drugs to combat disease. We need to know what works and what does not work, given our shared purpose, and we need to discover and apply such insights as rapidly as possible. The rewards for achieving this goal are enormous.

To better meet this organizational learning challenge, we seek tools for organizational self-analysis and comprehension. We are not afraid to ask hard questions about ourselves and our progress. So-called *360-degree feedback* is a way of life. The audit function for regulatory and financial compliance is firmly in place, as is our benchmarking capability. But the number one enabler of effective organizational learning is presumably our organizational culture; yet appraising the culture of which one is a part is neither an easy nor a well-established task. Can we develop the ability to learn from ourselves about ourselves? Are we unintentionally creating invisible walls between work units that must share information? Are we rewarding those who take appropriate risks?

Of course, it is more difficult to find postbaccalaureate credentialling programs in organizational self-understanding than in chemistry or biology. Nevertheless, consultancies such as McKinsey, The Boston Consulting Group, and others specialize in providing "objective" (or at least "outsider") views of how an organization is managing intellectual assets. Our initial efforts in organizational learning, like those of many other organizations, were under-taken in collaboration with such partners.

These ubiquitous "brains for hire" provide a remarkable amount of intellec-tual horse power that is readily brought to bear on organizational issues. Like medieval minstrels, they carry the stories and cautionary tales of their most recent consults (anonymously, of course) and seed these lessons into other organizations. In so doing, they fulfill an important component of knowledge management, increasing the horizontal flow of knowledge across sectors and companies.

The major consulting organizations also model the principles of organiza-tional learning quite well and thus make excellent learning partners.[5] Their organizational structure is customer driven: "anywhere you want us, anytime, for as long as you need us." Despite, or rather because of, this almost complete decentralization, they have consciously developed cultures and infrastructures to support learning. Hoarding information in such organizations is a sure ticket to oblivion; sharing ideas with colleagues is the way to get noticed.

As "thinking partners," such organizations also have their drawbacks. They are expensive; but worse, the presence of consultants often demotivates the problem solvers among one's own employees. How can one explain that the organization that has been retained to help build a corporate culture that values trust and loyalty loses one out of three employees every year? How to explain that all the knowledge of our business developed through protracted interviews with employees will "walk out the door" when the consult is complete?

The continuous or frequent presence of consultants in the workplace clearly implies to many employees that their accumulated understanding of the work process and their tacit knowledge of how to do it better are underappreciated. However, building on Pfizer's commitment to respecting people, we are committed to respecting what those who have married their "personal" scientific knowledge to the organizational process of drug development have learned.

Effective knowledge management honors those who perform the work and seeks to mobilize what they know for the benefit of others. This places a refreshing premium on experience, long service, and even retirees whose accumulated wisdom and perspective should be brought to bear on contemporary issues. No excuse exists for overlooking any source of relevant knowledge. If we can do it well, balancing our continual experimentation with new science, new tools, and new technologies with the wisdom of experienced practitioners will prove a clear competitive advantage.

The first set of learning opportunities taught by our experienced practitioners is being finalized as this is written, and we look forward to the results of these efforts in the form of reduced dependence on outside consultants, cost savings, and greater efficiencies across organizational boundaries.

Thus, those long-term, mutually beneficial relationships between employees and employers are an essential component of successful organizational learning. The key ingredient is trust: that employees are working in the best interests of the organization and that the organization values employee insights. Our challenge is to equip all employees to be effective learners and teachers. This means developing the capacity and having the time to reflect on their experience so that important insights can emerge; it means providing the instructional design and technological support to leverage the insights; and it means respecting the specific needs of all employees as active learners and listeners.

Corporations and corporate universities may always seem biased toward the future, just as traditional universities often have seemed biased toward the past. Corporations seldom believe that the answer to a pressing problem lies in the past; rather, they believe in new circumstances, new solutions, innovation. But successful organizations, private or public, will actively manage the balance between wisdom and innovation, between individual employees' aspirations and the organization's collective needs.

A POSTSCRIPT ON COLLABORATION

As knowledge-dependent organizations have focused on knowledge management, they have come to appreciate the fundamental questions with which education institutions have wrestled for generations: How does one connect good "scholarship" and good teaching? What incentives are available to manage this balance effectively? How does an organization or institution address the diverse learning styles/intelligences of students/employees? What is worth capturing and learning for how long? How can one best measure the effects of learning and teaching?

A recent article by Phillip Dover and Thomas Moore documents the trend in executive education toward customized programs for business clients.[6] In fact, the authors assert that the design, delivery, and follow-up of programs are becoming fully shared by the client and B-school faculty. This is an important trend because it points to a fundamental characteristic of "adult education": learning/teaching among professionals is reciprocal. When we work together, we learn from and with one another.

I would welcome collaboration with any education institution that shares our passion for doing work better, for seeking ways to activate and engage what working professionals know, for developing instructional design principles for highly educated professionals. We already know that true insight and innovation come from discontinuity, a change in the internal or external environment that requires a response. Perhaps cross-sectoral exchanges would provide such stimulus.

General Electric (GE) frequently is cited in the literature for its direct approach to knowledge management. Learning from each other is good; more learning is better. GE achieves results by finding the commonalities in its disparate businesses, not by focusing on their distinctions or differences. This principle, if applied candidly to our mutual efforts to learn and teach better, seems certain to yield value on both sides. At present, communities of practice are hot topics as components of intellectual capital management.[7] Perhaps these deliberations will build just such a group for the future.

NOTES

1. David Ulrich, "Intellectual Capital = Competence + Commitment," *Sloan Management Review,* 39, no. 2, Winter 1998, pp. 15-25.
2. *Manpower Argus,* 360, September 1998, p. 11.
3. See B. Manville, and N. Foote, "Strategy as if Knowledge Mattered," *Fast Company,* April/May 1996, p. 66.

4. Anthony J. Fresina, "The Three Prototypes of Corporate Universities," *Corporate University Review*, January/February 1997.
5. See C. Bartlett, and S. Ghoshal, *The Individualized Corporation*. Cambridge, MA: Harvard University Press, 1997, Chapter 6, for a brief overview of McKinsey's knowledge management practices.
6. Philip Dover, and Thomas Moore, "Executive Education, A New Model for Changing Times," *Corporate University Review*, March/April 1998, pp. 24-27.
7. See William Graham, D. Osgood, and J. Karrren, "A Real-Life Community of Practice," *Training and Development*, May 1998, pp. 34-38.

CHAPTER 14

Higher Education's Changing Contours: The Policy Implications of an Emerging System

Patrick M. Callan and Joni E. Finney

A merican higher education is remarkably adaptive. A "system" only in the broadest sense of the term, it has been flexible enough to absorb and adapt to broad changes that, at the time, were outside the traditional purview of mainstream colleges and universities—for example, the land grant movement, the creation of community colleges, the passage of the GI Bill, and the need to serve increasing numbers of adult students. On the threshold of the twenty-first century, American higher education faces yet another new movement, one that has been described variously as "part-time," "postbaccalaureate," or "non-degree" education. But for public policy purposes, these characterizations are too narrow; the emerging, diverse aggregation of educational activities and interests beyond the boundaries of traditional higher education are too broad to be so described. "System of users" seems more appropriate—at least for preliminary policy analysis.

Although the emerging system of users is based on broader, more complex phenomena than those encompassed in the terms "part-time," "post-bacca-laureate," and "non-degree" education, the trends in these areas point toward a system that will have far-reaching implications for higher education generally.

Patrick M. Callan is president of the National Center for Public Policy and Higher Education.

Joni E. Finney is the vice president of the National Center for Public Policy and Higher Education.

People examine every new social phenomenon from different perspectives. The newly emerging system is no exception. Many employers see nontraditional educational venues—including employee training—as a cost of doing business, while state budget analysts hope that new delivery systems may help to control costs. Faculty at prestigious graduate schools do not see the emerging system at all, but their peers at other institutions often perceive it as a threat to their jobs. Entrepreneurs see it as a pot of gold. Continuing education specialists see it, of course, as comprising various forms of continuing education. Each of these interpretations is reasonable, but can they be aggregated to describe and help us understand the complexities of an emerging "system?" We believe the attempt should be made, since the congeries of nontraditional educational activities, accompanied by diverse interpretations and interests, are likely to have profound implications for higher education and for public policy generally.

Public policy analysts' perspective of these trends and changes is neither more nor less "correct" than that of employers, faculty, or any others. Yet it differs in that its primary concern rests with the public interest. We seek to identify and understand the varying interpretations and to bring order to the aggregation from a public policy perspective.

A NEW SYSTEM COMING INTO FOCUS

A new system of higher education is developing around us. It is elusive, its distinct dimensions only noticeable, we believe, when viewed from perspectives very different from those of traditional higher education. The conventional perspective encompasses a wide range of images: large public universities with noisy football stadiums, eastern liberal arts campuses with beautifully manicured lawns, even bustling urban institutions and the diversity that helps define them. The newly emerging system of higher education—still unrecognized by many but quickly taking shape before us—does not mesh easily with these traditional images or the perspectives they inform.

Blurred visibility and discomfort are to be expected. As yet, we know comparatively little about the emerging system that lies outside traditional higher education. Data are not regularly reported, and when they are, they are not completely reliable. Nevertheless, the emerging system appears to have the following five major characteristics:

- *The system is used by students (or customers) for practical purposes.* Many participants are adults returning to school because of the changing marketplace and the rapid pace of technological advances. The majority of the "customers" are part time, but some are full time. Most already have baccalaureate degrees, but some do not. Some, though not the majority, are seeking advanced degrees. The system is large and is growing rapidly. Conservative estimates document approximately 30 million users, compared to approximately 14 million enrolled in traditional higher education.[1]

- *The system consists of a wide range of educational providers.* These providers include traditional colleges and universities (primarily continuing education divisions and graduate programs), employers, professional associations, training centers, and independent for-profit colleges and universities.
- *The system uses a greater variety of educational delivery modes than is found on most campuses.* In addition to traditional classroom instruction, modes most frequently identified through surveys include job-site education, Internet-based learning, and other means of technologically delivered instruction.
- *Market forces, as opposed to public policy, appear to be the major drivers of educational change in the emerging system.* This trend is evident in the range of organizations offering education (from corporations to professional associations) and in who pays for the education. In 1994, 86 percent of the courses taken by employed persons with bachelor's degrees were paid for by employers.[2]
- *The system has developed at the margins or in the interstices of formal higher education.* The emerging system is at the periphery rather than at the core of the enterprise, at least in terms of institutional and public policy. However, the dollars supporting the emerging system are far from peripheral. The total dollars in the system far exceed state spending for higher education. Early estimates put the amount in excess of $55 billion annually, in contrast to the $42 billion per year that states spend on higher education.

"System of users" is an appropriate name for the aggregation of these phenomena because the system's most distinctive feature is that it is best viewed as a system from the perspective of the user (i.e., the student or customer). There is little commonality in the missions of the providers. Nor do common curricular elements define the delivery of educational services, as they do in many other areas of education. The system lacks a common faculty and the set of collective professional experiences that defines a faculty. However, what this aggregation has in common is an emphasis on students—the users. Students may not think of the education they receive in terms of a "system," but each of them is contributing to its development. Many are employees, while others seek an education that can help them become employed. Some are graduate or even undergraduate students enrolled at traditional campuses. Professionals, such as CPAs and lawyers, make use of this system. At least at this early stage, the system's single most important characteristic is that it is user-driven. Hence, it is a "system of users." The influence of the system of users is felt on the competitive edges of higher education—in professional programs, on the Internet, and in the more entrepreneurial academic enterprises.

THE CONTEXT FOR THE "SYSTEM OF USERS"

Like all higher education in the United States, the system of users will be shaped by its environment: by the economy, state and national; by changes in the growth and composition of the population; by technology; and by a wide variety of real though only dimly understood social and political forces. As the system of users has emerged over the past 10 years, the context in which higher education operates has changed significantly. It is not clear how ongoing changes will affect the system of users. Nevertheless, we can speculate about four major changes influencing all higher education and how they could specifically influence the system of users.

Erosion of Public Consensus on Paying for Higher Education

One of the most significant changes in the conditions affecting U.S. higher education is the slow but significant erosion of the 30-year consensus on how the costs of higher education should be shared by students, family, and government. The costs of higher education have shifted from government to students, a trend that was noticeable during the 1980s and that became more pronounced in the 1990s. In addition, government support appears to be shifting increasingly toward middle-class students and their families. The past decade has witnessed a dramatic shift in student financial aid, from grants to student loans, as students have had to borrow more to attend college. We cannot yet predict the effect of new, increased federal support through tax credits, but the impact will be significant.

For those students not at traditional campuses, the system of users has been supported primarily by employers and only secondarily by students. Corporations of a variety of sizes appear willing to invest in employee education that is perceived to have a clear payoff in terms of productivity and effectiveness. Continued erosion of government support for public higher education may strengthen the apparent trend toward corporate and individual financing in the system of users.

Competition Will Intensify

Financial support for traditional colleges and universities is likely to remain under pressure over the next decade. Projected student demand is growing in about half the states, but so are the demands of health care, the public schools, welfare services, and corrections. In just eight years, 39 states will face "structural deficits," that is, shortfalls in expected revenues needed to support projected spending.[3] States that combine inelastic tax systems with rapid spending growth show the largest structural deficits. The range is from a 0.1 percent deficit in Oregon to a 18.3 percent deficit in Nevada. The national average is approximately -4 percent.[4]

In traditional public higher education, competition for state funds most likely will lead to competition for students. Private, nonprofit campuses will compete also, as evidenced by New York University's recent plan to establish NYU On-Line, Inc. to compete with the University of Phoenix and other companies that sell training courses to working adults. Competition will increase the likelihood that public funds for the system of users will be scarce. After all, present data suggest that the system primarily benefits individuals and corporate employers and that it has grown largely without government support. But the system of users may well have experience from which the state could benefit—for example, serving geographically isolated professionals and technicians in whose continuing education the state and the public has an interest. Public investment would be justified where the public interest is clear.

Economic Stratification in the Population

It is clear that traditional higher education opportunities are much more available to the rich than to the poor. Over the past 20 years, the share of disposable income required to pay for college increased modestly—from 7 to 9 percent—for the wealthiest Americans (those above the 75th income percentile). For the least wealthy, however (those below the 25th percentile), the increase was from 17 to 25 percent. Thus, a young person from a family whose annual income is greater than $75,000 has an 86 percent chance of enrolling in college by age 18 to 24; those whose annual family income is less than $10,000 have only a 28 percent chance of doing so.

Early trends in the system of users indicate increasing participation levels, but a substantial proportion of the increase appears to be attributable to corporate support for education for employees who already possess significant educational credentials. These trends only exacerbate a difficult situation. Historically, higher education has been a force for ameliorating the gap between those with opportunity and those without. It is therefore appropriate to ask what role the system of users can play in the American goal of providing education opportunities beyond high school to *all* citizens.

Technology's Influence on the Educational Monopoly

Among the most important contextual changes affecting education has been the emergence of technology and its ability to influence how, when, and where instruction is delivered. For some time, technology has enhanced both the administrative and research capacities of colleges and universities. Only recently, however, has technology made more than incremental changes in traditional teaching and learning. Although traditional faculties express concern about the effect of educational technology on quality, corporations and others in the system of users are less hesitant to make the necessary technological investments and to experiment in this arena.[5] The majority of users in the emerging system tend to differ from those pursuing more traditional educational paths both in terms of their emphasis on learning (rather than a degree) and in their acceptance of technology as a means to that end. The use of technology in the system of users is likely to accelerate because it is favored by both providers and users.

PUBLIC POLICY AND THE ROLE OF GOVERNMENT

Traditionally, higher education has been a primary responsibility of the states, and each state has met this responsibility in its own fashion. In general, however, states have relied on the establishment and development of college and university campuses, "real" institutions in the sense of having distinct, readily identifiable geographic locations, faculties, and missions. Major federal policies have been more market sensitive, supporting students (e.g., through grants to veterans and Pell grants) rather than institutions. The system of users, meanwhile, has developed largely either outside of governmental higher education policy or, as in the case of continuing education, in the interstices of the academic enterprise.

As policy makers and others consider the role of public policy in this arena, it is crucial to consider—and question—the extent to which the educational services provided by the emerging system of users comprise a legitimate public as well as a private good. Although answers to that question will vary from state to state, several factors appear to have direct implications for public policy. For example, some states might find it in the public interest to address issues of equity regarding workforce access to ongoing education. That is, given the trend of corporations to pay for the education of their more highly educated employees, states may seek to enhance the education of other, less highly educated workers. Alternatively, states may find that there are specific public needs regarding the education and training of dislocated workers. Many states require continuing education in many professions; some may seek to enhance education and retraining in specific fields that are important to the state's economic and social fabric.

Yet another salient public need calls for policy makers to consider the role of government in relation to the emerging system—the system of users may be a glimpse into the future of American higher education generally. If it is, then state and federal policy makers face a substantial challenge. The present policy framework will require more than tinkering at the margins to shift the institutional focus to policies that are sensitive to users and their needs in a market-driven environment. The extraordinarily complex relationships between institutions, public and private, and the states in which they are located are not the least part of the challenge. Legitimate vested interests—both academic and political—in traditional governance and finance policies and practices will stand in the way of change.

A possible federal role is as yet unclear, but state policy makers cannot ignore the changes taking place. They have two alternatives: They can encourage colleges and universities to respond, positively and constructively, to the emerging system of users; or states themselves can enter the rapidly changing higher education market directly on behalf of their citizens.

State Policy Encouraging Institutional Response

If states elect to encourage their higher education institutions to respond to the system of users, what should be encouraged? Arthur Levine has speculated on institutional responses to what he sees as the "unprecedented" level at which the private sector (the system of users) is competing with traditional colleges and universities. He believes that a constructive response is required if higher education is to continue to be a viable force in American society. He suggests three options: (1) higher education can team up with the private sector, joining the traditional higher education product with the wider distribution available in the private sector; (2) higher education can reject the private sector and continue to offer its product primarily through on-campus courses; or (3) higher education can ignore the private sector and develop its own technology to more broadly distribute its products.

Of the three options, Levine believes that the first—teaming up with private enterprise—is the only reasonable course. "Higher education is making the mistake of thinking it is in the campus business, when in reality it is in the very, very lucrative education business."[6] Higher education cannot continue to rely on traditional on-campus instruction because providers in the system of users will develop their own courses by hiring expertise away from traditional campuses. Nor is it likely that a college or university will be able to compete successfully in the system of users on its own because of costs, current governance mechanisms, and other constraints.

Two recent developments, one in the southern states and the other in California, provide examples of the states encouraging a constructive response from higher education. Through the Southern Regional Educational Board, institutions in the South have been encouraged to cooperate in offering courses online and to rationalize tuition across state lines. The California Virtual University (CVU) is a similar effort.[7] Both efforts are structured within the existing institutional framework of degree programs, student credits, transfer, and degrees awarded. In California, for example, the CVU online catalog identifies courses offered electronically by participating, accredited, California colleges and universities. All the limitations of traditional higher education—particularly conditions for course transfer—are built into the new system. Although it is an extremely useful consumer tool for students, CVU is designed on institutional (albeit using technology) rather than user terms. Nevertheless, these efforts should not be disparaged, for they may be an important and necessary transitional step in adapting to what can best be described as market forces. At the very least, institutions in these states recognize the existence and importance of the market and are trying to respond to it, even if they seek to do so on their own terms.

Direct State Entry into the System of Users

Arthur Levine's analysis addresses institutional responses to the system of users, but how and whether states should enter the market directly are distinctly different questions. In contrast to the efforts in the South and in California, Western Governors University (WGU) is an example of states entering the market directly on behalf of their citizens. WGU has the potential to be more compatible with a system of users because it is designed around the needs of the potential users. Educational providers will vary, as will the range of educational offerings—from skill training and unrelated liberal arts courses to those leading to a degree. Learning, verified by assessment, will matter more than credits accumulated at a particular institution.

POLICY QUESTIONS AND OPTIONS FOR ADDRESSING THE SYSTEM OF USERS

Regardless of whether a state chooses to encourage higher education to respond to the system of users or enters that system directly, its action should be based on its higher education policy. Typically, such policy is more implicit in governing and finance practices than explicit as a framework for decision making. The emergence of the system of users is but one among several major changes in higher education's environment (e.g., projected enrollment growth and state revenue constraints) that provides compelling reasons to develop more explicit public policy. In the present context, each state's policy questions can be framed in a variety of ways: To what extent—and in what specific areas—are the educational services provided by the system of users a public as well as a private good? How can the market forces that are principally responsible for shaping the system of users be directed purposefully through policy? What is the most effective way to bring existing educational assets to bear on educational priorities or on unmet educational needs at the state level? However the questions are framed, they must relate the public purpose of higher education to a system of users that includes—at the least—existing public and private institutions, proprietary ones, corporate training, and technological delivery systems.

In answering these kinds of questions, states have many policy tools at their disposal. In choosing among them, they must consider the effects that any new policies will have on the system of users as well as on traditional higher education. For example, will new public policy make the system of users more or less agile in responding to state residents' changing educational needs? Will public policy make the emerging system more or less likely to innovate in the creation of new areas of professional study? Will public policy ameliorate or exacerbate the gaps between the haves and the have nots? If state policy makers simply adopt traditional educational policies for use in relation to the emerging system of users (e.g., policies that provide for equity among providers rather than the funding of users, or those that focus on inputs rather than outputs), then one of the primary effects of these actions—intended or not—will be to make the system of users less, rather than more, responsive to emerging educational needs.

The policy tools outlined below involve questions and options relating to finance, governance, and quality assurance.

Finance: Questions and Options

In what ways, if any, should government budgeting be changed to be more responsive to users than to traditional, institutional concerns? What government subsidies, if any, should go directly to students in pursuit of their educational goals? Should the state directly subsidize specific types of education? What public policy goals would be advanced by the answers to these questions?

States expend large sums of money for the construction of new campuses and for the maintenance and operation of existing ones. The emergence of the system of users raises the question of whether this pattern of investment should be continued. This question is particularly salient considering other factors affecting higher education finance: the prospect of constrained state revenues, technological advances, and increased variation in student needs. This issue should be considered regardless of the design of a state's higher education system. For example, in the Midwest and in the West, state monies have supported the development of large campuses and public higher education systems; they have relied on independent campuses only secondarily. In the East, on the other hand, public monies have supported small to mid-size public higher education systems, and, primarily through student financial aid, they have relied substantially on private colleges and universities. In both instances, state policies have supported the goals of college opportunity and choice. But the emergence of the system of users—as well as other important trends—requires that the policies be reexamined.

In many states (perhaps all), public funding has focused on issues of institutional equity rather than on public priorities. The perceived "fairness" of the resource distribution among institutions has been a high priority for states. Funding also is targeted overwhelmingly (in per student costs) to favor students of traditional college age. Budgetary procedures (formulas and less formal rules of thumb) perpetuate these institutionally based customs. State policy objectives may call for attention to changing student needs or to other unmet state needs.

Finally, state funding is driven largely by inputs, such as student/faculty ratios, rather than outputs, such as performance or learning outcomes. In contrast, the federal government invests in students (through financial aid) rather than in institutions. The federal government distributes monies for research on a competitive basis rather than through designated federal research universities or centers. These policies are more market sensitive than traditional state investment in institutions. As a result, federal investment mechanisms and structures can be adapted to a system of users more easily than those of the states. Adaptation would be required, for example, in determining the eligibility of providers and students, as well as programs or courses that are not degree oriented.

Governance: Questions and Options

Who should be responsible for decision making related to the system of users? Are traditional higher education governance structures able to respond to market forces?

By definition, state governing structures are oriented explicitly to individual institutions. Each state has its own unique arrangement of governing boards and state higher education agencies that relate state government to its public (and, to a lesser extent, private) colleges and universities. For the most part, state governance structures have balanced institutional priorities and goals with those of the public quite successfully. But a growing number of states are examining their governance arrangements to determine whether existing structures can meet present and future challenges. The relationship of these structures to the system of users must be explored.

Governing and, to a lesser extent, coordinating structures are the major players in state financing of higher education. Changes in financing policy in response to the system of users likely would have implications for governance. For example, a shift in state funding to students and away from institutions likely would strengthen market forces and also might require increased institutional flexibility, with more focus on institutional than systemwide governance structures. Funding institutional operations on a competitive basis to focus on public priorities, however, suggests the need for new or strengthened state capacity to judge performance. Deregulation also would be required to enhance institutional flexibility. In light of these transformations, many states may need to revise their governance structures to prompt institutions to become more sensitive to higher education markets.

Moreover, existing governing structures may obfuscate critical unmet educational needs, for example, effective higher education and K-12 relationships. Important participants in the system of users may not have a place in existing structures. For example, the National Center for Higher Education Management Systems argues that others outside of the formal "chain of command" or the provider-driven hierarchy perhaps should act directly on behalf of users. Structural change may allow states to facilitate user access to a wider range of educational providers than do existing structures. It also may offer ways to combine incentives for traditional higher education to be more sensitive to the system of users and, at the same time, to increase state capacity for new providers to address user needs.

Quality Assurance: Questions and Options

Should there be a system of quality control? If so, who should be responsible for it? The state and federal governments have, for the most part, deferred to institutions and institutionally controlled processes to verify institutional quality. State licensure and certification processes often set forth formal educational requirements for the professions. State policy can and does drive educational requirements beyond the baccalaureate degree for various professionals to stay current in their fields. Between 1981 and 1995, for example, 12 states implemented mandatory continuing education for certified public accountants (CPAs); every state but one now requires it. Similar trends exist for law, pharmacy, and real estate professionals.

The system of users may open up new and valuable avenues for exploring and assessing educational quality. Although the quality of higher education has not (yet) been subject to the public's harsh attacks, it has not been above criticism. Many have called attention to the inadequacy of the quantitative, institutionally based input measures used in budget negotiations and accreditation (e.g., proxies for quality such as the number of books in the library or student/faculty ratios). Likewise, the ranking of campuses by reputation as a measure of quality is increasingly criticized. State and educational leaders have been more vocal in calling for student learning outcomes and performance as true measures of quality. These trends toward more satisfactory assessment of quality may well be accelerated by the emerging system of users, most parts of which do not seem to be based on a single institution; whatever their adequacy, institutionally based criteria simply do not apply when students draw from various sources for their education.

Traditional institutions have been slow to address quality through the assessment of learning outcomes. In contrast, the system of users must rely more heavily on assessing learning outcomes to certify or verify results. Indeed, assessing student learning, publishing the results, and demonstrating effectiveness with students and employers could increase the image and visibility of the system of users.

Perhaps the most educationally significant change that this developing system of users can contribute to higher education generally is to be found in a revised assessment of quality. Western Governors University provides an example, for it has a separate and independent assessment process to verify that the desired learning has occurred. As WGU and others in the system of users experiment with quality measures, their efforts may well prove useful— indeed, transformational—for the overall system of higher education.

CONCLUSION: TWO OVERARCHING QUESTIONS

Much of this chapter is speculative, based only on data and events that have come to our attention. Such lack of precision and specificity always hinders accurate analysis of a new social phenomenon, particularly when a topic's nature and boundaries are as blurred as those of the system of users. But we urge early and serious attention to two questions that overarch the future of that system, the first pertaining to information and data and the second to the public purposes of education. Neither question is limited to the system of users, but consideration of that system highlights their importance for all of higher education.

Information and Data: How Do We Know What We Are Doing?

The states, the federal government, and many professional associations routinely collect data about higher education, but these data focus almost exclusively on traditional higher education. To the extent that information about users is collected, it almost always is from an institutional rather than from a user perspective. Reported information is rarely helpful to students as users or consumers, and sometimes it is not particularly useful for decision makers or policy analysts. As higher education enters more fully into the present era of changing demographic, economic, technological, and social conditions, every state will need more information about higher education than most have at present. NCHEMS describes information relevant to the system of users that, routinely collected, would be helpful to both students and policy leaders—the real costs of attendance, the likelihood of students with similar backgrounds and experience being successful in their educational choices, and the results of successful completion (e.g., job placement rates, expected income).[8]

There are many subsidiary questions: What information and data needs are most relevant for the system of users? Who should be responsible for collecting and reporting it? In what ways should the public be protected from educational fraud through regular data collecting and reporting? Who should monitor the data for accuracy? As the system of users continues to emerge and affect the higher education enterprise, it is clear that educational and state policy makers need to address these questions explicitly. States must rigorously examine their higher education information and reporting practices, and, as they do so, they should have a clear understanding of why specific information is necessary.

The Public Purposes of Higher Education: Where Are We Going?

Even with ideal information about higher education's present capabilities, the selection of options to stimulate change will be random unless policy leaders know where they want to go, unless they know the public purposes of higher education in their states. These purposes usually are found in state constitutions and are implemented through legislation. Too often, however, they become relics of rhetorical good intent, not ignored deliberately, but obscured by time and habit. We have argued elsewhere that the public purposes of all higher education should be reexamined because of the dramatically changed conditions the next century will bring. The emergence of the system of users will be an integral part of these changes, and it presents an opportunity for those of us in higher education—as well as for policy leaders—to consider fundamental changes in how we view higher education in the United States.

How our society incorporates the system of users into the existing higher education enterprise and how we respond to and learn from these changes will have enormous implications. The system of users encourages questions about students as users and learners rather than about institutions and institutional well-being. It also allows (in a powerful way, and perhaps sooner than expected) an opportunity to raise old but important questions about the public purposes of higher education. It gives us the opportunity to order policy priorities for the new century.

NOTES

1. U.S. Department of Education, National Center for Education Statistics, *Digest of Education Statistics 1997*. NCES 98-015. Washington, DC: U.S. Department of Education, 1999. Of the nearly 30 million students, approximately 3 million are enrolled in graduate and professional degree programs.
2. U.S. Department of Education, *Digest of Education Statistics 1997*, Tables 353 and 369.
3. Harold Hovey, *State Spending for Higher Education in the Next Decade: The Battle to Sustain Current Support*. Washington, DC: The National Center for Public Policy and Higher Education, 1999.
4. Ibid.

5. According to Laurie J. Bassi, Scott Cheney, and Mark E. Van Buren, *Training Industry Trends 1997*. Alexandria, VA: American Society for Training and Development, 1997, p. 13, companies are using more technology-delivered training. Between 1996 and the year 2000, most companies are expecting technology-delivered training to grow. The main areas of growth include the use of CD-ROM, text-based CBT, multimedia, the Internet, and videoconferencing.

6. Arthur Levine, *The State of American Higher Education*. Columbia University Annual Report, 1997, p. 11.

7. The California Virtual University ceased operating in early 1999. Nevertheless, its brief existence serves as a useful example of the difficulties higher education will encounter as it ventures into the digital world.

8. National Center for Higher Education Management Systems, *The Challenges and Opportunities Facing Higher Education: An Agenda for Policy Research*. Dennis Jones, Peter Ewell, and Aims McGuinness. Washington, DC: The National Center for Public Policy and Higher Education, December 1998.

SELECTED BIBLIOGRAPHY

Bassi, Laurie J., Cheney, Scott, and Van Buren, Mark E. *Training Industry Trends 1997.* Washington, DC: American Society for Training and Development <http://www.astd.org/virtual_community/comm_trends>.

Bassi, Laurie J., and Van Buren, Mark E. *The 1998 ASTD State of the Industry Report.* Washington, DC: American Society for Training and Development <http://www.astd.org/virtual_community/comm_trends>.

Callan, Patrick M., and Finney, Joni E., eds. *Public and Private Financing of Higher Education: Shaping Public Policy for the Future.* Phoenix: American Council on Education and Oryx Press, 1997.

Cervero, Ronald M. *Effective Continuing Education for Professionals.* Madison, WI: Jossey-Bass, 1988.

Conklin, Kristin D., and Finney, Joni E. "Access and Affordability: State Policy Responses to the Taxpayer Relief Act of 1997." In *Financing a College Degree: How It Works, How It's Changing*, edited by Jacqueline E. King. Phoenix: American Council on Education and Oryx Press, 1999.

Davis, Stanley M., and Botkin, Jim. *The Monster under the Bed.* New York: Simon & Schuster, 1994.

Galbraith, Michael W. *Confronting Controversies in Challenging Times: A Call for Action.* San Francisco: Jossey-Bass, 1992.

Gehres, Edward D., ed. *Lifelong Learning Trends.* Washington, DC: University Continuing Education Association, 1998.

Hovey, Harold. *State Spending for Higher Education in the Next Decade: The Battle to Sustain Current Support.* Washington, DC: The National Center for Public Policy and Higher Education, 1999.

Levine, Arthur. *The State of American Higher Education.* Columbia University Annual Report, 1997.

Mortenson Research Seminar. *Postsecondary Education OPPORTUNITY.* 1995-1998.

National Center for Higher Education Management Systems, *The Challenges and Opportunities Facing Higher Education: An Agenda for Policy Research.* Dennis Jones, Peter

Ewell, and Aims McGuinness. Washington, DC: The National Center for Public
Policy and Higher Education, December 1998.

Richardson, Richard C., Bracco, Kathy Reeves, Callan, Patrick M., and Finney, Joni E.
Designing State Higher Education Systems for a New Century. Phoenix: American
Council on Education and Oryx Press, 1999.

State Policy Reports. Hilton Head, SC. Volume 16, no. 14, July 1998.

Stern, Milton R. *Power and Conflict in Continuing Professional Education.* Belmont, CA:
Wadsworth, 1983.

U.S. Department of Education. National Center for Education Statistics. *Digest of Education Statistics 1997.* NCES 98-015. By Thomas Snyder. Washington, DC: U.S. Department of Education, 1997 <http://nces.ed.gov/>.

————. *Distance Education in Higher Education Institutions.* NCES 98-062. By Laurie Lewis,
Debbie Alexander, and Elizabeth Farris. Project Officer: Bernie Greene. Washington,
DC: U.S. Department of Education, 1997 <http://nces.ed.gov/>.

————. *Pocket Projections. Projections of Education Statistics to 2008.* NCES 98-017. By
William J. Hussar. Washington, DC: U.S. Department of Education, 1998 <http://
nces.ed.gov/>.

————. *Student Financing of Graduate and First-Professional Education, 1995-96, with Profiles
of Students in Selected Degree Programs.* NCES 98-083. By Susan P. Choy and Ron
Moskovitz. Project Officer: Andrew G. Malizio. Washington, DC: U.S. Department of
Education, 1998 <http://nces.ed.gov/>.

————. *Technology and its Ramifications for Data Systems: Report of the Policy Panel on
Technology.* By G. Phillip Cartwright. Washington, DC: U.S. Department of Education, 1998 <http://nces.ed.gov/>.

U.S. Department of Labor. Bureau of Labor Statistics. *1995 Survey of Employer Provided
Training.* Washington, DC: U.S. Department of Labor, 1995 <http://stats.bls.gov/
epthome/htm>.

CHAPTER 15

Postbaccalaureate Futures: Where Do We Go from Here?

Kay J. Kohl and Jules B. LaPidus

W e have entered a new era in which wealth is the product of knowledge. This transformation has changed the character of work. Whereas once land, seaports, and the physical labor of factories were the capital assets required to create wealth, today intellectual assets are becoming the most important factors of production. This new economy is affecting careers. Not only are more people earning college degrees, but they also are pursuing postbaccalaureate education in growing numbers. Old career paths are gone. Continuous acquisition of new skills and knowledge has become a strategy for maintaining employability in a short-term society. At the same time, dramatic advances in information technology are making it easier for those in the workforce to continually upgrade their knowledge and skills. It is not surprising, therefore, that modern postbaccalaureate education represents the fastest-growing and most rapidly changing sector of higher education.

The rise of postbaccalaureate education may be seen as a precursor of inevitable changes in the entire higher education enterprise—changes that loom just ahead. The forces promoting postbaccalaureate education derive principally from the knowledge economy. Postbaccalaureate education's constituencies have become demographically more diverse. In many places, the

Kay J. Kohl is the executive director of the University Continuing Education Association (UCEA).
Jules B. LaPidus is the president of the Council of Graduate Schools (CGS).

rapid rate of knowledge creation is making it exceedingly difficult for the faculty and libraries of individual institutions to keep up.

New networked delivery systems are altering the organization and financing of higher education. The quality measure in postbaccalaureate education is shifting from credit, or time spent in class, to competency. New competitors from the private sector are challenging higher education's credentialing monopoly even as they provide the impetus for new partnerships. In today's dynamic economy, the value of a college credential is increasingly timebound. It is no longer assumed that a baccalaureate degree will be adequate preparation for a lifelong career. With jobs changing and new jobs being created, postbaccalaureate learning has become a requirement for staying employable.

The expanded demand for postbaccalaureate learning serves to underline the significant environmental changes that are challenging traditional higher education institutions to examine their public purposes as well as their responsibilities to their graduates. Traditional colleges and universities are but part of a growing and more pluralistic system of higher education providers. This emerging system has close connections to the world that is external to the university. Higher education has long played an important economic role— one that has only been elevated by the economy's need to continually upgrade the knowledge and skills of the labor force. Higher education is also a critical societal agency for imparting our cultural inheritance and developing citizenship. If institutions are committed to advancing both economic and cultural objectives, they must seek to understand how components of this emerging higher education system relate to one another and to the whole and then make the necessary adaptations. Accordingly, we offer the following recommendations:

1. *Higher education institutions need to assume responsibility for preparing their students to become lifelong learners.* This implies ensuring that baccalaureate degree curricula require students to demonstrate acquisition of learning in general—as well as in narrow—knowledge areas. Further, the dramatic changes taking place in the way people acquire education means that baccalaureate education will have to develop students' capacity to explore and use information technologies critically and prepare them to be proactive lifelong learners.

    One of the significant changes occurring in postbaccalaureate education has to do with time. The traditional expectation has been that students would acquire most of their formal education during the early part of their lives. The issue is being defined in different terms. Students and employers realize that education on a continuous basis will be needed to help them keep up with rapid changes in the nature of work. This will place a high premium on students' ability to continue to learn. This is not a new notion, but it often gets lost in day-to-day efforts to be "practical" and "relevant." As Robert Hutchins pointed out many years ago, "All that can be learned in a university is the general principles, the fundamental propositions, the theory of any discipline. The practices of the profession change so rapidly that an attempt to inculcate them may merely succeed in teaching the student habits that will be a disservice to him when he graduates."[1]

2. *An institution that professes a commitment to postbaccalaureate learning needs to articulate this in its mission.* This implies that the leadership of an institution must be willing to initiate a planning process designed to evaluate how and in which areas the university might best respond to postbaccalaureate learning demands. Commitment at the top is key to establishing broad-based internal support and to ensuring that the resources required to assure delivery of high-quality programs are made available.

3. *Universities need to reduce barriers to articulation to succeed in an increasingly competitive national and international higher education market.* Distribution of education beyond the campus inevitably raises articulation issues. It becomes difficult to justify a requirement that all coursework be done at a "home" institution when learners have access to an array of high-quality, technology-mediated courses from diverse universities. Moreover, the growing global demand for higher education offerings in English and the formation of new international partnerships suggest that universities will need to adopt more flexible articulation policies once they decide to compete in this market.

4. *States need to promote cooperation among existing public and private universities to make optimum use of scarce resources, avoid redundancies, and extend learning opportunities to underserved populations.* Most Americans live and work in major metropolitan areas, but often they are not within convenient commuting distance of a university. Because access to postbaccalaureate learning resources is critical to economic development, governments need to find ways to combine institutional resources and deliver education conveniently to where it is most needed. This may involve development of suburban or center city learning centers.[2] Where regional population centers cross state boundaries, states may encourage several public and private universities to create a single regional learning center in lieu of building a new institution.[3] Still other states may seek to address postbaccalaureate education needs by committing resources to the development of a statewide virtual university, as Kentucky has done.

5. *States need to develop new funding formulas that take into account the impact of technology on learning.* Online education necessitates that states develop new funding models. For the most part, these models have involved concepts like "seat time," classroom utilization in square

footage and hours of use, support services and physical plant, and student credit hours, often expressed in terms of full-time equivalents (FTEs). These, as well as differential in- and out-of-state tuition rates make no sense in the age of the Internet. Students may satisfy graduation requirements through a variety of mechanisms, many of which will bear little or no relation to any of the above. Undoubtedly, universities will continue to provide education in the traditional manner while they are developing capabilities and capacities in distance education and online education, all at considerable cost. How these costs are assessed, how they affect tuition and state subsidies, and what costs will be borne by for-profit partners that contract with universities to provide educational services are all questions of the moment to which satisfactory answers must be found. Until recently, relatively little attention has been paid to the economics of postbaccalaureate education. This is changing rapidly.

6. *Universities must be willing to ensure the authenticity of the education they provide and establish assessment processes that evidence the learner's acquisition of new knowledge or skills.* Employers recognize that investing in upgrading their employees' knowledge and skills can yield substantial productivity gains. And individuals know that postbaccalaureate certificates are often required to make the transition from one job to the next. In both instances, consumers want universities to assume responsibility for ensuring that the education they deliver is of high quality and meets professional standards.

7. *Higher education institutions need to recognize that legitimate university postbaccalaureate learning can imply certificates as well as degrees.* Currently, certificates represent a completely unregulated segment of higher education, with no consensus—even within the academic community—on credit for effort, evaluation, and representation of the student's completed work on a transcript or related document. Some universities have developed internal procedures for review and approval of certificate programs. Once a certificate program is approved, a student's successful completion thereof is recorded on his or her transcript. Units that choose not to undergo this process may be able to offer "unofficial" certificates that do not carry the institution's imprimatur and do not appear on the student's transcript. Universities will be able to affect standards of non-university units (professional groups, private companies, etc.) through their willingness to accept credit for transfer to university programs. It would be in universities' best interest to arrive at some consensus about guidelines for postbaccalaureate certificates that include learning outcomes evaluation, acceptability for transfer credit, and official recognition of accomplishment in some documented form.

8. *Exponential growth in the amount of information available, together with the need to create accessible virtual libraries, means that universities must cooperate and share infrastructure development costs to ensure that students and scholars have access to affordable library resources.* Creation of accessible virtual libraries requires that universities cease viewing libraries in competitive terms and instead embrace interinstitutional cooperation. Ranking institutions according to the number of holdings in their campus libraries is counterproductive in an electronic environment. Rather, universities need to commit to shared investment in developing a new kind of library. Brian Hawkins has suggested that "the library of the future will be less a place where information is kept than a portal through which students and faculty will access the vast information resources of the world. . . the library of the future will be about access and knowledge management, not about ownership."[4]

9. *Higher education institutions and the federal government need to collect and analyze improved data about providers of postbaccalaureate programs and postbaccalaureate learners.* It is important for the federal government to gather data about how postbaccalaureate learners are being served by diverse higher education providers. Credible and reliable data are key to gaining support for any new legislation designed to offer financial incentives to consumers of postbaccalaureate learning.

   Data currently gathered by the Department of Education are inadequate because they focus on postbaccalaureate degree programs, whereas modular programs—often in the form of certificate programs— constitute much of postbaccalaureate learning. New strategies are required for gathering detailed information about postbaccalaureate certificate programs that are offered both by traditional universities and by non-university providers.

   Postbaccalaureate education providers also need to be encouraged to gather more extensive data about their students. It is essential to have data about the social, economic, and educational characteristics of postbaccalaureate learners to understand the true nature and scope of the postbaccalaureate phenomenon and formulate institutional strategies for serving this population.

10. *The federal government needs to create new incentives both to promote employer investment in education and training and to encourage individuals to update their knowledge and skills on a continuing basis.* In the interest of promoting the ongoing development of a high-quality workforce, the federal government should extend tax-free employer-provided educational assistance benefits to postbaccalaureate students on a permanent basis, make federal student financial aid available to distance learners, and provide education and training tax credits.

Universities are being challenged to extend their research and education to an expanding postbaccalaureate constituency. Addressing the program priorities of this constituency often requires institutions to develop new curricula, collaborate with other providers, and make substantial infrastructure investments. While the demands of postbaccalaureate learners are but one of the forces driving change in higher education, the extent to which universities are sensitive to this growing public demand—and the economic changes underlying it—could have a profound impact on their future.

NOTES

1. Robert Maynard Hutchins, *The Higher Learning in America*. New Haven and London: Yale University Press, 1936, p. 48.
2. In the late 1980s, officials in Montgomery County, a suburban area adjacent to Washington, DC, built the Shady Grove Life Sciences Center and persuaded The Johns Hopkins University and the University of Maryland to offer postbaccalaureate education there. Montgomery County leaders believed that the county needed graduate education opportunities if it were to attract and retain high-tech companies in a county where 43 percent of the residents already held at least a bachelor's degree.
3. The Quad Cities Graduate Center is a bi-state consortium of 13 public and private universities funded by monies from the states of Iowa and Illinois. The Center is an organizational unit that facilitates the delivery of the programs of the various institutions. It was created in response to the urging of the business community, which saw recruitment and retention of high-level professionals as being tied to the region's ability to offer graduate-level professional development and degree programs.
4. Brian L. Hawkins and Patricia Battin, eds., *The Mirage of Continuity: Reconfiguring Academic Information Resources for the 21st Century*. Washington, DC: Council on Library and Information Resources and Association of American Universities, 1998, p. 153.

APPENDIXES

....

APPENDIX 1

Certificate Program Snapshots

Wayne Patterson

Certificate programs are a rapidly growing and relatively new phenomenon in postbaccalaureate education. Although many universities have invested in the development of certificate programs, no comprehensive picture of their impact yet exists.

Over the past two years, I have conducted several studies designed to provide insight into this phenomenon. The initial studies were conducted while I served as dean-in-residence for, the Council of Graduate Schools (CGS). Further studies were conducted with the cooperation of the University Continuing Education Association (UCEA).

The interest of both organizations is indicative of the decentralized aspect of many university efforts in certificate program development. Certificate programs may reside in the graduate school, the continuing education school, a professional school, or indeed any other academic department. This is one reason that the collection of comprehensive data on certificate programs has been difficult. Another is that very similar short-term, non-degree programs may be given any of various names: certificate program, diploma, certificate of graduate study (COGS), certificate of advanced graduate study (CAGS), professional development program, and so on.

Here, I seek to address some of the questions that may arise when one contemplates the certificate phenomenon, particularly:

Wayne Patterson is senior fellow, Council of Graduate Schools (CGS).

- types of universities offering certificate programs;
- types of programs being offered;
- admissions criteria for certificate programs; and
- coexistence of certificates and degrees.

These discussions amount to only brief glances at a number of issues related to postbaccalaureate programs. Many other academic units, professional schools, professional associations, and corporations have data on certificate programs that have not yet been gathered systematically. (Interested readers are referred to this appendix's "References" section for information on several other articles on the subject of certificate programs.)

TYPES OF UNIVERSITIES OFFERING CERTIFICATE PROGRAMS

My initial study[1] had respondents from 113 universities. For the most part, the respondents were persons affiliated with the Council of Graduate Schools: deans and associate deans of graduate schools, other graduate school officers, or, occasionally, graduate program directors. A second study[2] had respondents from 86 universities—in this instance, the respondents being affiliated with the University Continuing Education Association. Nineteen universities participated in both studies, so information was gathered from a total of 180 universities, including 130 public universities (72.2 percent of the total) and 50 private universities (27.8 percent of the total).

To develop a profile of the types of universities involved in certificate programs, I classified the 180 respondents by locus of control (public or

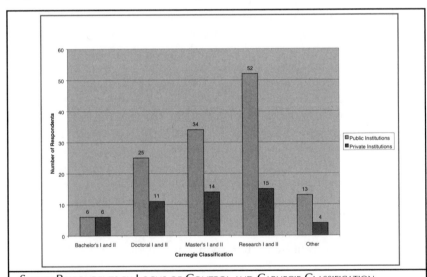

SURVEY RESPONDENTS BY LOCUS OF CONTROL AND CARNEGIE CLASSIFICATION

FIGURE 1

private) and also by Carnegie classification. Figure 1 indicates the distribution and demonstrates that interest in certificate program development is widespread.

The "Other" category in Figure 1 includes respondent international institutions (located in Canada, France, and Mexico) and respondent universities bearing the Carnegie classifications of medical, engineering, and tribal institutions.

TYPES OF PROGRAMS BEING OFFERED

The studies mentioned above looked at certificate policies and did not attempt to quantify the numbers or types of certificate programs at responding institutions. However, in further research, I have identified 1,288 certificate programs at 77 institutions. (For the most part, the 77 institutions are among the 180 institutions mentioned above.) Some of the lists of programs analyzed here were provided as part of the aforementioned studies; many were developed by examining university Web pages.

As is often the case in academe, there is not necessarily any consistency in how programs are named or in how programs with differing names relate to one another. Furthermore, universities may not attempt to use the so-called CIP codes to describe certificate programs. Thus, the categorization developed here is entirely the author's.

In my attempt to present a moderately focused picture of certificate programs, I have used two levels of differentiation: a "discipline" category wherein programs are classified by broad groupings of disciplines, which may correspond somewhat to the organization of academic colleges and schools (e.g., business, engineering, health sciences, education, etc.); and subcategories, which may correspond to individual academic units (such as departments or centers).

TABLE 1

NUMBER OF CERTIFICATE PROGRAMS BY BROAD DISCIPLINE CATEGORIES

Broad Discipline Categories	Number of Programs	Percent of Total
Agriculture	9	0.7%
Architecture	4	0.3%
Art	62	4.8%
Business	316	24.5%
Communications	34	2.6%
Education	106	8.2%
Engineering	49	3.8%
Environmental Studies	40	3.1%
Health Sciences	195	15.1%

TABLE 1 (CONTINUED)

NUMBER OF CERTIFICATE PROGRAMS BY BROAD DISCIPLINE CATEGORIES

Broad Discipline Categories	Number of Programs	Percent of Total
Humanities	43	3.3%
Information Science	204	15.8%
International Studies	22	1.7%
Law	28	2.2%
Pharmacy	2	0.2%
Sciences, Natural and Physical	45	3.5%
Social Sciences	83	6.4%
Technology	46	3.6%

TABLE 2

CERTIFICATE PROGRAMS BY CARNEGIE CLASSIFICATION

	Bachelor's	Doctoral	Master's	Research	Other
No. of Institutions	3	20	14	39	1
No. of Programs	7	242	99	934	1
Agriculture	0%	0%	0%	3%	0%
Architecture	0%	0%	0%	1%	0%
Art	0%	3%	9%	0%	0%
Business	0%	24%	26%	5%	0%
Communications	0%	2%	4%	25%	0%
Education	57%	3%	20%	3%	0%
Engineering	0%	8%	1%	8%	0%
Environmental Studies	0%	6%	0%	3%	0%
Health Sciences	14%	14%	12%	3%	100%
Humanities	14%	4%	0%	16%	0%
Information Science	0%	20%	7%	4%	0%
International Studies	0%	2%	1%	16%	0%
Law	0%	2%	2%	2%	0%
Pharmacy	0%	0%	0%	2%	0%
Sciences, Natural and Physical	14%	4%	2%	0%	0%
Social Sciences	0%	6%	12%	4%	0%
Technology	0%	3%	3%	6%	0%

It should not be surprising that the Carnegie research universities analyzed—typically larger institutions—should offer, on average, more than 20
certificate programs, whereas the doctoral institutions average about 10 and
the master's institutions even fewer. It also is not surprising that the three
largest broad groupings of disciplines are business, information science, and
health sciences, respectively. However, the observation that more certificate
programs are offered in education, social sciences, and art than in engineering

seems to belie the conception that certificate programs are being developed in fields which are "cash cows."

Number of Certificate Programs by Subcategories

In the fields of agriculture, architecture, and pharmacy, too few programs existed for subcategories to be developed. However, subcategories were developed in the other groups of disciplines. They are listed in Tables 3 to 16 below for each broadly defined category and are ordered by their frequency of occurrence.

TABLE 3

NUMBER AND PERCENTAGE OF CERTIFICATE PROGRAMS, BY SUBFIELD: ART

	No. of Programs	Percentage
Film and Television	7	11%
Graphic Design	7	11%
Music and Dance	7	11%
Studio and Photography	7	11%
Screenwriting and Writing	6	10%
Interior Design	4	6%
Medieval and Renaissance Studies	4	6%
Museum and Gallery Studies	4	6%
Art Therapy	3	5%
Arts Management	3	5%
Other	10	16%
TOTAL	62	98%*

*Total does not equal 100 because of rounding.

TABLE 4

NUMBER AND PERCENTAGE OF CERTIFICATE PROGRAMS, BY SUBFIELD: BUSINESS

	No. of Programs	Percentage
Human Resources Management and Career Counseling	29	9%
Marketing & Advertising	23	7%
International Business	22	7%
Management	18	6%
Project Management	16	5%
Business Administration	15	5%
Leadership & Supervision	15	5%
Public & NPO Management	15	5%
Accounting	13	4%
Public Relations	12	4%

TABLE 4 (CONTINUED)

NUMBER AND PERCENTAGE OF CERTIFICATE PROGRAMS, BY SUBFIELD: BUSINESS

	No. of Programs	Percentage
Training & Development	11	3%
Finance/Financial Management	10	3%
Purchasing	10	3%
Real Estate	10	3%
Office Computing	7	2%
Financial Planning	6	2%
Fundraising	6	2%
Total Quality Management	6	2%
Logistics & Transport	5	2%
Organizational Change	5	2%
Technical Writing	5	2%
Facilities Management	4	1%
Labor Relations	4	1%
Retailing	4	1%
Business & Econ Development	3	1%
Entrepreneurship	2	1%
Taxation	2	1%
Other	38	12%
TOTAL	316	101%*

*Total does not equal 100 because of rounding.

TABLE 5

NUMBER AND PERCENTAGE OF CERTIFICATE PROGRAMS, BY SUBFIELD: COMMUNICATIONS

	No. of Programs	Percentage
Journalism and Media	7	21%
Writing and Composition	7	21%
Marketing Communications	4	12%
Editing and Publishing	3	9%
Interpersonal Communications	3	9%
Conflict Resolution	2	6%
Organizational Communications	2	6%
Professional Communications	2	6%
Translation	2	6%
Other	2	6%
TOTAL	34	102%*

*Total does not equal 100 because of rounding.

TABLE 6

NUMBER AND PERCENTAGE OF CERTIFICATE PROGRAMS, BY SUBFIELD: EDUCATION

	No. of Programs	Percentage
English as a Second or Foreign Language	17	16%
Educational Technology	16	15%
Psychology and Counseling	9	8%
Reading and Language Arts	9	8%
Early Childhood Education	6	6%
Special Education	6	6%
Educational Leadership	4	4%
Gifted and Talented Education	4	4%
Health Education	4	4%
Library and Media Studies	4	4%
Community College Teaching	3	3%
Mathematics and Science Education	3	3%
Educational Facilities Management	2	2%
Teacher Education	2	2%
Other	17	16%
TOTAL	106	101%*

*Total does not equal 100 because of rounding.

TABLE 7

NUMBER AND PERCENTAGE OF CERTIFICATE PROGRAMS, BY SUBFIELD: ENGINEERING

	No. of Programs	Percentage
Mechanical Engineering	12	24%
Industrial Engineering	7	14%
Civil Engineering	6	12%
Electrical Engineering	6	12%
Manufacturing Engineering	4	8%
Transportation	3	6%
Communications Systems Engineering	2	4%
Engineering Management	2	4%
Systems Engineering	2	4%
Other	5	10%
TOTAL	49	98%*

*Total does not equal 100 because of rounding.

TABLE 8

NUMBER AND PERCENTAGE OF CERTIFICATE PROGRAMS, BY SUBFIELD: ENVIRONMENT

	No. of Programs	Percentage
Hazardous Materials and Waste Management	9	23%
Environment and Natural Resource Management	5	13%
Occupational Health and Safety	5	13%
Air and Water Quality	4	10%
Environmental Policy	3	8%
Land Use Planning	3	8%
Environmental Sciences	2	5%
Geographic Information Systems	2	5%
Other	7	18%
TOTAL	40	103%*

*Total does not equal 100 because of rounding.

TABLE 9

NUMBER AND PERCENTAGE OF CERTIFICATE PROGRAMS, BY SUBFIELD: HEALTH

	No. of Programs	Percentage
Gerontology	31	16%
Health Administration	16	8%
Family Nurse Practitioner	12	6%
Substance Abuse Prevention & Counseling	12	6%
Dental Care	10	5%
Human Performance and Fitness	9	5%
Public Health	9	5%
Emergency Medical Service & Trauma	7	4%
Pediatric & School Nurse	7	4%
Nursing Post-Master's	6	3%
Therapy (Physical & Occupational)	6	3%
Counseling	5	3%
Health Computing	5	3%
Other Nursing Specializations	5	3%
Post-Baccalaureate Premed.	5	3%
Childbirth Education	4	2%
Clinical Pathology	4	2%
Laboratory Science	4	2%
Dietetics and Nutrition	3	2%
Medical Coding	3	2%
Nurse Anesthetist	3	2%
Occupational Health & Safety	3	2%
Office Administration	3	2%
Legal Nurse Consulting	2	1%

TABLE 9 (CONTINUED)

NUMBER AND PERCENTAGE OF CERTIFICATE PROGRAMS, BY SUBFIELD: HEALTH

	No. of Programs	Percentage
Registered Nurse Assistant	2	1%
Women's Health	2	1%
Other	17	9%
TOTAL	195	105%*

*Total does not equal 100 because of rounding.

TABLE 10

NUMBER AND PERCENTAGE OF CERTIFICATE PROGRAMS, BY SUBFIELD: HUMANITIES

	No. of Programs	Percentage
Asian Studies	7	16%
Languages	7	16%
Latin American Studies	7	16%
European Studies	6	14%
Medieval Studies	5	12%
Renaissance Studies	3	7%
Translation	3	7%
Classics	1	2%
English	1	2%
Historic Preservation	1	2%
Religion	1	2%
Writing	1	2%
TOTAL	43	98%*

*Total does not equal 100 because of rounding.

TABLE 11

NUMBER AND PERCENTAGE OF CERTIFICATE PROGRAMS, BY SUBFIELD: INFORMATION SCIENCES

	No. of Programs	Percentage
Communications and Networks	16	8%
UNIX/C/C++ Programming	16	8%
Database Management Systems	13	6%
Telecommunications	13	6%
Web and Internet Technology	12	6%
Computer Information Systems	11	5%
Microsoft Applications	11	5%

TABLE 11 (CONTINUED)

NUMBER AND PERCENTAGE OF CERTIFICATE PROGRAMS, BY SUBFIELD: INFORMATION SCIENCES

	No. of Programs	Percentage
Graphics	9	4%
Multimedia	8	4%
Advanced Software	7	3%
Computers in Education	7	3%
Information Resource Management	7	3%
Software Engineering	7	3%
Computer and Computational Science	6	3%
Systems Computing	6	3%
Programming	5	2%
Java Programming	4	2%
Geographic Information Systems	3	1%
Information Technology Management	3	1%
Object-Oriented Programming	3	1%
Visual BASIC	3	1%
Computer-Aided Design	2	1%
Digital Signal Processing	2	1%
Human Computer Interface	2	1%
Very Large Scale Integration	2	1%
Other	26	13%
TOTAL	204	95%*

*Total does not equal 100 because of rounding.

TABLE 12

NUMBER AND PERCENTAGE OF CERTIFICATE PROGRAMS, BY SUBFIELD: INTERNATIONAL

	No. of Programs	Percentage
International Business	14	64%
International Administration	1	5%
International Education	1	5%
International Science and Technology	1	5%
International Security	1	5%
International Studies	1	5%
Other	3	14%
TOTAL	22	103%*

*Total does not equal 100 because of rounding.

TABLE 13

NUMBER AND PERCENTAGE OF CERTIFICATE PROGRAMS, BY SUBFIELD: LAW

	No. of Programs	Percentage
Paralegal and Legal Assistant	13	46%
Court Management	2	7%
Juridical Science	2	7%
Legal Interpretation	2	7%
Legal Secretary	2	7%
Regulatory Affairs	2	7%
Court Reporting	1	4%
Other	4	14%
TOTAL	28	99%*

*Total does not equal 100 because of rounding.

TABLE 14

NUMBER AND PERCENTAGE OF CERTIFICATE PROGRAMS, BY SUBFIELD: SCIENCE

	No. of Programs	Percentage
Biological Sciences and Biotechnology	15	33%
Physical and Chemical Sciences	12	27%
Earth Sciences	6	13%
Premedical Postbaccalaureate Sciences	4	9%
Science Policy	2	4%
Mathematical Sciences	1	2%
Other	5	11%
TOTAL	45	99%*

*Total does not equal 100 because of rounding.

TABLE 15

NUMBER AND PERCENTAGE OF CERTIFICATE PROGRAMS, BY SUBFIELD: SOCIAL SCIENCES

	No. of Programs	Percentage
Women's Studies	9	11%
History	7	8%
Criminal Justice and Law Enforcement	6	7%
Conflict Management	5	6%
Geographic Information Systems	4	5%
Latin American Studies	4	5%

TABLE 15 (CONTINUED)

NUMBER AND PERCENTAGE OF CERTIFICATE PROGRAMS, BY SUBFIELD: SOCIAL SCIENCES

	No. of Programs	Percentage
Chemical Dependency	3	4%
Social Research	3	4%
Social Welfare	3	4%
Survey Design	3	4%
American Studies	2	2%
Asian Studies	2	2%
Demography	2	2%
Diversity	2	2%
Domestic Violence	2	2%
Family Studies	2	2%
Political Science	2	2%
Public Administration	2	2%
Urban Development	2	2%
Other	18	22%
TOTAL	83	98%*

*Total does not equal 100 because of rounding.

TABLE 16

NUMBER AND PERCENTAGE OF CERTIFICATE PROGRAMS, BY SUBFIELD: TECHNOLOGY

	No. of Programs	Percentage
Building Technologies	10	22%
Electrical and Electronic Technologies	6	13%
Manufacturing Technologies	6	13%
Biotechnology	4	9%
Technology Management	4	9%
Educational Technology	3	7%
Other	13	28%
TOTAL	46	101%*

*Total does not equal 100 because of rounding.

ADMISSIONS CRITERIA FOR CERTIFICATE PROGRAMS

Admissions criteria for certificate programs need to be examined carefully. In addition, because the term *certificate program* may imply a program conducted at the undergraduate level, the postbaccalaureate level, the graduate level, not for credit, for professional development, or for many other purposes, the admissions process for each such type of program may also differ considerably.

Detailed survey responses address admissions criteria for certificate programs that are deemed to be at the postbaccalaureate or graduate level; in other words, the certificate courses carry graduate credit and, in many cases, may be transferable to a master's or doctoral program. Even within this category, there is considerable divergence in the views of the academy as to what should be considered when admitting a student to a certificate program. Admissions policies range from no requirements whatsoever to admission restricted to already enrolled doctoral degree students at the institution. Between these two extremes are programs that require only the completion of a bachelor's degree, those that have a conditional graduate student admission category (as is the case at many universities), and those that require full graduate school admission. Table 17 indicates some of the differences in requirements, with responses grouped by Carnegie classification.

TABLE 17

ADMISSIONS CRITERIA FOR POSTBACCALAUREATE/GRADUATE-LEVEL CERTIFICATE PROGRAMS, BY CARNEGIE CLASSIFICATION PROGRAMS, BY CARNEGIE CLASSIFICATION

	No Entrance Requirements	Bachelor's Degree Only	Master's Degree Only	Regular Graduate Admission	Graduate Admission with Qualifications	Already in Graduate School	Other
Bachelor's	0%	0%	0%	50%	50%	0%	0%
Doctoral	3%	40%	14%	13%	22%	6%	3%
Master's	3%	40%	13%	23%	13%	0%	7%
Research	10%	31%	3%	16%	18%	5%	16%
Other	6%	50%	0%	19%	19%	0%	6%
Total	6%	37%	7%	18%	18%	4%	10%

Further study will examine similar admissions issues for certificate programs at other levels.

COEXISTENCE OF CERTIFICATES AND DEGREES

One question raised at many institutions contemplating the initiation of certificate programs pertains to the impact of the certificate program on related master's or doctoral degree programs. Some speculate that initiating a certificate program in a particular discipline could have the effect of "cannibalizing" the existing degree program. In other words, prospective students might find the certificate program more valuable to their development (and requiring only a fraction of the time and money) and elect to enroll in the certificate program rather than pursue the degree.

The contrary position avers that the certificate program may strengthen the degree program. For example, the certificate program could prove to be a fertile recruiting ground for the related degree program.

According to practitioners (those who administer certificate programs), fears of "cannibalization" are almost entirely groundless. Following are the remarkably consistent results from the respondents in the CGS and UCEA studies.

The results given above provide only a brief look at the complexity of the emerging phenomenon of certificate programs. As this phenomenon continues to develop, it will be useful to conduct more careful analysis into its ramifications for postbaccalaureate—and indeed for all—higher education.

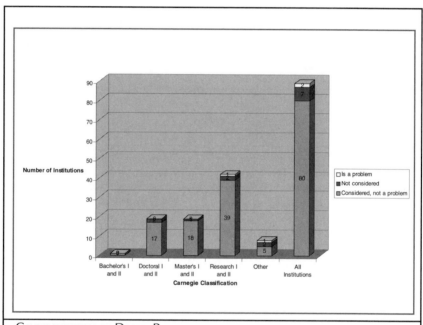

CANNIBALIZATION OF DEGREE PROGRAMS

FIGURE 2

NOTES

1. Wayne Patterson, "Summarizing Data on Certificate Programs," Council of Graduate Schools, March 1999 <www.cgsnet.org/summary.pdf>.
2. Wayne Patterson, "Summarizing Data on Certificate Programs at UCEA Institutions," forthcoming.

REFERENCES

"Certificates: A Survey of Our Status and Review of Successful Programs in the U.S. and Canada," CGS Occasional Papers, Council of Graduate Schools, 1998 <www.cgsnet.org/certif.htm>.

Alice J. Irby, "Certificates: The New Twist," *Change*, March–April 1999.

Wayne Patterson, "Analyzing Policies and Procedures for Graduate Certificate Programs," Council of Graduate Schools, July 1999. <www.cgsnet.org/pdf/analysis.html>.

Wayne Patterson, "A Survey of Graduate Certificate Policies, Procedures, and Programs," University of Charleston, 1997. <www.cofc.edu/~wayne/gradcerts.html>.

Wayne Patterson, "A Model of Shared Leadership for Graduate Certificate Programs," *University Continuing Education Review*, Fall 1999: 69–80.

Stephen Welch and Peter Syverson, "Post-Baccalaureate Certificates," *CGS Communicator*, November 1997 <www.cgsnet.org>.

APPENDIX 2

Creating Postbaccalaureate Programs to Meet Workforce Needs: Participating Institutions

T he following institutions were selected to send two representatives to one of three national workshops organized by the Johns Hopkins University School of Professional Studies in Business and Education in conjunction with this W.K. Kellogg Foundation-sponsored project. The workshops were held in Baltimore (February 4-6, 1999), San Diego (March 11-13, 1999), and Chicago (April 22-24, 1999).

American University

Angelo State University

Arizona State University

Aurora University

Ball State University

Baylor University

Boston College

Bradley University

Buffalo State College

California State University—
Bakersfield

California State University—Fresno

California State University—
Hayward

Carnegie Mellon University

City University of New York

Clarion University of Pennsylvania

Cleveland State University

College of William and Mary

Coppin State College

DePaul University

East Carolina University

East Tennessee State University

Eastern Illinois University

Ferris State University

George Washington University

Indiana University—Purdue
University Indianapolis

Indiana University

Kansas State University

Kent State University

Louisiana State University

Loyola Marymount University

Massachusetts Institute of
Technology

Marquette University

MCP Hahnemann University/
Drexel University

Miami University

Michigan State University

Middle Tennessee University

Minneapolis College of Art and
Design

Montclair State University

National University

New Jersey Institute of Technology

North Carolina A&T State University

Northern Arizona University

Northwestern University

Ohio State University

Ohio University

Oklahoma State University

Pace University

Pennsylvania State University

Portland State University

Rochester Institute of Technology

San Jose University

South Carolina State University

Southwest Missouri State University

Southwest Texas State University

St. John's University

SUNY Empire State College

Texas Tech University

Texas Women's University

Towson University

University of Albany SUNY

University of California, Davis

University of California, Los
Angeles

University of California, Merced

University of California, San Diego

University of Houston—Clear Lake

University of Illinois at Springfield

University of Maryland Baltimore
County

University of Massachusetts,
Amherst

University of Michigan

University of Missouri

University of Nebraska, Lincoln

University of Nevada, Las Vegas

University of North Carolina at
Charlotte

University of North Carolina—
General Administration

University of Northern Iowa

University of Notre Dame

University of Pennsylvania

University of Richmond

University of South Dakota

University of Southern California

University of Southern Indiana

University of St. Thomas

University of Texas at Arlington

University of Texas at Austin

University of Texas at Brownsville

University of Texas at El Paso

University of Washington

University of Wisconsin—Stout

University of Wyoming

Villanova University

Virginia Commonwealth University

Washington State University

Washington University

APPENDIX 3

"Postbaccalaureate Futures" Colloquium Participants

The "Postbaccalaureate Futures" Colloquium was held at The Aspen Institute in Aspen, Colorado, November 1-3, 1998. The following is a list of individuals who participated in the Colloquium.

Bernard Ascher, Director, Service Industry Affairs, Office of the U.S. Trade Representative

Judith D. Auerbach, Prevention Science Coordinator and Behavioral and Science Coordinator, Office of AIDS Research, National Institutes of Health

Alan R. Bassindale, Pro-Vice-Chancellor, Open University, United Kingdom

Carole A. Beere, Vice President of Academic Affairs, Walden University (formerly Dean, Graduate Studies, and Assistant Vice President for Research, Central Michigan University)

Stephen A. Bieglecki, Director, Technical Education and Training, United Technologies Corporation

Howard M. Block, a Managing Director, Banc of America Securities (formerly Vice President, Education/Training, BancBoston Robertson Stephens)

Myles Brand, President, Indiana University

David G. Burnett, Head of Pfizer Research University, Central Research Division of Pfizer, Inc. (formerly Director, Employee Resources, Central Research, Pfizer, Inc.)

Patrick M. Callan, President, National Center for Public Policy and Higher Education

Steven D. Crow, Executive Director, Commission on Institutions of Higher Education, North Central Association of Colleges and Schools

Sir John Daniel, Vice-Chancellor, Open University, United Kingdom

Joni E. Finney, Vice President, National Center for Public Policy and Higher Education

Stanley C. Gabor, Dean, School of Professional Studies in Business and Education, Johns Hopkins University

Michael B. Goldstein, Attorney, Dow, Lohnes & Albertson

Michael G. Hansen, Senior Vice President for Organizational Capability, Veridian Corporation

Gerald A. Heeger, President, University of Maryland University College (formerly Dean, School of Continuing and Professional Studies, New York University)

Peter W. Hegener, Senior Vice President of Alliances and Acquisitions for Thomson Learning (formerly Chairman, Peterson's)

Alice J. Irby, President Emeritus, Chauncey Group International

Kay J. Kohl, Executive Director, University Continuing Education Association (UCEA)

Jonathan Kotler, Dean, Graduate School, University of Southern California

Thomas F. Kowalik, Director, Continuing Education and Summer Programs, SUNY-Binghamton

Charlotte V. Kuh, Executive Director, Office of Scientific and Engineering Personnel, National Research Council, National Academy of Sciences

Donald N. Langenberg, Chancellor, University of Maryland System

Jules B. LaPidus, President, Council of Graduate Schools (CGS)

Peter Lyman, Professor and Associate Dean, School of Information Management & Systems (SIMS), University of California, Berkeley

Alan R. Mabe, Dean, Graduate Studies, and Vice President for Program Development and Faculty Support, Florida State University

Sue C. Maes, Senior Development Officer, Education Communications Center, Kansas State University

Theodore J. Marchese, Vice President, American Association for Higher Education

Gordon H. Mueller, Director, Center for Austrian Culture and Commerce and Professor of History, University of New Orleans, and Chairman of the Board for the National D-Day Museum (formerly President, Research and Technology Park, and Vice Chancellor for Extension and Research Park, UNO)

Michael J. Offerman, Executive Director, Learning Innovations Center, and Dean, Continuing Education Extension, University of Wisconsin

Robert M. O'Neil, Professor of Law, University of Virginia, and Director, Thomas Jefferson Center for the Protection of Free Expression

Betty J. Overton-Adkins, Program Director and Director of Higher Education Programming, W.K. Kellogg Foundation

Wayne Patterson, Scholar-in-Residence, Council of Graduate Schools

Leonard K. Peters, Vice Provost, Research, and Dean, Graduate School, Virginia Polytechnic Institute and State University

Robert M. Rosenzweig, President Emeritus, Association of American Universities

Michael Schrage, Co-Director of the E-Markets Initiative of the Media Lab at the Massachusetts Institute of Technology and Executive Director of the Merrill Lynch Innovation Grants Competition for Doctoral Students

Daniel W. Shannon, Dean, Graham School of General Studies, University of Chicago

Michael Shinagel, Dean, Continuing Education and University Extension, Harvard University

Debra W. Stewart, Vice Provost and Dean, Graduate School, North Carolina State University

Catharine R. Stimpson, Dean, Graduate School, New York University

Steadman Upham, President, Claremont Graduate University

James D. Van Erden, Director, Workforce Development, Goodwill Industries International, Inc. (formerly, Senior Vice President, Workforce Development, National Alliance of Business)

Vivian A. Vidoli, Dean, Division of Graduate Studies, California State University, Fresno

Mary L. Walshok, Associate Vice Chancellor, Extended Studies and Public Programs, University of California, San Diego

Staff

Mary Burke, University Continuing Education Association

John W. Hager, University Continuing Education Association

Amy Yerkes, Johns Hopkins University

Note: Bernard Ascher and Patrick Callan contributed written analyses to the Colloquium but were unable to participate in the discussions in Aspen.

INDEX

by Kelly R. Stern